D1283535

Getting the Most Out of IEPs

An Educator's Guide to the Student-Directed Approach

by

Colleen A. Thoma, Ph.D.
Virginia Commonwealth University
Richmond

and

Paul Wehman, Ph.D.
Virginia Commonwealth University
Richmond

with invited contributors

·P A U L·H·
BROOKES
PUBLISHING Co.®

Baltimore • London • Sydney

Paul H. Brookes Publishing Co.
Post Office Box 10624
Baltimore, Maryland 21285-0624
USA

www.brookespublishing.com

Typeset by Spearhead Global, Inc., Bear, Delaware.
Manufactured in the United States of America by
Sheridan Books, Inc., Chelsea, Michigan.

The individuals described in this book are composites or real people whose situations are masked and are based on the authors' experiences. In most instances, names and identifying details have been changed to protect confidentiality. Real names are used with permission.

Library of Congress Cataloging-in-Publication Data

Thoma, Colleen A.
  Getting the most out of IEPs : an educator's guide to the student-directed approach/by Colleen A. Thoma and Paul Wehman; with invited contributors.
    p.   cm.
  Includes bibliographical references and index.
  ISBN-13: 978-1-55766-944-5 (pbk.)
  ISBN-10: 1-55766-944-9 (pbk.)
  1. Individualized education programs—United States.   2. Youth with disabilities—Education—United States—Decision making.   3. Student participation in curriculum planning—United States.   I. Wehman, Paul.   II. Title.
  LC4031.T44 2010
  371.9'043—dc22
                                                                                            2010001814

British Library Cataloguing in Publication data are available from the British Library.

2021   2020   2019   2018

10   9   8   7   6   5   4   3

Contents

About the Authors

Colleen A. Thoma, Ph.D., Professor, Department of Special Education and Disability Policy, School of Education, Virginia Commonwealth University (VCU), 1015 West Main Street, Richmond, Virginia 23284

Dr. Thoma earned her doctoral degree from Indiana University, where she began her research on self-determination in transition planning. She is Director of Doctoral Studies in the School of Education at VCU and teaches courses on disability policy, transition and secondary education, curriculum and instruction, and characteristics of students with intellectual and/or developmental disabilities. Her research interests include preparation of teachers to support self-determined transition planning, student-directed individualized education program development, and the impact of student self-determination on transition and academic outcomes. She has mentored doctoral candidates at VCU in their own research on self-determination, teacher preparation, and transition services. She was also the recipient of VCU School of Education's Award for Distinguished Scholarship in 2007. Her leadership in the field of transition services included 5 years on the executive board of the Division on Career Development and Transition, a division of the Council for Exceptional Children, including 1 year as President of the executive board. Dr. Thoma began her 3-year term as a member at large on the Board of Directors of the Council for Exceptional Children in January 2010.

Paul Wehman, Ph.D., Chairman, Division of Rehabilitation Research, Department of Physical Medicine and Rehabilitation, Virginia Commonwealth University (VCU), 1314 West Main Street, Richmond, Virginia 23284

Dr. Wehman is Professor of Physical Medicine and Rehabilitation at VCU, with joint appointments in the Department of Special Education and the Department of Rehabilitation Counseling. He pioneered the development of supported employment at VCU in the early 1980s and has been heavily involved in the use of supported employment with people who have severe disabilities. He has written extensively on issues related to transition from school to adulthood and special education as it relates for young adulthood. Dr. Wehman has published more than 200 articles and 77 book chapters and has authored or edited 40 books. He is a recipient of the Joseph P. Kennedy, Jr. Foundation International Awards in Mental Retardation, was a Mary Switzer Fellow for the National Rehabilitation Association in 1985, and received the Distinguished Service Award from the President's Committee on Employment for Persons with Disabilities in October 1992. Dr. Wehman was recognized as one of the 50 most influential special educators of the millennium by a national survey coordinated by the *Remedial and Special Education* journal (December 2000) and received the VCU Distinguished Service Award on September 6, 2001. He is also Editor-in-Chief of the *Journal of Vocational Rehabilitation*. Dr. Wehman has been the Principal Investigator of more than 35 million dollars worth of federal grants since he started working at VCU.

Contributors

Beth A. Bader, Ph.D.
Rehabilitation Research and Training
    Center on Workplace Supports
    and Job Retention
Virginia Commonwealth University
Richmond, Virginia

Christina C. Bartholomew, Ph.D.
Exceptional Education Department
James Madison University
Harrisonburg, Virginia

Kimberly S. Boyd, M.T.
Chesterfield County School Division
Chesterfield, Virginia

Renee Z. Bullano, M.Ed.
Virginia Department of Education
Training and Technical Assistance Center
    at VCU
Richmond, Virginia

Ann Deschamps, Ed.D.
TransCen, Inc.
Baltimore, Maryland

Mary Fisher, Ph.D.
Indiana University School of Education
Indiana University–Purdue University
Indianapolis, Indiana

Elizabeth Evans Getzel, M.Ed.
Rehabilitation Research and Training
    Center on Workplace Supports
    and Job Retention
Virginia Commonwealth University
Richmond, Virginia

Mary Held, Ph.D.
Indiana Institute on Disability and
    Community
Center on Community Living and
    Careers
Indiana University
Bloomington, Indiana

Dawn R. Hendricks, Ph.D.
School of Education
Virginia Commonwealth University
Richmond, Virginia

Sharon Jones, M.Ed.
Virginia Department of Education
Training and Technical Assistance Center
    at VCU
Richmond, Virginia

Shannon McMannus, M.Ed.
Rehabilitation Research and Training
    Center on Workplace Supports
    and Job Retention
Virginia Commonwealth University
Richmond, Virginia

Barbara Purvis, M.Ed.
Technical Assistance Center for
    Deaf-Blindness
Helen Keller Institute
Shawnee Mission, Kansas

Mark Richardson, M.A.
School of Education
Virginia Commonwealth University
Richmond, Virginia

Patricia Rogan, Ph.D.
Indiana University School of Education
Indiana University–Purdue University
Indianapolis, Indiana

Sterling Saddler, Ed.D.
College of Education
University of Nevada, Las Vegas

Carol Schall, Ph.D.
Virginia Commonwealth University
and Virginia Autism Resource Center
Richmond, Virginia

LaRon A. Scott, M.Ed.
Henrico County School Division
Henrico, Virginia

Frances Smith, Ed.D.
Virginia Department of Education
Training and Technical Assistance Center
    at VCU
Richmond, Virginia

Ronald Tamura, Ph.D.
Department of Special Education
    and Reading
Southern Connecticut State University
New Haven, Connecticut

Pamela S. Targett, M.Ed.
Rehabilitation Research and Training
    Center on Workplace Supports
    and Job Retention
Virginia Commonwealth University
Richmond, Virginia

Marsha S. Tennant, M.Ed.
Horry County Schools
Conway, South Carolina

Judith E. Terpstra, Ph.D.
Department of Special Education
    and Reading
Southern Connecticut State University
New Haven, Connecticut

Katherine M. Wittig, M.Ed.
Virginia Department of Education
Training and Technical Assistance Center
    at VCU
Richmond, Virginia

Yaoying Xu, Ph.D.
Department of Special Education
    and Disability Policy
Virginia Commonwealth University
Richmond, Virginia

Preface

When the Education for All Handicapped Children Act (PL 94-142) was signed into law by President Gerald Ford in 1975, there were many outstanding, and yet controversial, aspects of this entitlement for children with disabilities, including due process, free appropriate public education, nondiscriminatory assessment, least restrictive environment, and the individualized education program (IEP). Over time each of these parts of the law have been tested in the courts and written about extensively. Perhaps none has defined this groundbreaking disability law more than the IEP.

The IEP is an extremely important document to parents and educators because it defines what is going to be taught to the student, where the material will be taught, and what services and supports will be used. The IEP has all too often become the lightning rod for conflict between families and schools as there are disagreements about accountability for services and the best services or curriculum for the child. Fortunately, the IEP more often than not is a means of bringing the educational team and family together to meaningfully plan what is in the best interest of the child educationally.

Historically, the IEP was developed by the educational team with input from the family and very infrequently the student. Arguably this was the normal practice for the first 20 years that the law was in place. However, in the early 1990s, there began to be an increasing swell of interest and demand for self-determination on behalf of students and adults with disabilities. This philosophical movement grew out of the passage of the civil rights law, the Americans with Disabilities Act of 1990 (PL 101-336), and was buttressed by the writings of researchers such as Michael Wehmeyer, who introduced the idea of self-determination for students with disabilities and targeted the IEP meeting as a practical way to help students practice those skills (Wehmeyer, 1992). Increasingly, people began to ask, "Why isn't Margaret at the meeting? It's about her life, anyway," or "Where is Robert? Why is he not attending and participating in this meeting about his education?"

Initially, there was a large amount of skepticism about how children and youth with disabilities could possibly make meaningful additions to an "important" meeting like the IEP meeting. Like most innovative practices, there was distrust and confusion about how this practice could really be helpful and effective for the process. In fact, the entire IEP planning was missing the most important ingredient of all: the student! And it took almost a quarter century to figure that out.

With that said, there is an art to how to include students meaningfully in repeated IEP meetings, how to include their family, how to prepare them to communicate effectively, and ultimately how to get them to move into a leadership role either by themselves or through a designate. This book is about how to bridge that gap. It helps teachers, administrators, moms, dads, students, counselors, and others know how to set up a meeting, plan for it, and follow through so that the IEP is effective.

When we first entertained the idea of writing this book, we did not realize how many special educators were already working to implement one or more of the student-led IEP processes that have made their way into our field. Some used components of curricula designed to teach self-determination skills to transition-age youth like *The Next S.T.E.P. Curriculum* (Halpern et al., 1997) or *Life-Centered Career Education* (Brolin, 1997); others used stand-alone student-led IEP processes available on the Internet (e.g., *Student-Led IEP* available through the National Dissemination Center for Children with Disabilities [NICHCY]); and still others created their own. We were inspired and energized as we spoke with these teachers and they shared their enthusiasm for the process.

However, as we began the task of writing the chapters (or asking others to contribute chapters), we found that while there was a great deal of information about it, there were some problems. First, we didn't find a standard definition of student direction, involvement, or leading of the IEP process. Some used these terms interchangeably; others also included person-centered IEP processes as a strategy that could facilitate student involvement in their IEP. Despite these complications, we found that the focus of the information out there was on the meeting itself and preparing the student to participate in the meeting in a meaningful way. We knew that, to be useful for teachers, this book needed to clarify terms, begin with the IEP itself, and address the entire IEP process from the assessment of student strengths and needs, to preparation for the meeting, to the meeting and IEP document itself, to the day-to-day implementation of IEP goals and evaluation of student progress that leads directly into the preparation for the next IEP.

We organized the book to accomplish these objectives. We start with a chapter that defines student-directed IEPs as including a range of ways that students can be involved and set the direction for their educational plans by introducing a continuum to describe different levels of student involvement. Chapter 1 introduces you to five students who have very different support needs and are of different ages; these students are used as examples to illustrate strategies introduced in subsequent chapters. Kathy's example is included in each chapter. Chapter 2 describes the ways that teachers can involve families in the process and tailor the student-directed IEP process for students from diverse backgrounds. The rest of the book is divided into three sections: premeeting, meeting and IEP document, and implementation/evaluation activities that together make up the full IEP process.

After the introductory chapter, each chapter in these sections follows a similar format. The chapters start with an overview of the legal requirements and evidence-based and/or promising practices for the topic to increase the level of student involvement and direction (e.g., assessment, present level of performance). Then, Kathy's example is shared and followed by a Listening to the Experts section that includes the perspectives of Kathy, her teacher (Mr. Scott), and her mother (Ms. Abbott) regarding their experience in implementing that strategy. Lastly, chapters include tips and strategies you can use to get started and/or to adapt the process for students with different needs (i.e., students like Max, Alejandra, Susan, and Dwight). These tips and strategies were generated by teachers who have implemented student-directed IEP procedures. The authors ran a series of focus group interviews with teachers who were very generous in sharing their knowledge and skills with all of us.

Since this book is designed to be teacher friendly, each chapter primarily focuses on strategies that you can use with the students for whom you are responsible. These examples will help you identify how you can tailor a student-directed IEP approach to meet the needs of the students with whom you work.

References

Americans with Disabilities Act (ADA) of 1990, PL 101-336, 42 U.S.C. §§1201 *et seq.*

Brolin, D. (1997). *Life-Centered Career Education: A competency-based approach* (5th ed.). Arlington, VA: Council for Exceptional Children.

Education for All Handicapped Children Act of 1975, PL 94-142, 20 U.S.C. §§1400 *et seq.*

Halpern, A., Herr, C., Wolf, N., Doren, B., Johnson, M., & Lawson, J. (1997). *The Next S.T.E.P. (Student Transition and Educational Planning) Curriculum.* Austin, TX: PRO-ED.

Wehmeyer, M.L. (1992). Self-determination and the education of students with mental retardation. *Education and Training in Mental Retardation and Developmental Disabilities, 27,* 302–314.

Acknowledgments

This book was possible because of the work of very dedicated teachers of students with disabilities who have embraced the concept of student-directed individualized education programs (IEPs) and implemented them in schools all around the country. We learned so much by talking with them about what works and how they adapted, modified, and "tweaked" the standard approaches so that more students could find their voice throughout the educational planning process. In fact, when we asked teachers to participate in a series of focus group interviews to help guide the development of this book, they not only agreed to the interviews, but they encouraged us to hold more of them so that they could have a forum for sharing with each other (and with us).

We want to thank Dr. Christina Bartholomew, Mr. LaRon Scott, and Mrs. DiAnne Davidsen for helping us organize, implement, and summarize the data from these meetings. We also want to thank the teachers who participated in these focus groups: Kimberly Boyd, Carol Giles, Mary Anne Huband, Jennifer Hampton, Dan Irwin, Paula Penick, and Jennifer Warner. Many of these teachers are former students of the authors, and we are thrilled that they have implemented much of what they learned in their classes and now serve as models for their former university professors.

We also want to thank the contributing authors, who were willing to share their expertise with the field by contributing to the writing of one or more chapters of this book. We know that this earns you a line on your curriculum vitae, but the other "rewards" for writing or co-writing a book chapter are much less tangible. We recognize that and therefore are very appreciative of the efforts of our contributing authors, who worked on initial drafts, made revisions, and looked for examples of "what works" to share with the field. Thanks to Beth Bader, Christy Bartholomew, Renee Bullano, Kimberly Boyd, Ann Deschamps, Mary Fisher, Elizabeth Evans Getzel, Mary Held, Dawn Hendricks, Sharon Jones, Shannon McMannus, Barbara Purvis, Patricia Rogan, Sterling Saddler, Carol Schall, Fran Smith, Ron Tamura, Pamela Targett, Marsha Tennant, Judy Terpstra, Kathe Wittig, and Yaoying Xu. You all helped so much…but a special thanks goes to Barb and LaRon, who helped at the 11th hour to create forms and examples when we needed them. You are the best!

We also want to acknowledge the work of others in the field who are the trailblazers in efforts to involve students with disabilities in educational planning, assessment, and implementation. These leaders in the field of transition and educational planning include Dr. Sharon Field, Dr. Moira Konrad, Dr. James Martin, Ms. Marcia McGahee, Dr. Ann Nevin, Dr. David Test, and Dr. Michael Wehmeyer. Your collective efforts served as the foundation for this book, and we wanted to acknowledge your contributions to the field and to this important work. You inspired and guided our work on this project.

Lastly, we want to acknowledge the support of the Brookes Publishing Co. team who helped pull this work together despite competing priorities, shortened (or extended) timelines, and the inevitable challenges of pulling together a cohesive product that includes the work of so many different authors and contributors. Thanks to Rebecca Lazo, Steve Plocher, Janet Wehner, and the other members of the Brookes production staff who worked so hard to make this book a reality. We are pleased with the final product and hope the readers are as well.

To our families, who keep us grounded;
our colleagues, who keep us reaching for the stars;
and individuals with disabilities and their families,
who keep us moving forward each and every day

1

....

Essentials of the Student-Directed IEP Process

Colleen A. Thoma, Sterling Saddler, Barbara Purvis, and LaRon A. Scott

Your job as a teacher of students with disabilities is not easy; you are often challenged with finding ways to incorporate new, evidence-based practices into your classroom, particularly when the students for whom you are responsible have different strengths, needs, and preferences. The students in your classroom come to you with a range of support needs: significant intellectual disabilities, limited communication skills, autism, and disruptive behavior. You might be struggling with prioritizing all that is necessary to prepare students academically while still meeting their functional, behavioral, and communication goals. How do you find a way to balance these seemingly competing priorities, particularly in developing individualized education programs (IEPs) for each of your diverse students? How can you build on the legal requirements as well as existing policies and procedures for IEP development to increase student involvement in the process?

This book provides a guide to help not only increase student involvement or direction of the process but also ensure that IEP development adheres to legal requirements and evidence-based practices while meeting the needs of students such as Dwight, Susan, Max, Alejandra, and Kathy, who are described in the following paragraphs.

Dwight is a 19-year-old man with multiple challenges. He has autism and very limited expressive communication skills. He has a laptop computer with a voice output software program that he is learning to use in the classroom to participate in instructional activities. Dwight also sometimes uses the software at home in more functional ways. His teacher identified goals for the coming year that she thought were critical in multiple domains, such as transition (employment and community living), academics (earning high school academic credits and passing statewide academic assessments), and functional skills (communication, advocacy, and financial).

Susan is a 9-year-old girl who is attending her neighborhood elementary school for the first time this year. She and her teacher are both struggling with the transition. Susan is legally blind with a moderate hearing loss and has been in a deafblind classroom at the state school for the blind and visually impaired since preschool. Adaptations, modifications, and accommodations that were routine in the previous setting are not readily available in this public school, and Susan's teacher lacks the training to put them into place. Susan's needs for the coming year include 1) learning new routines and becoming comfortable in her new environment and 2) identifying appropriate accommodations including assistive technology (AT); alternative assessments; differentiated instruction; and social skills training at school, with peers, and at home.

Max is a 14-year-old young man who qualifies for special education services to help him with overcoming challenging behavior that affects his ability to learn. He can disrupt a classroom quickly by refusing to participate in instructional activities (particularly in math or science classes), swearing at teachers and his peers, and ignoring teacher direction. Max's attendance at school is becoming increasingly unpredictable, and his mother has been unable to meet with the teacher due to her work schedule. Max has multiple needs for the coming year; he is at risk for dropping out of school and/or entering the juvenile justice system. His IEP team must find ways to identify the function of his behavior and then supports such as positive behavior supports, stress management, and possibly medical intervention to help him focus and attend to academic instruction.

Alejandra is a 12-year-old girl with autism who has limited communication skills. Her goals focus primarily on functional, self-help skills such as learning to take her medication safely on a schedule, cooking simple meals using a microwave oven, and using money to make purchases. Alejandra has had limited experiences in the community and has few friends. She comes from a family who identifies themselves as Hispanic, and her parents speak Spanish as their primary language. Alejandra has been able to respond to simple instructions presented to her in either language, but she needs her IEP team to help her increase her expressive communication skills in English to help her participate more fully in school and her broader community.

Kathy is a 17-year-old young woman with an intellectual/developmental disability that affects her educational and functional abilities. She requires an intermittent level of support in educational, home, and community settings. She attends her neighborhood high school and is currently in the 11th grade. Kathy has strong social and verbal skills that contrast with cognitive, reasoning, and attention support needs. She has strong skills in expressive language, listening comprehension, and conceptual thinking. Her IEP goals must address her inclusion in general education classes as well as strategies to address functional skills she will need to make a successful transition to adult life.

Does using a student-directed IEP process offer any benefit for these students? Of the five students introduced previously, Kathy most resembles students for whom a student-directed IEP process has become a reality. She has strong communication skills, expresses an interest in being an advocate for herself, and has a teacher who understands the link between increased student motivation, goal attainment, and academic achievement that occurs when students are actively involved in setting their own goals. But what about the other four students? Are there ways to involve students who are not yet ready to lead the entire process themselves (and may never do so)? And, if so, how can teachers make it real for students who need supports to understand the process and communicate their preferences?

This book provides a step-by-step guide that organizes your efforts in promoting student-directed IEP processes, regardless of the level of support students need to make it a reality. It helps provide direction for you, whether you are working with students who can learn to do it all themselves (from preparing for the meeting, to running the meeting themselves, to managing the implementation process), with students who need more support, or with students who will always need (and want) the help and support of others. This book considers *student direction of the IEP process* as an evolving, fluid continuum in which students increase their self-determination skills by participating to the degree to which they are capable in developing their IEPs. When done well, student direction can also improve the process when students need additional instruction, support, and/or motivation to take control of the process, while still assuring that all legal requirements for IEP development are met. For example, although Kathy is able to and interested in leading the entire process, Dwight needs some technological supports to communicate his long-range goals for the future and his decisions about how he will reach them, and Alejandra needs to learn how to solve problems and needs support to explore options and possibilities.

This chapter introduces you to the concept of a continuum of a student-led IEP process by making a clear connection between it and the legal requirements for quality IEP development. Subsequent chapters provide examples, tips, and strategies for applying the continuum to the various critical components of the IEP process (from planning and assessing through the meeting itself, to implementing the goals and evaluating student progress). Throughout this book, you will follow the experiences of one student, Kathy; her teacher, Mr. Scott; and her mother, who together implemented a student-directed IEP process. Kathy's experiences will demonstrate how a student-directed IEP process can work for a student who has the ability and support to fully participate in leading the way. In addition, each chapter highlights first steps, strategies, and approaches that you can use with students such as Max, Dwight, Alejandra, and Susan, who each need different levels of support from teachers, parents, and other participants in the process.

IEP 101: The Basics of the Special Education Planning Process

Students with disabilities are entitled to an individualized, free appropriate public education according to the Education for All Handicapped Children Act of 1975 (PL 94-142). The cornerstone of this specialized education is the IEP, developed as a method for collaborative educational planning based on student strengths and needs. It is important to remember that the IEP is a program and, thus, is not a piece of paperwork but rather the set of content, instruction methods, assessment, and long-term planning that is used with an individual student. The requirements for IEPs have evolved as the law has been reauthorized throughout the years, but the underlying principles of collaborative planning, choosing educational goals that address students' needs and build on their strengths, and evaluating student progress annually have remained critical components of IEP development. You are probably aware of your own school district's policy and procedures for IEP development, but you need to know more in order to make changes in the process to support student direction. You will need to know that the law does not require a specific form to complete; instead, the Individuals with Disabilities Education Improvement Act (IDEA) of 2004 (PL 108-446), like most federal policy, is written to provide grey areas so that states, local school districts, schools, and even individual teachers can tailor the process to meet the needs of students and respond to the changes in practice developed through ongoing research in the field. Table 1.1 outlines some of the major components of IEP development as mandated by the most current federal education policy (IDEA 2004).

This book is divided into sections that correspond to the three components of IEP development (premeeting preparation, the meeting itself, and implementing and

Table 1.1. Individualized education program (IEP) regulations

Requirement and section	Details
Definition of *individualized education program* (§300.320)	a) General. As used in this part, the term individualized education program or IEP means a written statement for each child with a disability that is developed, reviewed, and revised in a meeting in accordance with §330.320 through §300.324, and that must include—
	(1) A statement of the child's present levels of academic achievement and functional performance, including—
	(a) How the child's disability affects the child's involvement and progress in the general education curriculum.
	(2) (i) A statement of measurable annual goals, including academic and functional goals designed to—
	(A) Meet the child's needs that result from the child's disability to enable the child to be involved in and make progress in the general education curriculum; and
	(B) Meet each of the child's other educational needs that result from the child's disability;
	(ii) For children with disabilities who take alternative assessments aligned to alternative achievement standards, a description of benchmarks or short-term objectives;
	(3) A description of—
	(i) How the child's progress toward meeting the annual goals described in paragraph (3) of this section will be measured; and
	(ii) When periodic reports on the progress the child is making toward meeting the annual goals (such as through the use of quarterly or other periodic reports, concurrent with the issuance of report cards) will be provided;
	(4) A statement of the special education and related services and supplementary aids and services, based on peer-reviewed research to the extent practicable, to be provided to the child, or on behalf of the child, and a statement of the program modifications or supports for school personnel that will be provided to enable the child—
	(i) To advance appropriately toward attaining the annual goals;
	(ii) To be involved in and make progress in the general education curriculum in accordance with paragraph (a)(1) of this section, and to participate in extracurricular and other nonacademic activities; and
	(iii) To be educated and participate with other children with disabilities and nondisabled children in the activities described in this section.
	(5) An explanation of the extent, if any, to which the child will not participate with nondisabled children in the regular class and in the activities described in paragraph (a)(4) of this section.
	(6) (i) A statement of any individual appropriate accommodations that are necessary to measure the academic achievement and functional performance of the child on State and districtwide assessments consistent with section 612(a)(16) of the Act; and
	(ii) If the IEP Team determines that the child must take an alternative assessment instead of a particular regular State or districtwide assessment of student achievement, a statement of why—
	(A) The child cannot participate in the regular assessment; and
	(B) The particular alternative assessment selected is appropriate for the child.

Requirement and section	Details
	(7) The projected date for the beginning of the services and modifications described in paragraph (a)(4) of this section, and the anticipated frequency, location, and duration of those services and modifications.
	(b) Transition services. Beginning not later than the first IEP to be in effect when the child turns 16, or younger if determined appropriate by the IEP Team, and updated annually, thereafter, the IEP must include—
	(1) Appropriate measurable postsecondary goals based upon age appropriate transition assessments related to training, education, employment, and where appropriate, independent living skills; and
	(2) The transition services (including courses of study) needed to assist the child in reaching those goals.
	(c) Transfer of rights at age of majority. Beginning not later than one year before the child reaches the age of majority under state law, the IEP must include a statement that the child has been informed of the child's rights under Part B of the Act, if any, that will transfer to the child on reaching the age of majority under §300.520.
IEP team (§300.321). *IEP team* means a group of individuals who are responsible for developing, reviewing, or revising an IEP for a child with a disability.	(a) The public agency must ensure that the IEP team for each child with a disability includes:
	1. The parents of the child;
	2. Not less than one regular education teacher of the child (if the child is or will participate in the regular education environment);
	3. Not less than one special education teacher of the child;
	4. A representative of the public agency who
	i. is qualified to provide, or supervise the provision of, specially designed instruction to meet the unique needs of children with disabilities;
	ii. is knowledgeable about the general education curriculum; and
	iii. is knowledgeable about the availability of resources of the public agency;
	5. An individual who can interpret the instructional implications of evaluation results, who may be a member of the team described in paragraphs (a)(2) through (a)(6) of this section;
	6. At the discretion of the parent or the agency, other individuals who have knowledge or special expertise regarding the child, including related services personnel as appropriate; and
	7. Whenever appropriate, the child with a disability.
IEP team *transition services participants* (§300.321)	(b) Transition services participants.
	(1) In accordance with paragraph (a)(7) of this section, the public agency must invite a child with a disability to attend the child's IEP Team meeting if a purpose of the meeting will be the consideration of the postsecondary goals for the child and the transition services needed to assist the child in reaching those goals under §300.320(b).
	(2) If the child does not attend the IEP Team meeting, the public agency must take other steps to ensure that the child's preferences and interests are considered.

(continued)

Table 1.1. *(continued)*

Requirement and section	Details
	(3) To the extent appropriate, with the consent of the parents or a child who has reached the age of majority, in implementing the requirements of paragraph (b)(1) of this section, the public agency must invite a representative of any participating agency that is likely to be responsible for providing or paying for transition services.
Development, review, and revision of IEP (§300.324)	(a) Development of IEP. (1) General. In developing each child's IEP, the IEP Team must consider— (i) The strengths of the child; (ii) The concerns of the parents for enhancing the education of their child; (iii) The results of the initial or most recent evaluation of the child; and (iv) The academic, developmental, and functional need of the child.

Source: IDEA 2004 (PL 108-446).

evaluating IEP goals; see Figure 1.1). Each section is divided into chapters that describe the major activities that are part of each component of quality IEP development, assuring that using a student-led approach not only supports the involvement of students in their own educational assessment, planning, and implementation processes, but also meets legal and evidence-based standards.

The IEP Process Is More Than an Annual Meeting

A good student-directed IEP approach needs to begin with a good IEP process, which means that it is critical to understand the legal requirements for IEP development as well

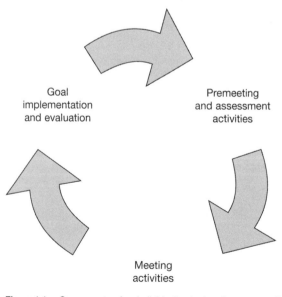

Goal implementation and evaluation

Premeeting and assessment activities

Meeting activities

Figure 1.1.   Components of an individualized education program (IEP) process.

as the local, state, and national recommendations designed to enhance the process. This assures that collaboration and the design of an annual plan for a student starts with his or her educational and functional needs determined by a comprehensive assessment of his or her present level of performance, builds on student strengths and preferences, and uses the best of instructional design.

Many teachers and school personnel erroneously think of the IEP process, including a student-directed process, as consisting of the activities that take place during the hour (or so) meeting. A successful IEP, however, can include three distinct components (premeeting preparation, the meeting itself, and the postmeeting implementation and evaluation; see Figure 1.1), each of which should be viewed as opportunities for students to direct and/or lead the process and each of which must be considered essential for educational decision making. These components build on each other, and their dividing lines are fluid. For example, the process of implementing current IEP goals and collecting data on student progress is also a part of the premeeting assessment for the next year. It is, and should be, difficult to separate one year's implementation and evaluation from the next year's premeeting preparation. Of course, when viewing an IEP process as comprehensive of all pre- and postmeeting activities, it is easier to identify multiple ways to involve students in the process and find ways throughout the year to enhance their self-determination as well. Students may make significant contributions to developing the IEP through a variety of means. They may help draft their IEP, present information about themselves at the IEP meeting, and even lead the meeting. At the very least, in a student-directed IEP, they understand the purposes of the IEP and are involved in the process through more basic activities such as sharing examples of their work from the previous year or sharing their preferences, interests, strengths, or needs.

Too often, a focus on the legal requirements of completing the paperwork involved in IEP development can overshadow the *process* of educational planning as well as the logistics and evaluation of instructional delivery. The danger in trying to implement a student-directed IEP process is that teachers can underestimate the amount of time it takes to really prepare students for assuming a role or be unprepared to implement the goals that are agreed to during the meeting. It is cruel to provide an educational planning meeting process in which students are asked for their preferences and interests for educational goals or long-range plans but these suggestions are not implemented. Remember that part of acquiring self-determination skills includes learning the realities of one's situation, not having everything that one desires. You need to be realistic about adequately preparing students to be part of the team, and team members need to understand how their roles might need to change to involve the student in the goal-setting process. The following reflects what can happen when a teacher tries to involve a student without adequate preparation of the team.

Teacher:	So, Dwight, what do you want to tell us as we start your IEP meeting?
Dwight:	Is this the time to talk about graduation?
Teacher (to team members):	Oh, yes. Dwight wants to talk about graduating at the end of this year at 19 years old.
Teacher (to Dwight):	We'll get to that at the end of the meeting. Right now we're going to talk about your long-term goals.

The meeting goes on to discuss Dwight's long-range goals and plans for the next 2 or 3 years to get him there. The discussion was person centered, discussing the goals that Dwight had for his life, but was not student directed or student led. Dwight agreed with the goals but did not understand the effect on his previously stated goal: graduation.

Teacher (to Dwight): Okay, do you have anything else that you would like to add?

Dwight: Oh, yeah. I want to graduate this year.

Teacher: But Dwight, we just made all the plans to help you do what you want to do. Those goals have you staying in school 2 more years. So, graduation this year won't work. We can talk about it again next year.

This example illustrates the danger of trying to increase student participation in the IEP process without a vision of the student's involvement throughout the entire process and without an understanding of the process for the student or the other participants in the meeting. It does not work to just have students attend their meetings and expect that they will understand what is happening or the effect that their choices (or lack thereof) might have on their long-range plans. Students need concrete direction on how to participate, and the focus of the adult participants should be on increasing students' abilities to direct the process during all three components of educational planning, implementation, and evaluation.

Think of how this process could have gone differently with clear expectations in place.

Teacher: So, Dwight, you prepared some information to share with your team during this IEP meeting.

Dwight: Yes, and I want to talk about my goal to graduate at the end of this year.

Teacher (to team members): Oh, yes. Dwight met with his guidance counselor to look at the requirements for graduation and whether he has enough credits to meet that goal.

Teacher (to Dwight): Dwight, do you want to share that checklist with everyone? And then do you want to explain it to us? Then we can talk about it in relation to your long-range goals.

Dwight explained the graduation checklist, with his teacher helping to explain some of the technical aspects of meeting graduation requirements. The meeting then focused on Dwight's long-range goals and what he would need to do to not only meet graduation requirements but also his goals for his adult life. The discussion was student directed in that it not only focused on Dwight's goals (or the team members' understanding of Dwight's goals), but it also included Dwight in the discussion and allowed him to set the parameters of the discussion. Although the team could come up with a plan for the year that would provide Dwight with an opportunity to graduate, it would not also provide him with the opportunity to include goals related to work. Dwight and his team decided that it was better to develop a plan that would have him graduate 1 year later, giving him a better opportunity to meet both objectives.

What Is a Student-Directed IEP Process?

Many authors use the terms *student directed* and *student led* interchangeably. In this book, a *student-directed IEP process* refers to a range of methods, strategies, and approaches that are designed to provide support to students with disabilities in participating in the IEP process to the maximum extent possible. A *student-led IEP process* in this book refers to the most independent example of a student-directed process in which the student takes an active role in organizing, running, implementing, and evaluating his or her progress in the process of annual educational planning and implementation. Student direction can focus on one part of the IEP process or on multiple steps.

It is easier to identify opportunities for student direction or involvement, as well as student leadership, when an IEP is viewed as an annual process and not just a meeting. Opportunities include 1) describing strengths, needs, legal rights, and present level of performance; 2) evaluating progress, weighing alternative goals, and engaging in goal-setting and goal-attainment activities; 3) preparing for a formal presentation and advocating for oneself in formal settings; 4) communicating preferences and interests; 5) accepting responsibility for areas where improvement is needed; 6) participating in discussions regarding postschool plans and needs; and 7) determining accommodation needs and securing appropriate accommodations (Konrad & Test, 2004).

Although some teachers are more comfortable using commercial and web-based materials that are designed to help implement a student-directed IEP approach, successful implementation does not rely on using these materials. You can start with the process you currently use and modify one or more of the steps to enhance student direction and involvement. Creative teachers may find this approach works best because it begins with their school, district, state, and national policies and procedures. As another option, teachers who are confident in their understanding of IEP policies and procedures can start with a generic student-directed IEP process and add or adapt it to assure that they meet all requirements. This guide is designed primarily for those teachers who wish to start with their current IEP process and adapt it to provide opportunities for student direction and/or involvement, but it will also offer suggestions for teachers who have already taken steps to establish student-directed IEP processes. The appendix at the end of this book includes a list of existing student-directed IEP resources and curricula for those who prefer to start with that kind of template.

Why Implement a Student-Directed IEP Process?

Although the special education field has been moving toward implementing evidence-based practices, it is important to note that there is little research or evidence that developing an IEP is an effective approach to improving the education provided to students with disabilities (see Konrad & Test [2004] for a review of the literature related to IEP effectiveness). Nevertheless, it is required under current federal and state laws pertaining to the education of students with disabilities and reflects the underlying principle of special education that it should meet students' unique educational, functional, and emotional needs that affect their ability to learn. The IEP process brings together educational experts to develop a plan that addresses annual goals, assessment needs, and accommodations and modifications, as well as other services needed by a student to gain access to and progress in the general education curriculum. In addition, the parents of students with disabilities must be invited to be part of this planning process, and, when appropriate, the student must also be part of the process.

Research on IEP development describes challenges in implementing the process, particularly in regard to collaboration and student involvement. Consider the following problems with IEP development as it is practiced:

1. IEP development typically focuses on a deficit model that fails to result in an educational plan that builds on student strengths (Vandercook, York, & Forest, 1989).

2. IEPs do not foster individually designed educational practices (Smith, 1990).

3. Teachers do not use IEPs for daily educational activities (Smith, 1990).

4. Educational personnel engage in a number of behaviors that act as deterrents to student involvement (Thoma, Rogan, & Baker, 2001).

5. Parents are often passive during IEP meetings (Smith, 1990).

These research findings are not new, yet they persist in spite of revisions to IDEA as well as recommendations for changes to the process. Some of the earlier recommendations for IEP development included person-centered planning strategies such as Personal Futures Planning (Mount & Zwernik, 1989), MAPS (Forest & Lufthaus, 1990), Group Action Planning (Turnbull & Turnbull, 1996), PATH planning (Pearpoint, O'Brien, & Forest, 1993), and Lifestyle planning (O'Brien, 1987). Vandercook et al. (1989) referred to these approaches as "vision-based" planning as they create a vision of an integrated school and community life. These approaches were created to be used with students with a range of disabilities but have been used only to support students with more significant support needs as they participate in their IEP process (Miner & Bates, 1997). Student-directed IEP strategies have been developed to help students with disabilities actively participate in, and possibly lead, their IEP development process (i.e., Halpern et al., 1997; McGahee, Mason, Wallace, & Jones, 2001). These strategies were developed in many cases as part of curricular packages to increase student self-determination and to do it within the context of planning for their transition to adult life. Although participation in an IEP meeting is insufficient to teach self-determination skills, it is an effective place to start as students learn to identify their strengths and weaknesses; communicate their long-range goals; and advocate for instructional strategies, supports, modifications, and adaptations that will help them reach their goals.

Using student-directed IEP processes has been examined by researchers in the fields of education (i.e., Niemiec & Ryan, 2009), psychology (i.e., Deci & Ryan, 2000), and special education (i.e., Martin et al., 2006). Their findings indicated that not only can these processes address the legal requirement for involving students with disabilities in developing their educational programs, but they also can do the following:

- Enhance student motivation (Deci & Ryan, 2000; Dweck, 1986; Niemiec & Ryan, 2009)

- Help students understand the IEP process (Allen, Smith, Test, Flowers, & Wood, 2001)

- Improve student academic achievement (Test et al., 2004)

- Increase the IEP team's understanding of student preferences, strengths, and challenges (Martin et al., 2006)

- Increase student self-determination in general (Test et al., 2004; Thoma, Held, & Thomas, 2004)

- Increase student and parent participation and opportunities to communicate at the IEP meeting (Martin et al., 2006)

Continuum of Student Direction in IEPs

The level of student involvement and control of the IEP meeting process can exist along a continuum. Figure 1.2 illustrates the progression from a school-directed to a student-directed IEP process. It is important to remember that the IEP meeting itself is but one piece of an entire IEP process. Much of the potential for student involvement and control presents itself in what comes before and after the actual IEP meeting. This big-picture view of an IEP provides a wealth of possibilities and opportunities for a starting point to increase student involvement, direction, and/or leadership beyond the annual one-shot meeting many people equate with an IEP and which many students would find particularly stressful.

Progress toward the type of student-directed IEP process described in this book requires evidence of movement along the continuum. Although total student direction of the entire IEP process may be unrealistic or ill advised for some students, it must nevertheless be the ideal for which you strive. Effective schools and classrooms recognize not only the students who come closest to reaching the highest standards set, but also those who show the greatest effort and improvement. Progress should be the aim of all those working to implement the practices this book describes. It is not acceptable to let yourself "off the hook" by saying a student is "too this" or "too that" to participate meaningfully. Instead, it is your task to determine where each student lies on the continuum and identify strategies to move that student ever closer to the ideal. Likewise, it is not acceptable to be content with a level of involvement that seems positive in relationship to where other students are on the continuum. The goal must always be to know where a student is and work to assure that the level of participation and student direction increases at and between each formal IEP meeting.

It is also important that you do not fall into the trap of believing that all students must start a student-directed IEP approach at Stage 1. All students should start at a stage that is right for them, meaning that they believe that performing the task is difficult, but not impossible, for them. If it is too difficult, then students may give up too quickly and lose faith that they ever could be competent participants in the process. If it is too easy, then students may become frustrated or feel that teachers and parents have little belief in their ability to be active contributors in the process. They then may choose not to participate. Either one can become a barrier to student direction of the IEP process.

Stages of the Continuum

This section provides a narrative description of the seven stages of a student-directed IEP continuum. Each stage provides an opportunity for students to be involved in their IEP

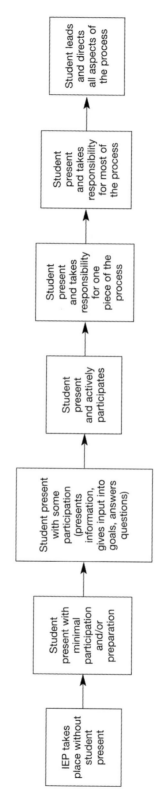

Figure 1.2. Student-directed individualized education program (IEP) continuum.

process and to learn skills to help them give voice to their preferences, interests, and educational needs. Table 1.2 describes the kinds of activities that may be occurring in each stage of the student-directed IEP continuum. As you read through this section and the table, think about where your students currently function on the continuum. What strategies do you currently use, and where do they fit on the continuum? Do you have students who could be functioning at a higher stage on the continuum? As the stages of the continuum are explained, the students introduced previously in this chapter will be used to illustrate the level of functioning necessary at that stage. It is important to bear in mind, however, that the stages are tied more to functional skills than they are to age or disability categories.

For the majority of students with disabilities, particularly those who are not in the transition years (older than age 14–16), their level of participation in the IEP process is at Stage 1 of the continuum, which is characterized by "no participation in the full range of IEP development and implementation and not being present during the IEP meeting itself." This is not because they cannot function at a higher stage of the continuum but because they have few opportunities or their teachers and parents do not expect them to be active participants in the process.

Kathy, for example, experienced Stage 1 participation in her early school years. She knew that her mother attended a meeting about her education, but she did not understand the purpose of the meeting and was not invited to attend. In premeeting preparations, Kathy's teachers assumed responsibility for identifying assessments, scheduling meetings, inviting key participants, and drafting a tentative plan. At the meeting, school officials presented the plan to the team (including Kathy's mother) and worked to refine and finalize it. Once the team developed a consensus IEP, Kathy's special education teacher assumed responsibility for sharing the plan with those who would implement the goals, collect data about her progress, and communicate that progress to her mother. Although the plan was developed specifically for Kathy, she had no opportunity to have input into its inception, development, implementation, or evaluation. A process such as this is the status quo for many schools, and you have probably experienced or organized a similar IEP process.

You can work to move out of this stage by talking with team members about student involvement, direction, and/or leadership in the process. Look for one student to start making changes or for one change that you can make for all students with whom you work. For instance, Mr. Scott started his efforts with Kathy in her junior year because she was both interested in participating in the IEP process and possessed skills such as oral communication, goal setting, advocacy, and self-assessment that would support her involvement. Another teacher chose to focus on having students learn to set one educational goal and then share that goal as part of the IEP meeting. Yet another teacher used her district's alternative assessment process to involve students in evaluating their progress on current educational goals and summarizing that in the meeting during the focus on present levels of performance.

Stage 2 of the continuum is characterized by student presence at the IEP meeting itself with little or no participation in the other components of the process. A student with even strong self-advocacy skills can find him- or herself at this stage of the continuum if not prepared for meaningful participation in the process by members of his or her

Table 1.2. Stages on the continuum of a student-directed individualized education program (IEP) process

Continuum stage	Premeeting activities	Meeting activities	Postmeeting activities
Stage 1 Student *not present* at IEP meeting *No participation* in overall IEP process	Assessments identified by school personnel with some input from parent Assessments administered, scored, and summarized by school personnel Meeting organization, scheduling, and preparation are responsibility of school personnel Focus is on compliance with district, state, and federal policies, laws, and procedures	School personnel run meeting with a focus on compliance with district, state, and federal laws, policies, and procedures There is little opportunity for the student to interact Meeting venue is not conducive to dialogue (either too many distractions or key people are not present)	School personnel assume responsibility for implementing IEP as written, collecting data on student progress, and modifying goals as necessary and agreed Critical information about IEP goals is shared between teachers but can be lost or forgotten without consistent, ongoing dialogue Summary information is shared with parents but this sharing does not include/involve students
Stage 2 Student present at IEP meeting, but with *minimal participation* *Little or no participation* in overall IEP process	Student is invited to meeting No premeeting activities take place	There is an attempt to be more student centered during the meeting, possibly by implementing a person-centered planning approach Emphasis is on school's agenda, including paperwork/compliance with regulations Student presence does not equal student participation Student may be asked a few questions about issues not critical to the process or not included in the dialogue as decisions are made	No follow-up postmeeting activities with student
Stage 3 Student present at IEP meeting, with *some participation* *Some participation* in overall IEP process	Teacher or parent may have discussed goals in advance, rehearsed, or otherwise prepared for student participation in meeting Some participation in identifying assessment goals	Student may have attended prior IEP meetings with little or no participation Student has some knowledge of what the meeting is about Questions are directed to student throughout the meeting Team members elicit student input into goals	Student may be included in collecting some self-assessment data through using simple checklists, tally sheets, and/or self-correction of homework assignments

Stage 4

Student present at IEP meeting, *participates actively*

Some participation in overall IEP process

School personnel and/or parent(s) put thought into how to structure the meeting to promote meaningful participation by student

Student has input into who to invite to the meeting

Student presents information prepared ahead of time and has input into appropriate accommodations and support for meaningful participation

Premeeting takes place

Student is involved in making decisions and presenting/using information

Necessary and appropriate accommodations and support are available for student to use during the meeting

Student asks questions as well as answers them

Supports and accommodations are designed to help student make a connection between IEP goals as developed and daily classroom activities and available accommodations, adaptations, and supports

Student collects data on progress

Stage 5

Student *actively participates* in IEP meeting

Directs *at least one piece* of the IEP meeting

Some participation in overall IEP process

Student participates in meeting preparations such as inviting participants and choosing location, day, and time

Student understands the IEP process

Student and teacher identify a component of the IEP meeting process that student can direct/lead; student rehearses and prepares for that part of the meeting

Appropriate accommodations, adaptations, and supports are identified by teacher and/or parent to help student participate in IEP meeting

Student directs one part of the IEP process with appropriate accommodations, adaptations, and supports in place

Student is asked questions throughout meeting and attempts are made to incorporate those answers into IEP when possible or appropriate

Attempts are made to direct information to student as well as parent throughout meeting

Information is shared in ways that encourage collaboration and dialogue with student

Supports and accommodations are designed to help student make a connection between IEP goals as developed and daily classroom activities and available accommodations, adaptations, and supports

Student collects data on progress, and teacher or school personnel helps student understand the significance of the data

(continued)

Table 1.2. *(continued)*

Continuum stage	Premeeting activities	Meeting activities	Postmeeting activities
Stage 6 Student *actively participates* in IEP meeting Directs *major portion* of the IEP meeting *Active participation* in overall IEP process	Student participates in meeting preparations such as inviting participants and choosing location, day, and time Student works with his or her teacher and IEP team to identify ways to enhance involvement in the meeting Appropriate adaptations and accommodations are identified and prepared for the meeting Student rehearses or otherwise prepares for the meeting Student collects assessment information and finds ways to share the results with team members	Student is able to direct and participate actively in most parts of the meeting Appropriate accommodations, adaptations, and/or supports are available to help student participate to greatest degree possible Student participates somewhat in the dialogue during which decisions are made, although some preferences are not included in the final IEP Most team members share information in a positive way and interact directly with student during the majority of the meeting	Student is involved in the day-to-day implementation of IEP goals through collecting data on progress and advocating for the use of approved adaptations, accommodations, and/or supports Student helps with identifying steps when IEP goals and objectives are not being met or next steps when IEP goals are met quicker than anticipated
Stage 7 Student *actively participates* in IEP meeting Directs *entire* IEP meeting Plays *major role* in direction of the overall IEP process	Student, with appropriate adaptations, accommodations, and/or supports, is able to actively participate in and/or leads the critical premeeting preparations for the IEP	Student, with appropriate adaptations, accommodations, and/or supports, is able to direct the IEP meeting	Student, with appropriate adaptations, accommodations, and/or supports, is able to track his or her progress on IEP goals and objectives, make decisions about possible revisions to IEP goals, and communicate progress with teachers, parents, and/or other team members

IEP team. When students attend the meeting but do not understand its purpose or their roles, rights, and responsibilities in the meeting, their presence may not contribute to achieving the overall purpose of the IEP meeting. Students might voice preferences or goals that are not in line with the general education curriculum and/or their educational, functional, or transition needs. Students also might feel uncomfortable or unprepared to share goals that are in disagreement with adult members of the team, especially adults who play significant roles in their lives or who have strongly held ideas that differ from the students' ideas.

Alejandra, who is 12 years old and diagnosed with autism, will be an example used to illustrate strategies and tips for working with students in Stages 2 and 3 of the continuum. Her limited expressive language ability and difficulty in focusing on the process at hand for an extended period of time makes it impossible for Alejandra to direct her IEP throughout all three components of the process. Yet, there are certainly parts of the process in which she can participate, direct, and/or lead. For example, during the premeeting stage, a teacher could work with her on assessing different communication methods that she could potentially use to help with her academic work. She could indicate her preference by pointing or nodding her head, and her teacher could bring that information to the team meeting. Alejandra could choose samples of her work to share with team members during the section that outlines her present levels of performance. She could also choose a friend to attend the meeting with her to help her feel more comfortable. These are small ways to help students understand the reason for the meeting and feel more comfortable to assume a bigger role in the future.

You can help the student make the most of his or her presence at the meeting by providing an outline of the major portions of the IEP meeting and making sure the student knows what to expect during each section. A written or picture-based outline that students can check off can help them stay focused. Other considerations can help the student feel more comfortable in the meeting, including having the student choose who will sit next to him or her, being sure that everyone introduces themselves to the student, helping the student prepare for the meeting by practicing what he or she might be asked to share, and providing other accommodations for the student to help facilitate his or her participation in the meeting itself. For example, a picture schedule can help the student understand and follow the various parts of the meeting or a PowerPoint slideshow can be used to describe the student's long-range plans (for transition IEP meetings) or to communicate his or her present levels of performance. Help the student play the role of host (greeting people as they arrive, showing them to their seats, starting or ending the meeting); share examples of his or her academic accomplishments from the past year; highlight his or her strengths, needs, and/or preferences as identified from premeeting assessments; and choose when, where, or how goals will be infused throughout the school day. Person-centered planning meeting processes (e.g., MAPS, PATH) can support your efforts to involve students in a meeting process that is welcoming.

The students' level of participation reaches Stage 3 when students are involved in more than just the meeting itself. Stage 3 activities can include attendance in the meeting itself in addition to one or more pre- or postmeeting activities. For instance, Alejandra chose participants, sent invitations to the IEP meeting, and collected examples of her work over the past year to demonstrate her progress in working on IEP goals. Recommendations for supporting student involvement in the meeting itself should be supplemented by recommendations that support student involvement in one or more premeeting activities (e.g., assessment, meeting preparation, preparing a section of the IEP draft document including identifying one or more goals) as well as one or more postmeeting implementation and evaluation activities (e.g., choose the specific class or classes in which it is appropriate to implement a specific IEP goal, participate in self-assessment of IEP goal implementation).

Students can be encouraged to increase their involvement in the components of the premeeting activities, including assessments, as well as the postmeeting implementation of IEP goals and evaluation of their progress to lead into identifying goals they would like to include in the next year's IEP meeting. A systematic approach to increasing students' involvement in the major components of the IEP process will lead the student into Stages 4, 5, and 6 of the student-directed IEP process.

In Stage 4 of the student-directed IEP process, students are more actively engaged in the IEP meeting itself, taking greater responsibility for such key components of the agenda as introducing participants, identifying the purpose of the meeting, summarizing assessment and present levels of performance information, and sharing components of the draft IEP. In addition, they are somewhat involved in some of the pre- and/or postmeeting steps of the process. For example, Susan and her teacher worked together to develop an invitation to the meeting that provided an overview of the goals on which she had been working over the past year and to identify people that Susan wanted to invite in addition to those who were legally required to attend. A braille agenda was created to help Susan follow along during the meeting and know when it was time for her to share her progress on the previous year's IEP goals. Last, a braille printer was set up so that Susan had a record of the goals she and the team agreed to include in the IEP for the coming year. To move from Stage 4 to Stage 5, teachers can help students build on their current level of participation to increase the level of their direction of the process.

Stage 5 of the student-directed IEP continuum is characterized by a student's involvement, at least minimally, throughout the entire three components of their IEP process. In addition, the student directs or leads at least one of the primary steps of the meeting. Students with good communication skills who learn best through an active, hands-on approach often start at this level. For instance, Dwight used a computer with voice output to share his long-range transition goals and his preferences, interests, strengths, and needs. He practiced giving other team members an opportunity to have input as well and led the team in a discussion of the annual goals that could help him achieve his long-range goals. His teacher recorded the goals generated by the group and developed a way that Dwight could record his progress on those goals through the year.

Team members can help students progress to the next level by identifying appropriate supports and, in particular, technologies that can help. Many students who direct their IEP process use PowerPoint slides to help them organize the meeting, assuring that key points are addressed. Adding pictures or music and using the templates that are available with the program help integrate the student's personality in the presentation. Although using a presentation software program does not ensure that the IEP process is student directed, many teachers and students find it helpful to facilitate student direction of the process. Kathy's role in the IEP process was facilitated through presentation software, and some of her slides are included elsewhere in this book to help you use this tool. The tips and strategies at the end of each chapter will include directions for using technology to enhance student participation and direction in the various components of IEP development and implementation.

In Stage 6 of a student-directed IEP process, students are actively directing the meeting itself and are involved in all components of the complete IEP process. Students are not completely leading the entire process, but their involvement provides direction to the IEP team members who are working through the process. For example, in the premeeting process, Max helped identify a component of the assessment process, chose whom to invite to be members of the IEP team, drafted goals to bring to the IEP meeting, organized information onto PowerPoint slides, and practiced in preparation for the meeting itself. After the meeting, he shared a list of IEP goals with teachers unable to attend the meeting, followed through on IEP goals, collected data to document performance, and worked with his special education teacher to organize the quarterly progress reports of progress on IEP goals. Additional steps of the process were added gradually to continue to increase Max's participation in and leadership of the entire IEP process.

Stage 7 of the student-directed IEP process is the ultimate goal of student participation in educational program development, implementation, and evaluation. Not all students, however, will reach this level. Very few people want to do all things independently; the goal at Stage 7 is to still facilitate the degree of interdependence that a student wants for his or her life (Condeluci, 1991). Students do value the input of adults (parents, teachers, and others who serve a mentorship role), but they do not want someone to take complete control over their lives. This is particularly true for adolescents who are developmentally asserting their roles as adults in the world; it is no less true for elementary-age students who want to assert some control over their daily lives.

 # Listening to the Experts

Throughout this book, you will learn about one example of a student-directed IEP process. Kathy is one student with a disability who is able to successfully participate in Stage 6 or 7 of the continuum: She has sufficient communication skills, self-advocacy skills, and the support of her mother and teacher to learn to lead the IEP process throughout the premeeting assessment and preparation, meeting, and postmeeting implementation processes. In each chapter, examples of how the student-directed IEP approach was used for Kathy will be included in detail, followed by her thoughts about her involvement in the process. The perspectives of her mother and teacher will also be included to highlight their role in supporting Kathy at specific tasks along the way. Finally, strategies that can address the needs of students at different stages of the continuum will also be highlighted.

About Kathy

Kathy is 17 years old and in her junior year at her neighborhood high school. Her interests are common for most young women her age. Her favorite leisure activities and interests include music, dancing, and reading. She enjoys listening to the same musicians as her peers. She craves foods that most teenagers prefer, including pizza, strawberries, milkshakes, ice cream, and an occasional soft pretzel. Kathy enjoys spending time "chilling" with her friends, traveling, and talking on the telephone. She does not enjoy cleaning her room (what teenager does?), but she does it because her mother holds her responsible for contributing to the family chores. Like many teenagers, she increasingly desires autonomy. Though she lacks self-advocacy skills that may come naturally to her peers without disabilities, she has expressed interest in taking a more active role in her education and future planning. In all, Kathy really is your average everyday fun-loving teenager. Yet, Kathy has more challenges to face in preparing for her life after high school than students without disabilities.

Although the majority of Kathy's education will focus on meeting the standards of the general education curriculum, she has an IEP, which also needs to include other annual goals identified based on her educational, functional, and transitional needs as well as the supports, services, accommodations, and AT she will need to gain access to and progress in her education program. Her strengths are reading, expressing herself verbally, paying attention to detail, and conducting vocational tasks. Her weaknesses are writing, generalizing skills to new settings, and doing mathematics. For example, although it is clear in class that Kathy has the math skills to correctly make change, she will forget to wait for change when making a purchase at a local store. She is enrolled in the following courses: cooperative work experience, keyboarding, history, English, and math. In addition, Kathy receives occupational therapy services targeted to improve her penmanship and other fine motor skills. Currently, her IEP goals include improving her math skills, transition assessment goals to help her set goals for her future, and self-advocacy training. Although Kathy has good work skills, she needs to increase her performance in the area of independent living, including laundry, grocery, and personal safety skills. These goals are also part of her IEP.

Kathy and her IEP team have discussed her experience in self-advocacy and leadership and agree that she can and should improve her skills in these areas. Although every student can improve in this area, Kathy's desire to improve made her an ideal candidate for a student-directed IEP process and a great example to share throughout this book. No two students are the same; neither will their experiences or perspectives of the process be exactly alike. Teachers learn best from others, however, through sharing their perspectives and experiences. In addition to Kathy, her teacher, Mr. Scott, will be contributing to each chapter as well.

Teacher's Perspective

I first learned about the student-directed IEP process in my training at the university. I remember reading an article that described its role as the cornerstone of an advocacy program for students with disabilities. What struck me the most about this article was its description of the lifelong skills (self-determination, advocacy, leadership) that students can acquire by participating in the student-directed process—skills that can help them in their daily lives. Yet, there were not many schools implementing this initiative. I knew that this process was one that I wanted to use to guide students in my classroom.

The school district in which I work is very supportive of trying new, evidence-based practices. In fact, the student-directed IEP process was not an entirely new concept for the district, but their current implementation of the approach for high school students during transition planning was not as comprehensive as I wanted it to be. It did become an important part of the district's overall efforts designed to improve students' level of participation in the IEP meeting process. I remember sitting in staff training about improving the IEP process as special education colleagues pushed for the student voice to be included in the IEP process. That support assured me that my efforts would be acceptable to both my colleagues and my supervisors. I knew I could move forward with plans to initiate student direction of the IEP process with the high school students on my caseload.

The transformation from the traditional IEP process to a more student-directed process was not as difficult as I expected. The school district had a process in place that was already in compliance with the legal requirements for IEP development, so a majority of my efforts to make this change centered on convincing my students, their families, and other IEP meeting participants that student-directed IEPs were the way to go. One of the first decisions I made was choosing the first student to implement this new approach. Starting with a student who would have a high likelihood of success would give me confidence to draw on later if the process was more challenging to implement as well as provide a role model for other students (McGahee et al., 2001). With that information in mind, I knew just the student for my first student-directed IEP—Kathy.

I felt that Kathy would be a great candidate for beginning the process. I knew we already had a great rapport; that is, she trusted me and would be more likely to transfer that trust to finding her voice in a student-directed IEP process. I also knew that with a little guidance she had the skills to be more involved in her own IEP process. Kathy happens to be a bright, intelligent, open-minded, and extremely motivated student. At the time, she was going into her junior year of high school.

Student's Perspective

In an interview about implementing the student-led IEP process, Kathy articulated that she "always wanted to participate more in my meetings and find out what all of those people were talking about." She went on to explain that she knows what she wants to do in life and would like to tell others her likes or dislikes, and that is something that can happen if she participates in these meetings. Kathy's excitement for collaborating on the student-led approach was seen as soon as she was asked about participating. This excitement would continue as she worked with her teacher and IEP participants on making the process one that finally centered on her.

Conclusion

You learned in this chapter that an effective IEP process is more than just a 1-hour meeting. It consists of premeeting assessments, planning, and preparing; the meeting itself; and implementing and evaluating annual IEP goals. Student involvement in educational planning can focus on one or more of these parts of the process. You were introduced to the concept of student direction of the process as a way to begin to conceptualize a continuum of student involvement from just being present to assuming leadership for each and every part of the process. Several student examples were also provided to illustrate this concept. Subsequent chapters will include the examples and will also add tips and strategies that you can use to tailor the information to your specific situation and the strengths and needs of the students with whom you work. Are you ready to get started?

References

Allen, S.K., Smith, A.C., Test, D.W., Flowers, C., & Wood, W.M. (2001). The effects of self-directed IEP on student participation in IEP meetings. *Career Development for Exceptional Individuals, 24,* 107–120.

Conduluci, A. (1991). *Interdependence: The route to community.* DelRay Beach, FL: St. Lucie Press.

Deci, E.L., & Ryan, R.M. (2000). The "what" and "why" of goal pursuits: Human needs and the self-determination of behavior. *Psychological Inquiry, 11*(4), 227–268.

Dweck, C.S. (1986). Motivational processes affecting learning. *American Psychologist, 41,* 85–101.

Education for All Handicapped Children Act of 1975, PL 94-142, 20 U.S.C. §§ 1400 *et seq.*

Forest, M., & Lufthaus, E. (1990). Everyone belongs with the MAPS action planning system. *Teaching Exceptional Children, 22*(2), 32–35.

Halpern, A., Herr, C., Wolf, N., Doren, B., Johnson, M., & Lawson, J. (1997). *The Next S.T.E.P. (Student Transition and Educational Planning) Curriculum.* Austin, TX: PRO-ED.

Individuals with Disabilities Education Improvement Act (IDEA) of 2004, PL 108-446, 20 U.S.C. §§ 1400 *et seq.*

Konrad, M., & Test, D.W. (2004). Teaching middle-school students with disabilities to use an IEP template. *Career Development for Exceptional Individuals, 27,* 101–124.

Martin, J.E., Van Dycke, J.L., Greene, B.A., Gardner, J.E., Christensen, W.R., Woods, I.L., et al. (2006). Direct observation of teacher-directed IEP meetings: Establishing the need for student IEP meeting instruction. *Exceptional Children, 72,* 187–200.

McGahee, M., Mason, C., Wallace, T., & Jones, B. (2001). *Student-led IEPs: A guide for student involvement.* Arlington, VA: Council for Exceptional Children.

Miner, C.A., & Bates, P.E. (1997). The effect of person centered planning activities on the IEP/transition planning process. *Education and Training in Mental Retardation and Developmental Disabilities, 32,* 105–112.

Mount, B., & Zwernik, K. (1989). *It's never too early; it's never too late. A booklet about personal futures planning.* St. Paul: Minnesota Governor's Planning Council on Developmental Disabilities.

Niemiec, C.P., & Ryan, R.M. (2009). Autonomy, competence, and relatedness in the classroom: Applying self-determination theory to educational practice. *Theory and Research in Education, 7,* 133–144.

O'Brien, J. (1987). A guide to life-style planning: Using the activities catalog to integrate services and natural support systems. In B. Wilcox & G.T. Bellamy (Eds.), *A comprehensive guide to the activities catalog* (pp. 175–191). Baltimore: Paul H. Brookes Publishing Co.

Pearpoint, J., O'Brien, J., & Forest, M. (1993). *PATH (Planning Alternative Tomorrows with Hope): A workbook for planning positive futures.* Toronto: Inclusion Press.

Smith, S.W. (1990). Individualized education programs (IEPs) in special education: From intent to acquiescence. *Exceptional Children, 57*(1), 6–14.

Test, D.W., Mason, C., Hughes, C., Konrad, M., Neale, M., & Wood, W. (2004). Student involvement in individualized education program meetings. *Exceptional Children, 70,* 391–412.

Thoma, C.A., Held, M.F., & Thomas, K. (2004). The John Jones show: How one teacher pulled it all together to facilitate self-determined transition planning for a young man with autism. *Focus on Autism and Developmental Disabilities, 19*(3), 177–188.

Thoma, C.A., Rogan, P., & Baker, S. (2001). Self-determination in transition planning: Voices unheard. *Education and Training in Mental Retardation and Developmental Disabilities, 34,* 16–29.

Turnbull, A.P., & Turnbull, H.R. (1996). Group action planning as a strategy for providing comprehensive family support. In L.K. Koegel, R.L. Koegel, & G. Dunlap (Eds.), *Positive behavioral support: Including people with difficult behavior in the community* (pp. 99–114). Baltimore: Paul H. Brookes Publishing Co.

Vandercook, T., York, J., & Forest, M. (1989). The McGill Action Planning System (MAPS): A strategy for building the vision. *Journal of The Association for Persons with Severe Handicaps, 14,* 205–215.

2

....

Involving Families in the Process and Multicultural Considerations

Yaoying Xu, Barbara Purvis, and Judith E. Terpstra

Involving families is critical for the success of individualized education program (IEP) development, implementation, and progress monitoring, particularly in a student-directed IEP process. Chapter 1 introduced the concept of such a process and provided an overview of its key components. This chapter examines the role of school–family partnerships in the student-directed IEP process, examines evidence-based practices for working with families, and identifies multicultural aspects that may affect school–family partnerships. In addition, the chapter presents strategies for increasing family involvement in the student-directed IEP process and engaging in effective communication with families from diverse backgrounds. As educators, you are well aware of the critical role that parents and families play in the development of a child and of a successful educational program. Now you must ask yourself how to effectively incorporate parents and families into the student-directed IEP process in ways that best support the student and the process.

The family is a child's smallest and most immediate social group. It provides early socialization, represents each individual unit with a family identity, and plays the most important and lasting role in the development of children (Dmitrieva, Chen, Greenberger, & Gil-Rivas, 2004; Fuligni & Flook, 2005). For children with disabilities, the family system often plays a larger role over a longer period of time between the child and the various systems that affect the child. Often, families become accustomed to taking the lead in making educational decisions for their child. As children get older, it becomes the teacher's task to identify strategies for increasing student involvement in the IEP process while continuing to support the role of the family in educational decision making. School–family partnerships that view IEP planning as a holistic process, recognize the family as the constant in a student's life, value family input, and respect family culture are partnerships that are best positioned to facilitate student-directed practices.

Active family involvement is an important factor related to better outcomes in educating children and students with and without disabilities in inclusive programs (Berger,

1995; Levy, Kim, & Olive, 2006; Pérez Carreón, Drake, & Calabrese Barton, 2005). Research has shown that high levels of parental involvement correlate with improved academic performance, higher test scores, more positive attitudes toward school, higher homework completion rates, fewer placements in special education, academic perseverance, lower dropout rates, and fewer suspensions (Christenson, Hurley, Sheridan, & Fenstermacher, 1997; Hoover-Dempsey & Sandler, 1997; Pérez Carreón et al., 2005). The importance of establishing positive partnerships between families and professionals in education has long been recognized (Summers, Gavin, Hall, & Nelson, 2003). Parental involvement at school fosters positive, collaborative relationships.

In special education, schools and teachers have looked to the IEP process as a place to involve parents in educational decision making, as mandated through the Individuals with Disabilities Education Improvement Act (IDEA) of 2004 (PL 108-446; Turnbull & Turnbull, 2001). IDEA 2004 states that schools must ensure that IEP teams include parents. Parents are identified first on the list of those named to make up the IEP team, and parental attendance at IEP meetings is required. Parents can invite others who have knowledge of their child's educational needs, and parental concerns for enhancing their child's education must be considered.

Family involvement is an ever-changing series of interactions that vary depending on the context in which they occur, the disciplines from which the collaborative team members are drawn, the resources parents bring to the interactions, and the particular needs of the student and the family. Traditionally, the education agency or school has created structures and activities intended to support parental involvement. As parents become involved, they do so with limited power to define their roles and actions (Fine, 1993). According to several studies, many parents do not feel that activities organized by the school constitute real opportunities for family participation, and many of them actually feel powerless in the decision-making processes (e.g., Weiss & Edwards, 1992; Williams & Stallworth, 1984). They are often expected to agree with and support the structures and dynamics already in place. Tables 2.1 and 2.2 provide suggestions for strategies to facilitate improved interactions with parents.

Traditionally, family involvement in the special education process was limited, and families were treated as passive recipients of special education services. As special education services have evolved since the 1980s, however, family involvement has shifted from a model that emphasized family problems or deficits to a model that emphasizes individual family values, family empowerment, and family strength (Cartledge, Kea, & Simmons-Reed, 2002). The concept of family empowerment has received considerable attention in recent years and has been seen as a critical component of services for families of children with disabilities (Freund, 1993; Singh et al., 1995; Staples, 1990). Empowering and enabling families has become a goal of special education services, with family in the center and the child with special needs as the focus (see Table 2.3). The field of early intervention provides valuable insights into effective techniques for building positive partnerships between families and educational and social services professionals. Professionals who work with children with disabilities from birth to age 3 years and their families have developed a body of evidence related to *enabling* and *empowering* families, terms that denote much more than mere family *involvement* in educational planning. A brief review sheds light on how to move from school-directed to family- and student-directed processes.

Table 2.1. Changing interactions to promote family involvement

Changing interactions depending on	What this means	Strategies
Context	Formal meetings Conferences Team meetings Informal school conversation	Create situations where parents have multiple opportunities to express ideas, opinions, or concerns
Disciplines of team members	Special education teacher General education teachers Therapists Counselors Administrators	Parents should have equal access to communicate with all team members in a variety of contexts Team members may have to initiate such interactions because parents frequently feel most connected with the primary teacher
Resources	Self-advocacy or advocacy Emotional resources Internal support for family (family members) External support for family (extended family, community support) Insurance/financial resources	Empower parents to recognize their existing resources within the process and to develop new resources for areas where none exist
Needs of family/ student	Degree of disability Medical needs Learning needs Behavioral needs Economic/employment status	Maintain high expectations regardless of disability Identify the student's ability to participate in the student-directed IEP process Think outside the box to develop a plan, resources, and accommodations

Although the importance of identifying family priorities and resources is self-evident, how to identify and obtain family resources is individualized and not always obvious. As Dunst, Trivette, Davis, and Cornwell (1988) examined, how you define a family concern or need has much to do with the approach that you use to address that need. Your role is

Table 2.2. Research-based strategies for increasing parent involvement

Specifically invite the parent to participate in a structured event in the classroom or school. A general invitation is often not enough. Replace, "You are welcome to come in to help any time" with, "Can you please come to the classroom next Friday afternoon to help with (reading, cooking, field trip, math activity, etc.)?" Build on parent and family strengths during the invitation by asking a parent to participate in an area of talent he or she may possess (Anderson & Minke, 2007).

Demonstrate your value of parental input and family involvement in the education of the child by engaging in specific behaviors. Always return telephone calls or e-mails within 24 hours. Take the time to listen to parent concerns, questions, or issues. If you do not have time right away, then schedule a specific time. Instead of saying, "I can't talk right now; I have (bus duty, faculty meeting, personal appointment, etc.). Call me later," say, "Let's meet (tomorrow morning at 8 a.m., tomorrow at pick-up time, telephone conference at 12:30)." Be specific and parents will know that their concerns are important to you (Brown & Medway, 2007).

Always respond to parent issues each day/week for daily/weekly home–school communication logs or progress reports. Ask questions to elicit information from the parent that will enhance the learning experiences of the child in the school and increase the feeling of value and empowerment of the family (e.g., providing feedback about homework assignments, class projects, positive/negative behavior issues).

Table 2.3. Empowering and enabling families

Definition	Strategies
Empowering families is to carry out "intervention in a manner in which family members acquire a sense of control over their own developmental course as a result of their own efforts to meet needs" (Allen & Cowdery, 2005, p. 168).	Recognize families know their children best Teach families to advocate in a variety of settings Teach families to recognize and gain access to supports
Enabling families is to create "opportunities for family members to become more competent and self-sustaining with respect to their abilities to mobilize their social networks in order to get their needs met and attain goals" (Allen & Cowdery, 2005, p. 168).	Offer parent training Offer parent support groups Develop and set goals for the child, immediate family, and extended family

to acknowledge and support each family's ability to identify its own concerns relative to the development and education of the child (empowerment) and to assist the family in acquiring both the skills and resources that may be necessary to effectively address those concerns (enablement).

Family empowerment includes recognizing that the family is the constant in the child's life, family members really do know their child best, and partnerships are strengthened when families are given the opportunity to provide information about and advocate for their child in a variety of settings. This family-directed approach can begin the shift away from a traditional school-directed approach. Empowered families learn to more fully utilize natural supports and existing family resources, rather than placing full responsibility on schools and teachers. The shift is further facilitated when teachers help parents understand that family support is comprehensive and ongoing in nature, reaching beyond the school setting and encompassing all areas of life. By beginning in the early years to engage families in IEP preparation, meetings, and follow up, teachers provide a model for meaningful participation by both student and family. Families who understand the IEP process and have established positive school partnerships are valuable allies in your efforts to increase student participation in the IEP process.

Parents, siblings, and other relatives know about what works and what does not work with the student, what the student likes and dislikes, and student behaviors and interactions at home and in the community. When given the opportunity, parents usually share openly and honestly about the hopes, dreams, and fears they hold for their child. For such communication to take place, however, a relationship of trust and respect must first be established (see Table 2.4). Working to build such relationships must be a high priority for teachers and school personnel.

Table 2.4. Strategies for developing open communication between teachers and families

Acknowledge families as important contributors
Treat families as equal partners
Engage in joint planning
Engage in joint decision making
Engage in joint problem solving
Respect family values and perspectives
Think outside the box for effective communication strategies

A student-directed IEP process requires looking at IEP planning, IEP meetings, and student progress monitoring from a holistic perspective. A traditional, school-directed IEP process often operates from a deficit-based model, containing detailed reports primarily concerned with student shortcomings and advancing the perception that school personnel are the experts. It should not come as a surprise when parents and students are reluctant to become active and invested participants in such situations. Embracing the notion that the IEP process is much broader than what happens at the annual meeting opens up a myriad of opportunities for family participation.

There is no prescribed age or time at which to start such a process; however, student involvement at an earlier age can increase confidence, organizational skills, and self-determination. Initially, facilitating student involvement will require considerable direction by the family, and you will need to support and empower the family to be able to support and empower the child in assuming a larger role.

Preparing for an IEP meeting by creating a person-centered plan (sometimes known as *mapping*) provides the team with a positive and holistic picture of the student. It helps assure that team members begin their annual planning meeting "on the same page" with clear information about what is most important to the student and the student's family. Knowledge about student preferences and interests can assist in setting goals, developing benchmarks, planning effective instruction, and designing methods for involving students in their own progress monitoring. Most important, though, the person-centered plan becomes the property of the student and family. It can serve as a guide not only for educational planning but also in planning for independent living, employment, and community participation. Parents can assist their child, beginning at a young age, in making choices and reasonable decisions. Later, efforts can be focused on understanding options and selecting goals, as well as explaining goals to others and reviewing or revising them as needed. As students grow, mature, and take more control of their lives, families (and teachers) need to pay increased attention to what students think and want and then respect and support their goals and decisions. This is not always easy, even for families and teachers of children without disabilities; however, it is an important step toward increased independence and one that must be afforded to students with disabilities in order to achieve a truly self-directed IEP process.

Multicultural Implications for Families in the Student-Directed IEP Process

The increasing diversity in the United States requires a pluralistic view that recognizes the multiple cultures contributing to American society. In school settings, cultural pluralism takes the form of multicultural education. Recognizing individual characteristics and values, multicultural education teaches the contributions of all cultural or subcultural groups to the development of our nation (Gollnick & Chinn, 2009). Multicultural education should not be narrowly understood with the addition of an instructional unit or a course on a specific culture or ethnicity. Instead, it is a philosophical orientation that permeates the curriculum across all educational programs including general and special education. See Table 2.5 for more information about multicultural curricula.

Table 2.5. Characteristics of multicultural curricula

Infusing multiple cultures throughout the curriculum, *not* cultural night where students and families eat snacks from other countries
Reflecting culture in academic subjects by providing culturally responsive teaching so that subject matter becomes meaningful to students
Including multiple perspectives by respecting and understanding differences such as religion, diet, ability, and family structure

Source: Gollnick & Chinn (2009).

Multicultural education is emphasized by the Council for Exceptional Children (CEC) through the Division for Culturally and Linguistically Diverse Exceptional Learners (DDEL). As special and general educators, you may need to change the way you think about culture and its effect on disabilities, students and families, appropriate education, and your role in the schools and community.

The population of students and families in the United States who receive special education is becoming increasingly diverse. Working with students with disabilities and their families from culturally and linguistically diverse backgrounds can be challenging for general and special education professionals. Because of the complexity of composition and sensitivity of cultural issues, it is risky or even dangerous to overgeneralize about family needs, priorities, values, and beliefs. No two families are exactly alike, even if they are from the same cultural backgrounds (Cartledge et al., 2002). The environmental and social settings of families throughout the world have been changing over the last several decades, especially in the United States.

As Filler and Xu noted,

> The realities of a multi-racial, multi-ethnic and multi-ability student population demand a unique and nontraditional approach characterized by an individualization sensitive to both inter and intra group identity. On the one hand educators must pay individual attention to the appropriate content and strategy and on the other hand, support each family's membership in a class loosely defined by common values, methods of adornment, and views regarding the role of the family in the formal educational process. (2006, p. 93)

The task is no more apparent than including students with disabilities in the general education curriculum through collaborative teamwork that involves family members as partners (Xu, Gelfer, & Filler, 2003). As a group, these students not only reflect the racial and ethnic diversities of their typically developing peers but may also present an additional aspect of individuality. See Table 2.6 for a listing of family and cultural barriers to participation in the IEP process.

Diversity exists not only between groups but also within cultural groups. Culturally appropriate services in special education must embrace and incorporate different aspects of diversity, such as accepting a family's ethnic background as their cultural identity, allowing for language preferences (primary or home language versus English), and respecting religious beliefs by including someone from a faith community at the IEP meeting. Providing culturally competent services benefits the family as a unit and as individual family members, including the child with disabilities. The focus of culturally competent services is on strengths and needs of both the family system as well as individual members of the family, whereas all aspects of service delivery remain sensitive to the unique racial, ethnic, geographical, and social makeup of the family.

Table 2.6.   Family and cultural barriers to participation in the individualized education program (IEP) process

How families define stress could be different from how professionals define stress. For example, attending an IEP meeting could be stressful for the parents if their first language is not English, even with an interpreter provided by the school.

Language can be a barrier if one or more parents do not speak English as their first language and an interpreter is not provided.

Families may perceive their resources differently from how professionals perceive them. For example, a family from a culturally diverse background may perceive internal family support or extended family support as their primary resources, whereas the professionals may see formal support as the primary resource.

Some cultures may lack familiarity with school or have different perspectives on school/teacher roles, responsibilities, expectations, and use of technology.

Employment situations in which both parents work outside the home may cause barriers to regular participation in school activities.

Availability for traveling to school for meetings or conferences may be limited (lack of car, lack of access to public transportation in suburban or rural areas).

Child care issues for the child with a disability and/or other siblings may prevent parents from participating in the process.

Different family members may take responsibility, which may vary for families with diverse backgrounds.

The primary caregivers in the family may be other family members besides the parents (e.g., grandparents).

Whether the student should be present when being discussed could be viewed differently by different families.

Sources: Bruder (2000); Noonan & McCormick (2006).

Strategies for Working with Families from Culturally Diverse Backgrounds

Effective communication between school and family is essential to ensure a successful student-directed IEP process. This is especially true for families with diverse backgrounds. The following section discusses strategies for working with families from culturally diverse backgrounds in a student-directed IEP process. Barrera, Corso, and Macpherson (2003) proposed a Skilled Dialogue approach to effective interaction between professionals and families from culturally diverse backgrounds. Three qualities are emphasized in Skilled Dialogue—respect, reciprocity, and responsiveness. These three qualities can be applied to school–family partnerships in the student-directed IEP process for any school-age students because effective communication is the key to the process.

Respect is the foundation for any relationship or interaction. It is essential that professionals respect and value the family's voice throughout the process of IEP development and implementation. The professionals need to focus on the family's strengths, discuss with family members their perceptions and changes of perceptions regarding the special needs of the child with a disability, and respect the family's perceptions even if they are different from those of the professionals. The professionals may want to reflect on their own backgrounds and share them with the family. This reflective process helps everyone recognize and understand differences of perceptions.

Reciprocity is built on respect. Being reciprocal is to acknowledge that each member in the interaction is equal in terms of capability and decision making. In the student-directed IEP process, reciprocity requires that everybody, including the student with a disability, contribute equally in choice making. Reciprocal interaction values diverse points of view and any one point of view should not dominate over others (Barrera et al., 2003). Although the professional may have a special expertise in a specified area (e.g., occupational therapy), reciprocal interaction also recognizes that the family contributes equally to the process (e.g., provides critical information about the child's behavior or skill at home).

Responsiveness is further based on respect and reciprocity. With deep respect and reciprocal interactions, professionals have the opportunity to know who the child really is instead of trying to shape who they want him or her to be (Barrera et al., 2003; Remen, 2000). This is the time that the professionals focus on taking to heart the family's input and getting to know their reality with their unique strengths. In other words, being responsive to individual families is the process of professionals being willing to give up their own ideas about a reality and to accept the unique reality that makes sense to the individual family. This is critical for families with diverse backgrounds because professionals may find each family is more than who they appear to be. For example, when parents do not seek professional assistance in the IEP process, it does not necessarily mean that they are inactive; instead, it could be that they already have established a strong extended family support system as part of their coping strategies.

Other strategies for working with families who are culturally diverse include offering families a choice of language for communication, both at school and between home and school, and offering a variety of levels at which to participate in the educational and student-directed IEP process. Some families will feel more comfortable and confident interacting with school staff than others, and some families will have more available time or resources for participating in specific programs or communication strategies. You should also seek out culturally appropriate language (e.g., avoid using terms with negative connotations such as *limited English proficient student;* instead, use *English language learner*) and linguistically appropriate materials to use with the family (translated newsletters, forms, memo, other documents) and with the student (supplemental materials, testing in the child's native language). Finally, involve the family (at their level of comfort) in all levels of planning and implementation of the educational planning, especially at the transition planning stage for the child.

Communicating with Families Who Are Linguistically Diverse

Much of the student-directed IEP process involves effective communication between school and family, as you have seen throughout this chapter. Without effective communication, important meetings could be missed or end up unproductive; miscommunication could cause confusion, frustration, and even resentment. As a result, expectations might not be established consistently, and progress tracking might get muddled. Consequently, parents, families, and students are not collaborating for the benefit of the students.

Certain accommodations must be made so that families who are linguistically diverse can effectively communicate with the school staff. Many schools have students from families who speak a variety of languages in their homes and communities. It is often impossible to be completely prepared for all of the translation needs that a school district may encounter. Some realistic and functional options must be discussed by the team to ensure effective communication by all members of the team. Barrera et al. (2003) suggested some strategies for effective communication that include 1) seeking bilingual/multilingual practitioners who are proficient in English and other language(s) the student and the family speak; 2) identifying nonfamily members who are proficient in the desired language and culture; 3) meeting beforehand with the person who is identified as the translator and the person who is to assist the translator; and 4) allowing for sufficient time for the student and family to respond (e.g., after a question is asked, wait for 10 seconds for the student or parents to respond). Additional solutions that have occurred in real life to create effective communication systems include 1) a fully equipped translation department in your school district, including access to translators for a large variety of languages; 2) hiring an outside expert in the particular language to translate verbal and written materials; 3) hiring/recruiting a local university student to translate in his or her area of study or native language; 4) having a parent fluent in English translate for a parent who is not fluent; 5) having another relative fluent in English translate for a parent who is not fluent; 6) using pictures, graphs, and organizational charts to demonstrate the IEP process; and 7) always using clear language that everybody can understand and avoiding jargons.

 Listening to the Experts

Teacher's Perspective

A first step in implementing a student-directed IEP approach involved explaining the process to others and making sure they were on board with the new method. In particular, I knew that I should discuss the new approach with Kathy's family and knew her mother would be interested in learning about anything that involved helping Kathy take charge of her life. Having her mother on board was essential for moving forward with the meeting. I knew that Kathy's success would be enhanced by having her mother as a partner in supporting Kathy's efforts.

I shared the specifics of this approach with Kathy's mom, and we made decisions together about how to best approach the process. For example, she decided that she would work with Kathy to identify people to invite to the meeting and think about Kathy's long-range goals. I volunteered to coordinate the logistics of the meeting with Kathy (arranging for the room, organizing the agenda and a PowerPoint of her long-range goals, and sending out the invitations). We also agreed that it would be best for both of us to talk with Kathy to help her understand her rights in the IEP and the steps of the process so that we could reinforce her learning. Collaborating with Kathy's mom and involving her in every step of the process was critical to our success.

Student's Perspective	I was so excited that my mother was okay with me leading my IEP meeting. Having my mother there with me, helping me through it all, was a good feeling to have. I would go home and tell her things that I learned about myself. I would also go home and tell her how the process was going to go. Sometimes my mother would go to my IEP meetings and she would tell me everything that was decided; now it was my turn to tell her everything that she once knew.
Parent's Perspective	Kathy was so excited when her teacher asked her to lead her IEP meeting. She came home and told me all about it. Working with Mr. Scott made me feel at ease about what she was doing. I was used to showing up at the IEP meeting where the document was oftentimes completed. In that sense, I would only work with Kathy's previous teacher at the meeting to make adjustments. Kathy leading her entire meeting process gave me a sense that I was involved with her, her teacher, and in the actual IEP meeting.

Reflection on Kathy's Example

Mr. Scott found many ways for Kathy's mother to be involved in her student-directed IEP process. Mr. Scott decided to focus on implementing a student-directed IEP approach with Kathy and her mom because he had worked with Kathy for a few years, had a good sense of her abilities and interests, and knew that her mother would be a supporter of the process given her past encouragement of Kathy's self-determination. How did he solicit support from Kathy's mom? First, he took the time to send information home to explain the process. He used a parent information brochure that was developed to explain the student-directed IEP process (see Figure 2.1) and presented information in a way that looked different from much of the paperwork typically sent by the school to parents.

Mr. Scott's next step was to meet with Kathy and her mother to discuss the process specifically for Kathy. Kathy's mother completed the first half of a Parent Planning Tool that provided her with the opportunity to think about ways that Kathy could be involved in her IEP meeting (see Figure 2.2). Mr. Scott had developed a list of the skills and strengths that would help Kathy direct her IEP, as well as those things that she would need to learn or have support to complete. He and Kathy's mom used the list and the Parent Planning Tool to guide their discussion about how they could work together to prepare Kathy for this change in role. Kathy's mom volunteered to give Kathy some practice time at home and to work with Kathy to complete some of the initial transition assessment surveys and community-based assessments.

As they practiced for Kathy's IEP meeting, Kathy's mother noticed that Kathy became distracted when asked a question during the presentation of her information. They came up with some strategies for dealing with this. First, Kathy would attempt to answer questions, and her mother would provide an agreed-on prompt to redirect her attention to the presentation. Second, if Kathy still could not redirect her attention back to the meeting, then she would say something such as, "Mom (or Mr. Scott), would you

---

Introducing the Student-Directed IEP Process...

The IEP is going to be different this year. Students are going to direct the process!

What does this mean?

- A student-directed IEP process means that your son or daughter will be more fully involved in the IEP meeting and what happens after it than ever before.
- *It does not mean* that your son or daughter will be expected to run the entire meeting. *It does mean* that your son or daughter's role will be matched to his or her abilities and comfort level.

Why are we doing this?

- We know that student-directed IEPs are a great way for students to increase an important life skill called self-determination.
- Self-determination includes letting people know what you think, making decisions for yourself, and setting goals and working toward them. It is linked to increases in academic skills, employment, wages, postsecondary education, and an improved quality of life.

How can I help?

- You can help your son or daughter make a list of his or her preferences, interests, strengths, and needs.
- You can help your son or daughter think about the kinds of supports he or she needs to talk with others about in a meeting. Use lists, drawings, note cards, technology—whatever works!
- You and your son or daughter can also invite friends or relatives to help you feel more comfortable and to share their ideas.
- If your son or daughter is 16 or older, think about postschool outcomes when preparing for the meeting. Planning for transition should focus on all the areas related to life after your student leaves school: employment, postsecondary education, recreation, living choices, transportation, health care, community involvement, finances, friendships, and how to advocate for what is needed.
- You can help your son or daughter make a list of suggestions that would be good to include in the IEP.

What will my role be?

- Your participation in the meeting is no less important than it has been before. You should think ahead of time about the things you think are most important to talk about during the meeting.
- Remember that you'll be wearing two hats: sharing your own thoughts and supporting your son or daughter in sharing his or her thoughts. Don't forget to do both!
- Look for signs that your son or daughter wants or needs things explained differently or might need a break.
- Listen during the meeting for things you will want to talk about with your son or daughter afterward.
- After the meeting look for ways to help your student follow-up on items discussed and how to track his or her progress.

 Write your questions, thoughts, suggestions, and important information here and bring this brochure with you to the premeeting planning session.

Your son or daughter's IEP meeting is scheduled for:
April 22 at 4:00 p.m.

Figure 2.1. Parent information brochure.

take a turn?" and she or Mr. Scott would know that she needed a break from being the center of attention. They would introduce the next item or topic on the agenda, with Kathy jumping back in when she was ready.

Kathy and her mother also reviewed the draft goals that she established for her transition outcomes, as well as the educational goals of the IEP to determine which ones were priorities and which were negotiable. This separate list provided a way for Kathy to prepare for the inevitable negotiations that take place in any IEP meeting, as well as a way for Kathy's mother to support her during that process. They agreed prior to the meeting that it would be okay for her to be the one to remind the other IEP team members about those priorities as they discussed educational goals, supports, and services.

Mr. Scott also knew that family involvement in a student-directed IEP process extends beyond the meeting preparations and meeting itself. He organized a way that Kathy could share her progress on IEP goals with her mother on a regular basis, as well as opportunities for everyone to share their perceptions about the IEP meeting itself and ways they could improve. Kathy's mom was able to share her perceptions of the meeting by completing the second half of the Parent Planning Tool (see Figure 2.2). In addition, Mr. Scott used an "exit survey" to determine the perceptions of all team members, and he used that information to make changes for the next year's meeting.

Tips and Strategies

When asked about what they do to involve parents and family in a student-directed IEP process, teachers spoke about the importance of educating parents about the IEP process, finding effective ways to obtain their input, and involving them beyond the IEP meeting. Parents of a student such as Alejandra (introduced in Chapter 1) may be accustomed to taking what professionals say without question, even if the goals suggested by teachers do not match what the parents feel is important. For example, Alejandra's previous IEP included a goal for learning to cook a simple meal using a microwave. Alejandra's teacher learned late in the year, in a chance conversation with Alejandra's cousin, that the family did not own a microwave and almost always cooked in large pots, preparing meals that were shared with the entire extended family. When preparing for Alejandra's next IEP meeting, the teacher asked to meet with Alejandra's mom ahead of time. Alejandra's cousin translated, which was comfortable for both the parent and teacher. The teacher asked Alejandra's mom what kinds of things they could work on at school that would help Alejandra at home. At the next IEP meeting, the microwave meal goal was removed and replaced with goals for Alejandra to learn to cut a variety of foods safely and to identify picture vocabulary cards of ingredients used often in family cooking.

Teachers shared these additional tips and strategies for increased family involvement.

- Use a variety of strategies to change families' expectations by introducing families to the three-part IEP process. Try a Family Night, but consider individual conversations for families whose primary language is not English or for families that find it difficult or uncomfortable to attend formal meetings.

- Find a parent who is a "veteran" of a student-directed IEP approach to explain the process.

- Involve students in hosting a Family Night presentation. They could assemble and distribute handouts, introduce speakers (using voice, sign, or a voice output device), assist with a PowerPoint presentation, serve refreshments, or help set up and clean up. Instructional assistants could be used to engage students for certain periods, if needed.

- Send invitations to any informational meetings (group or individual) and make sure there is ample time to reply. Be prepared to follow up if parents do not respond. Do the same for IEP meetings.

Student: _____ Date: _____

Preparing for the meeting

Please tell about how you think your child might participate in his or her IEP meeting in terms of readiness and support.

Readiness (R): 1, knows about or has done before; 2, new skill or knowledge; 3, not at this time.

Support (S): 1, could do on own; 2, would need some help; 3, would need lots of help.

Who will help? List individuals who can provide support.

R	S		Who?
__	__	Learn what the meeting is about	____
__	__	Help decide who to invite to the meeting	____
__	__	Make invitations for the meeting	____
__	__	Send/deliver invitations	____
__	__	Photocopy materials for the meeting	____
__	__	Set up/clean up meeting room	____
__	__	Make/serve snacks for the meeting	____
__	__	Introduce people at the meeting	____
__	__	Distribute papers during the meeting	____
__	__	Write goals ahead of time to recommend	____
__	__	Review and update goals from previous IEP	____
__	__	Read goals during the meeting	____
__	__	Role-play how to act and what to say	____
__	__	Talk about likes/dislikes	____
__	__	Prepare a notebook or portfolio about self	____
__	__	Prepare a PowerPoint presentation	____
__	__	Share samples of work from class	____
__	__	Show pictures of self doing activities	____
__	__	Talk and ask questions during the meeting	____
__	__	Talk about/recommend accommodations	____
__	__	Lead the IEP meeting	____

Student: _____ Date: _____

Thinking about the meeting

How did it feel to have your child at the IEP meeting?

What did he/she say about it? or How do you think your child felt about it?

What surprised you most? Pleased you most? Concerned you most?

Compare this IEP meeting to others in which you have participated:

Preparing for the next meeting

What worked in your son/daughter's meeting?

What did not work in your son/daughter's meeting?

What would you like to see stay the same in terms of your son/daughter's participation?

What would you like to see changed in terms of your son/daughter's participation?

What suggestions do you have for increasing participation?

Figure 2.2. Parent planning tool. (Reprinted by permission from Barb Purvis.)

- Have students write the invitations for information meetings and any related IEP meetings. One teacher recommended having a student dictate a letter, describing the meeting process in his or her own words and why his or her parent's participation is important.

- Do not assume you know what a family needs. Parents should be able to request any accommodations (e.g., translators, large print, special meeting time) to assure their participation in the meeting.

- Make sure you have enough time to have materials, forms, and/or documents translated.

- Make yourself available to meet separately when one or two of the families cannot make it to a group information night.

- Become culturally competent: Find out how disability, education, and support services are viewed by different ethnic and religious groups. Talk to students, family members, fellow staff members, and other teachers to learn more about cultural aspects of the students with whom you work.

- Learn about the beliefs, rituals, and/or traditions of people who come from backgrounds similar to your student, but be careful not to make generalizations. Use the information to guide your questions and increase your understanding while avoiding stereotypes.

- Ask parents to help students with collecting information, practicing for the IEP meeting, problem solving when progress is not being made, or other tasks that the student directs or leads.

- Talk with parents to learn more about student support needs and/or communication difficulties. Parents can provide information about a student's past experiences and his or her skills in settings other than the classroom.

- Provide families with tools that include questions/items to think about before the IEP meeting.

- Ask families for specific ideas for including the student more fully in the process, and then be sure to incorporate their suggestions.

Conclusion

To successfully collaborate with families in the student-directed IEP process, you must work with fellow team members to make the values and strategies discussed in this chapter your own. Fostering open, honest, and effective two-way communication between school and home builds trust and allows ideas to be shared freely. Treating family members with respect, in a comfortable, culturally sensitive atmosphere with people who acknowledge their individual values and make every effort to put them at ease, encourages full participation and the desire to work together. Seeking family members' opinions and ideas lets them know you value their input and recognize the importance of the information they have to offer. Focusing on strengths, listening to what families have to say, and encouraging their efforts breaks down barriers and builds a stronger team.

With a strong partnership in place, you can more easily facilitate movement along the student-directed IEP continuum. Maintaining a positive attitude and focusing on strengths encourages greater participation by both child and family and begins the shift from school-directed to a student-directed IEP process. Admitting to families that you do not have all the answers and being willing to let go of some of the control you typically hold empowers students even more. Sharing knowledge and providing tools to families for understanding the process, preparing in advance, and monitoring progress will make for productive meetings and follow through. Having high expectations yourself, and encouraging families to share their expectations, will keep the process moving and increase family involvement, which will ultimately benefit the child and the whole family. These benefits begin as soon as the student, family, and school personnel begin preparations for the IEP meeting, utilizing strategies that ensure full and meaningful participation by everyone (see Chapter 3).

References

Allen, E.K., & Cowdery, S. (2005). *The exceptional child: Inclusion in early childhood education.* Albany, NY: Delmar.

Anderson, K.J., & Minke, K.M. (2007). Parent involvement in education: Toward an understanding of parents' decision-making. *Journal of Educational Research, 100,* 311–323.

Barrera, I., Corso, R.M., & Macpherson, D. (2003). *Skilled dialogue: Strategies for responding to cultural diversity in early childhood.* Baltimore: Paul H. Brookes Publishing Co.

Berger, E.H. (1995). *Parents as partners in education: Families and schools working together.* Upper Saddle River, NJ: Prentice Hall.

Brown, K., & Medway, F.J. (2007). School climate and teacher beliefs in a school effectively serving poor South Carolina African American students: A case study. *Teaching and Teacher Education, 23*(4), 529–540.

Bruder, M.B. (2000). Family-centered early intervention: Clarifying our values for the new millennium. *Topics in Early Childhood Special Education, 20*(2), 105–115.

Cartledge, G., Kea, C., & Simmons-Reed, E. (2002). Serving culturally diverse children with serious emotional disturbances and their families. *Journal of Child and Family Studies, 11*(1), 113–126.

Christenson, S.L., Hurley, C.M., Sheridan, S.M., & Fenstermacher, K. (1997). Parents' and school psychologists' perceptive on parent involvement activities. *School Psychology Review, 26*(1), 111–130.

Dmitrieva, J., Chen, C., Greenberger, E., & Gil-Rivas, V. (2004). Family relationships and adolescent psychosocial outcomes: Converging findings from Eastern and Western culture. *Journal of Research on Adolescence, 14*(4), 425–447.

Dunst, C.J., Trivette, C.M., Davis, M., & Cornwell, J. (1988). Enabling and empowering families of children with health impairments. *Children's Health Care, 17*(2), 71–81.

Filler, J., & Xu, Y. (2006). Including children with disabilities in early childhood education programs: Individualizing developmentally appropriate practices. *Childhood Education, 83*(2), 92–98.

Fine, M. (1993). [Ap]parent involvement: Reflections on parents, power, and urban public schools. *Teachers College Record, 94,* 683–710.

Freund, P.D. (1993). Professional role(s) in the empowerment process: "Working with" mental health consumers. *Psychosocial Rehabilitation Journal, 16,* 65–73.

Fuligni, A.J., & Flook, I. (2005). A social identity approach to ethnic differences in family relationships during adolescence. *Advances in Child Development and Behavior, 33,* 125–152.

Gollnick, D.M., & Chinn, P.C. (2009). *Multicultural education in a pluralistic society* (8th ed.). Boston: Allyn & Bacon.

Hoover-Dempsey, K., & Sandler, H. (1997). Parental involvement in children's education: Why does it make a difference? *Teachers College Record, 97,* 310–332.

Individuals with Disabilities Education Improvement Act (IDEA) of 2004, PL 108-446, 20 U.S.C. §§ 1400 *et seq.*

Levy, S., Kim, A., & Olive, M.L. (2006). Interventions for young children with autism: A synthesis of the literature. *Focus on Autism and Other Developmental Disabilities, 21*(1), 55–62.

Noonan, M.J., & McCormick, L. (2006). *Young children with disabilities in natural environments: Methods and procedures.* Baltimore: Paul H. Brookes Publishing Co.

Pérez Carreón, G., Drake, C., & Calabrese Barton, A. (2005). The importance of presence: Immigrant parents' school engagement experiences. *American Educational Research Journal, 42*(3), 465–498.

Remen, R.N. (2000). *My grandfather's blessings.* New York: Riverhead Books.

Singh, N.N., Curtis, W.J., Ellis, C.R., Nicholson, M.W., Villani, T.M., & Wechsler, H.A. (1995). Psychometric analysis of the family Empowerment Scale. *Journal of Emotional and Behavioral Disorders, 3,* 85–91.

Staples, L.H. (1990). Powerful ideas about empowerment. *Administration in Social Work, 14*(2), 29–42.

Summers, J.A., Gavin, K., Hall, T., & Nelson, J. (2003). Family and school partnerships: Building bridges in general and special education. In F.E. Obiakor, C.A. Urley, & A.F. Rotatori (Eds.), *Advances in special education: Psychology of effective education for learners with exceptionalities* (pp. 417–445). Stamford, CT: JAI Press.

Turnbull, A.P., & Turnbull, H.R. (2001). *Families, professionals, and exceptionality: A special partnership.* Columbus, OH: Charles E. Merrill.

Weiss, H.M., & Edwards, M.E. (1992). The family-school collaboration project: Systemic intervention for school improvement. In S.L. Christenson & J.L. Connolly (Eds.), *Home-school collaboration: Enhancing children's academic and social competence* (pp. 215–244). Silver Spring, MD: National Association of School Psychologists.

Williams, D.L., & Stallworth, J.T. (1984). *Parent involvement in education: What a survey reveals.* Austin, TX: Parent involvement in Education Project, Southwest Regional Educational Development Laboratory.

Xu, Y., Gelfer, J.I., & Filler, J. (2003). An alternative undergraduate teacher preparation program in early childhood education. *Early Child Development and Care, 173*(5), 489–497.

Prior to the Meeting

3

....

Student Awareness of the IEP Process

LaRon A. Scott and Colleen A. Thoma

As Chapter 1 stated, a student-directed individualized education program (IEP) process can be thought of as three component parts that interconnect and flow into each other. Although your first instinct might be to focus solely on the actual meeting itself, pre- and postmeeting components are just as critical to the overall success of your educational planning efforts. This chapter addresses one of the critical premeeting components of the process—introducing the concept of a student-directed IEP process to students and helping them understand and exercise their rights and responsibilities throughout the steps.

The literature has shown that it is not enough to simply have the student be present at his or her meeting to assure student involvement and/or direction of the process. Studies have demonstrated that when students attend their IEP meetings without specific IEP meeting instruction they do not know what to do, lack understanding of the meeting's purpose or language, feel like no one listens to them when they talk, do not know the goals or other outcomes of the meeting, and think that attending the IEP meeting is meaningless (Lehmann, Bassett, & Sands, 1999; Lovitt, Cushing, & Stump, 1994; Morningstar, Turnbull, & Turnbull, 1995; Powers, Turner, Matuszewski, Wilson, & Loesch, 1999; Sweeney, 1996; Thoma, Rogan, & Baker, 2001). These studies recommended that teachers help students understand the IEP process and their educational rights. It is critical for premeeting work to teach students about the IEP process, their rights and responsibilities in the process, and the identification of supports (including communication supports) that help them participate more fully in all stages of the process.

Student Rights and Responsibilities

Students have a number of rights and responsibilities when it comes to their education as well as the development of their IEPs. It is important that you review these rights and responsibilities with your students or make arrangements for someone else such as a counselor or student advocate to talk with them. Some students might prefer that their parents serve this role. The key is to find someone with whom the students feel comfortable and who also has a good understanding of their rights. Legal rights for students with disabilities are defined by the Individuals with Disabilities Education Improvement Act (IDEA) of 2004 (PL 108-446) as follows.

- **The right to receive a free appropriate public education (FAPE)**

FAPE is the legal requirement that "all disabled children receive a free and appropriate education, and that a school district must provide special education and related services to the child or his/her parents." This information is important to cover so that students are fully aware that they have the same right to an education as their peers without disabilities.

- **The right to be educated in the least restrictive environment (LRE)**

LRE means that a student with a disability has the opportunity to be educated with peers without disabilities to the greatest extent possible. He or she should have access to the general education curriculum, extracurricular activities, and any other programs that peers without disabilities would be able to access. The student should be provided with supplementary aids and services necessary to achieve his or her educational outcomes with peers without disabilities.

- **The right to have parental involvement in educational decisions**

An essential part of IDEA 2004 is the right of parents to be involved in making educational decisions on behalf of their child. These rights include, but are not limited to, requesting an evaluation if it is believed that the student is in need of special or related services, being fully informed of the rights and laws provided to the student and parents, participating in the development and placement decisions regarding the IEP, being kept informed of progress, and having the child educated in the LRE.

- **The right to fair assessment procedures**

Students who have or are suspected of having a disability are guaranteed the right to have a fair evaluation of their strengths, needs, and abilities in the educational environment. A thorough assessment of the students' special needs and regularly scheduled reviews to assure that services are provided appropriately are included in this provision.

- **The right to due process**

Due process ensures that both school agencies and parents/students have the right to request a hearing to resolve disagreements relative to the appropriateness of the special education programs and services offered or being provided to that student. There are specific rules and procedures that each party must follow in the event that such a disagreement cannot be resolved during the IEP meeting. Additional regulations regarding the right to due process, including a time line and safeguards for filing a due process complaint, can be found at the U.S. Department of Education's web site.

- **The right to an IEP**

Each student with a disability is required to have an IEP developed to meet his or her special education needs. As outlined in Chapter 1, an IEP is a written plan put together by a team designed specifically to address an individual student's needs and build on his or her strengths.

- **The right to assume the rights previously granted to their parents at the age of majority**

Finally, students have the right to have control of their IEP and services at the age of 18. Known as the *age of majority*, a student who reaches the age of 18 is presumed capable of making his or her own decisions, including educational decisions, in most states. "It just means that, by law, schools respect the educational decisions of every adult student" (Rockingham County Public Schools, 2008).

These rights are a brief summary of student and parent rights in regard to special education and its chief component, the IEP. It is important that you review your local state and school district policy and procedure when evaluating rights of students and parents.

After reviewing the rights involved in the IEP process, it is important to review with students their responsibilities during the IEP process. Student responsibilities during the IEP process include, but are not limited to, learning and understanding the purpose of their IEP, being an active member in the process, providing information regarding their preferences and interests to the IEP team, and working hard to meet their goals and objectives of the IEP.

You will also need to help students understand the IEP process and how it helps an educational team come together to plan the services, accommodations, modifications, and supports they need to benefit from their educational experience. For a student such as Max, who is in his first year of high school and has never attended an IEP meeting, this process begins with gathering information from his parents and past teachers to determine what was explained in the past (if anything) and what they perceive to be Max's understanding of the IEP process. There are a number of resources that you can use to determine a student's understanding of the IEP process. Figure 3.1 provides an outline of the three component parts of an IEP and the activities that are a part of each component (described as ways that the student can choose to be involved). Mr. Scott used this with Kathy to help her think about which activities she felt ready to do herself, which ones she needed some assistance to complete, and which ones she still needed to learn.

Of course, a younger student such as Susan, who has never been involved in her IEP meeting and who has more significant support needs, would need a combination of modifications, adaptations, supports, and instruction to take on just one or two aspects of the IEP process. She might not be able to comprehend all of her rights in the process, so her teacher might start with explaining that the IEP is a list of the supports she needs for school and the ways that her teachers, parents, and other school personnel are going to help her in the coming year. The lesson plan in Figure 3.2 can serve as a starting point for you to use to help students learn about the IEP process. It helps students learn about their learning style, which can be used to better understand themselves and the kind of support they may need to direct the IEP process. It uses the principles of Universal Design for Transition, or UDT (Thoma, Bartholomew, & Scott, 2009), which provides an opportunity for students to combine academic and functional/transition instructional goals in the same lessons. In this example, students learn about learning styles while increasing their writing/communication skills.

Roles of Participants at the Meeting

What does it mean to be an active member in the IEP process, and who are the other members? It is important for you to help students understand both aspects of this question.

The IEP process is not just the meeting, but it includes the activities that prepare for the meeting as well as carrying out the goals developed in the meeting and deciding if the goals are having the impact you want. You can and should have a role in each of these steps!

The premeeting

1. Collect information you need for the meeting about how you are doing now and what you might want to do in the coming years.

2. Plan for the meeting (who, what, where, when, why).

3. Practice for the meeting and organize the supports you need to have a successful meeting.

The meeting itself

1. Introduce the purpose for the meeting.

2. Participate in the meeting as practiced.

3. Share thoughts about goals for next year and/or transition goals.

4. Share what works and what doesn't work for supports, adaptations, and accommodations.

After the meeting

1. Share the goals you want to work on with your teachers so they can help you get where you want to be!

2. Send thank-you notes.

3. Advocate for the supports and adaptations that you need in your classes.

4. Learn to collect data on your goals to determine if you're making progress.

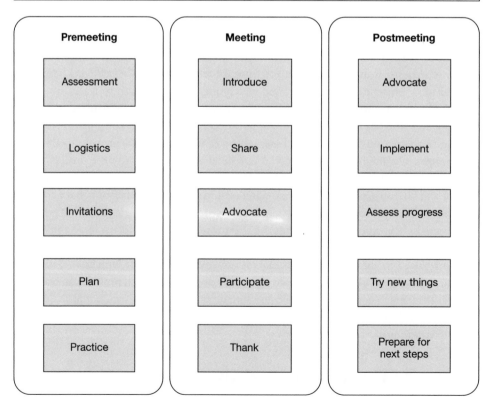

Figure 3.1. Student-directed individualized education program (IEP) process. Suggestions for participation in your IEP process.

What is my learning style?

Target group: *Secondary students*
Target curriculum: *English*

Goals and standards:
- Students will learn information about individual learning styles.
- Students will use a variety of learning strategies to organize ideas.
- Students will enhance vocabulary, determine meaning, and clarify the main idea.
- Students will communicate to the class at least one example of each way that they are similar to and different from their preferred learning style according to their learning style assessment. This must be communicated in an essay, collage, PowerPoint, video, or other creative way. The plan must be approved by the teacher within 1 week of the assignment. The plan must be in line with the student's preferred learning style as determined by his or her assessment.

Transition center:
Students will learn information about individual learning styles.
Students will evaluate the resources and information that they collect to determine how they learn best.
Students will use these skills to communicate their learning styles.

Self-determination:
Students will improve self-awareness, self-efficacy, and choice-making skills.

Materials:
"What Is My Learning Style" worksheet
Computer access
Various materials depending on how students present their learning styles

Procedure:
1. Students will be given the "What Is My Learning Style" worksheet and will be asked to visit http://www.healthcentral.com and search "learning styles" to research the several methods people use to learn information.
2. After completing the search, students will document the five styles of learning. They will write the five styles of learning that are used in Boxes 1–5 on the "What Is My Learning Style" worksheet.
3. Students will then be asked to eliminate one of the learning strategies that they feel does not work best for them. They will then list examples and representations for the four different learning styles in Boxes 6–9.
4. Students will then be asked to visit the online web quiz (http://www.educationplanner.org) and guide their way through the fun quiz that will help them determine what their unique learning style is. In the results section of the quiz, students will be presented with their unique learning styles. They will be asked to list the three unique learning styles in Boxes 10–12 on the "What Is My Learning Style" worksheet.
5. In Boxes 13 and 14, students will write their two lowest scoring learning styles and will give the percentages that they scored on each.
6. In the final "What is My Learning Style" worksheet box, Box 15, students will write their highest ranked learning style, according to the quiz, and what percentage they scored. Students will also describe in the box why they believe this learning style fits them best.

Assessment:
Students will express and represent their unique learning style to the class by formulating a unique method to explain to their classmates how they learn best. For example, a student who discovers that he or she is a "kinesthetic learner" may choose to create a sculpture or mold of his or her hands to clarify and present the learning style to classmates.

Evaluation:
Decide if students' assessments are true representatives of their learning styles.
Review and examine with students how they determined their learning styles.

Figure 3.2. What is my learning style lesson plan.

(continued)

What Is My Learning Style?

Learning styles

1.	2.	3.	4.	5.

Representation

6.	7.	8.	9.

Three learning styles

10.	11.	12.

Lowest scoring

13.	14.

My style

15.

Figure 3.2. *(continued)*

48

Preparing-Learning Styles Quiz results:

You are a visual learner!

Your test scores were:

Auditory: 25%   Visual: 60%   Tactile: 15%

You are a **visual learner,** so you learn by reading and seeing pictures. You understand and remember things by sight. You can picture what you are learning in your head, and you learn best by using methods that are primarily visual. You like to see what you are learning.

As a visual learner, you are usually neat and clean, you often close your eyes to visualuze or remember something, and you will find something to watch if you become bored. You may have difficulty with spoken directions and may be distracted by sounds. You are attracted to color and to spoken language (like stories) that is rich in imagery.

Visual learners can do the following to learn better:

- Sit near the front of the classroom.
- Have their eyesight checked on a regular basis.
- Use flashcards to study.
- Draw pictures to explain concepts.

People learn in different ways. Knowing how you learn will make it easier for you to learn and remember new information for the rest of your life.

Source: American Education Services web site (http://www.educationplanner.org).

Of course, it is much easier to teach them who needs to be there (besides themselves) than it is to teach them how to be an active member of their own IEP process. According to IDEA 2004, the required members of the IEP team include parents, general education teachers, special education teachers, test evaluators, administrators, related services staff/specialists (including a transition specialist for students ages 16–21), and the student, as appropriate. Of course, others can be invited, particularly when the parent or student requests an advocate or other participant. The IEP team members' roles are described in the following manner (U.S. Department of Education, 2000).

Parents

Parents know their child well and can talk about their child's strengths and needs as well as their ideas for enhancing their child's education. They can offer insight into how their child learns, what his or her interests are, and other aspects that only a parent can know. They can listen to what the other team members think their child needs to work on at school and share their suggestions. They can also report on whether the skills the child is learning at school are being used at home. Parents may also be able to work independently to prepare their child for the meeting.

Administrator or Individual Representing the School System

An administrator or individual representing the school system knows a great deal about special education services and educating children with disabilities. He or she can talk about the necessary school resources. It is important that this individual have the authority to commit resources and be able to ensure that whatever services are set out in the IEP will actually be provided.

General Education Teacher

If the child is (or may be) participating in the general education environment, then one of his or her general education teachers should be a member of the IEP team. This teacher has a great deal to share with the team. He or she is the person who can share information about the general education curriculum, expectations for students in the general education classroom, and teaching strategies and approaches already in place in his or her particular classroom. This information can help the IEP team make decisions about necessary supports for school staff that will ensure that the child can advance toward his or her annual goals, be involved and progress in the general curriculum, participate in extracurricular and other activities, and be educated with other children, both with and without disabilities.

Special Education Teacher

The special educator contributes important information about evidence-based practices for educating students with disabilities. Because of his or her training in the education of students with disabilities, this teacher can address issues such as modifying the general curriculum to help the child learn, identifying supplementary aids and services that the child may need to be successful in the general education classroom and elsewhere, adapting the testing and evaluation procedures so that the student can show what he or she has learned, and other aspects of individualizing instruction to meet the student's unique needs. Beyond helping to write the IEP, the special educator has responsibility for working with the student to implement the IEP and evaluate his or her progress.

Individual Who Can Interpret the Child's Evaluation Results

An individual who can interpret the child's evaluation results can be someone who fills another role in the meeting; for example, an administrator who understands standardized assessment would be capable of explaining those assessment results and how they can be used to design an appropriate IEP. In other cases, a special educator might be able to explain annual assessment results and the student's present levels of performance on the previous year's IEP goals to design the IEP for the upcoming academic year. Whoever fulfills this role must be able to talk about the instructional implications of the child's evaluation results, which will help the team plan appropriate instruction to address the child's needs.

Individuals with Knowledge or Special Expertise About the Child

The parent or the school system can invite individuals with knowledge or special expertise about the child to participate on the team. Parents, for example, may invite an advocate who knows the child, a professional with special expertise about the child and his or her disability, or others (e.g., a vocational educator who has been working with the child) who can talk about the child's strengths and/or needs. The school system may invite one or more individuals who can offer special expertise or knowledge about the child (e.g., paraprofessional, related services professional). Related services professionals are often involved as IEP team members or participants because an important part of developing an IEP is considering a child's need for related services. They share their special expertise about the child's needs and how their own professional services can address those needs. Depending on the child's individual needs, some related services professionals helping to develop the IEP in some manner might include occupational or physical therapists, adaptive physical education providers, psychologists, or speech-language pathologists.

Transition Specialist or Representatives from Transition Service Agencies

When the student reaches the age when a transition plan must also be part of the IEP, a transition specialist or representatives from transition service agencies become important participants. Whenever the purpose of a meeting is to consider needed transition services, the school must invite a representative of any other agency that is likely to be responsible for providing or paying for transition services. This individual can help the team plan any transition services the student needs as well as help explain different funding sources, criteria for qualifying to receive services, and/or the different laws and policies that outline the new roles, responsibilities, and rights. He or she can also commit the resources of the agency to pay for or provide needed transition services. If he or she does not attend the meeting, then the school must take alternative steps to obtain the agency's participation in planning the student's transition services.

Student-Invited Guests

Individuals who are invited by the student to be part of the IEP team may include, but are not limited to, friends, neighbors, relatives, teachers, coaches, club sponsors, and work-related personnel who may be able to speak to the work ethics or character of the student. These guests may increase the level of student comfort and confidence in participating in the meeting and also can provide insights about the student's interests and activities outside of school.

Student

The student may also be a member of the IEP team. If transition service needs or transition services are going to be discussed at the meeting, then the student must be invited to attend (U.S. Department of Education, 2000).

The IEP team members' roles are defined in accordance with the U.S. Department of Education. Your school district, however, might have different people who meet the requirements of one or more of theses categories who should be invited. For instance, an administrator might be a director of special education, a building principal, a special education department chair, or a specialist. The person who is qualified to interpret the assessment results might be the district administrator, a special educator, or a school psychologist. The idea that different individuals may meet the requirement to fill the roles of the meeting participants should be clarified for the student so that he or she can make an informed decision regarding whom to invite to the IEP meeting. For elementary-age students or students with more significant disabilities, such as Alejandra, it can be helpful to supply illustrations of the various categories of people who should be invited (see Figure 3.3). For example, Alejandra may have several general education teachers (physical education, music, and homeroom). Although only one is required for the IEP meeting, Alejandra may like to choose from any of those professionals to meet the requirement to include a general educator.

An older student such as Kathy, who has a better understanding of the process, could use a more detailed list such as Table 3.1. As Kathy was learning about the people who

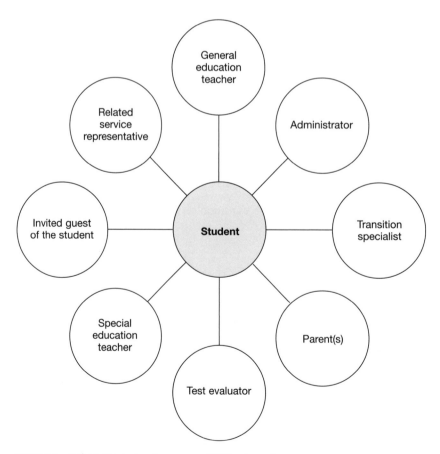

Figure 3.3. Individualized education program (IEP) team members.

Table 3.1. Individualized education program (IEP) participants

Federal requirements (IDEA 2004)	State/district requirements	My options
Special education teacher	Same	Mr. Scott
General education teacher	Same	Mrs. Rossi (history teacher)
Administrator	Principal or special education director	Mr. Kennedy (special education director) or Ms. Richardson (principal)
Assessment specialist	School psychologist	Ms. Pannozzo, Mr. Reinhardt, or Ms. Smith
Parent	Parent	Mrs. Abbott
Student	Student	Kathy Abbott
Support specialists	Speech-language pathologist (SLP), occupational therapist (OT), physical therapist (PT), and/or assistive technology (AT) specialist	Ms. Wright (SLP), Mr. Archway (PT), Mr. Jameson (OT), and/or Ms. Smyth (AT specialist)
Others	Others invited by school and/or parent	Ms. Jones (eighth-grade teacher), Grandma Abbott, Julie Wilson (friend), Beth Rolland (neighbor/friend), and/or Ms. Solomon (advocate)

Key: IDEA 2004, Individuals with Disabilities Education Improvement Act (IDEA) of 2004 (PL 108-446).

needed to be involved in her IEP meeting, Mr. Scott used a planning sheet with the information in Table 3.1 to help her identify the key people based on federal, state, and district policies (by category or title) and then determine those specific individuals who fit those categories. The first column outlines the requirements from IDEA 2004 in terms of the job titles/responsibilities of IEP team members. The second column outlines the state and district requirements. These are the job classifications of individuals who meet the requirements of the national regulations. The third column is a place to list the actual people who have that role or job title. Once those people are listed, the student can choose by circling the name of the person he or she wants to invite. Of course, you could also use pictures instead of the written names, and the student could point to the person he or she wants to invite. A modified format could be done using a computer program and voice output that says the name of each person who is an option for that role.

Assessing Student Skills

Gauging a student's skills is a critical component of preparing him or her for participating in his or her IEP. Remember, involvement stages range on a continuum where each student's level of participation depends on his or her skills and interest in the process. This initial assessment of student knowledge and skills is essential to target first steps as well as the instruction necessary to help the student increase involvement in the process. McGahee, Mason, Wallace, and Jones (2001) explained that it is imperative to assess student knowledge of the IEP process and evaluate his or her skills to communicate, set goals, engage in collaborative planning, and participate in implementing and evaluating the written plan. This assessment must answer the following questions.

- What skills does this student currently possess?

- What skills does this student need to learn?

- What supports are needed to facilitate student involvement?

How can you begin to answer these critical questions? Like any good evaluation, it is important to gather information in multiple ways, from multiple people, and in multiple settings. Pay attention to the ways that a student communicates with you and with other adults. Is he outgoing and assertive or introverted and uncertain? Does she feel comfortable in new situations, or does she appear nervous when faced with the unknown? Does he embrace a spirited discussion or shy away from disagreement? Does she have clear goals for the future or express confusion or disinterest when asked about those plans?

Of course, it is much easier to imagine the outgoing and assertive student who is comfortable in new situations and during spirited discussions and who has clear plans for the future being involved in his or her own IEP meeting. You probably already have a clear understanding of his or her skills and know that with some specific instruction, he or she would be able to learn what is necessary to be fully involved. It is more difficult to assess what students such as Susan, Dwight, and Alejandra know about their IEP as well as the skills they possess in order to be more fully involved. When you assess students with more significant disabilities, you will need to be more creative and, at the same time, more concrete with your assessment procedures.

Although you would be able to ask Kathy what she knows about her rights and responsibilities in the IEP process, and feel confident that her answer is an accurate description of what she knows, students with more significant disabilities with limited opportunities to be a self-advocate or to participate in educational planning would not be able to answer those questions with accuracy. Instead, your assessment could start by involving students in making choices, participating in a problem-solving process such as the Self-Determined Learning Model of Instruction (Agran, Alper, & Wehmeyer, 2002; Wehmeyer, Palmer, Agran, Mithaug, & Martin, 2000), or self-evaluating their progress in task completion. The Self-Determined Learning Model of Instruction involves a three-phase, self-regulated problem-solving process that will help students make choices, set goals, and solve problems for themselves. Once you identify student skills in these tasks, you can target those skills as the student's first step in a student-directed IEP process. For Alejandra, the first step was to provide a communication board so she had an opportunity to share her ideas and respond to the questions of her team. For Dwight, the first step was determining who would attend his meeting (giving him the opportunity to choose from the available people who would fill the required roles). And for Susan, the first step was asking her to choose a specific person she would like to invite to the meeting.

You can also assess students' self-determination skills by having them complete classroom exercises and lessons, observing them in situations that require them to use similar skills, having their former teachers and parents complete student information sheets, and conducting other informal and alternative assessments. Look through the student-directed IEP continuum from Chapter 1, particularly Stages 5–7: What skills are identified in these stages? Besides a student-directed IEP meeting, where else could students display or use communication or problem-solving skills? Taking time to consider these questions will help streamline your assessment process. If you already provide multiple opportunities for students to make choices, then you do not need to assess this skill. If you involve students in self-advocacy in the classroom, then you may only need to assess their ability to generalize that task to a new setting and with adults rather than their peers.

Activities useful for determining student understanding and awareness of the IEP may include fun but nontraditional methods of getting students to brainstorm and discuss the IEP process. In the next section, Mr. Scott talks about the lessons and activities he used to assess Kathy's understanding, motivation, and skills related to the IEP process. The activities were used as an introduction to more specific instruction of the components of the IEP process.

 Listening to the Experts

Teacher's Perspective

Introducing Kathy to the IEP process was not easy. There is so much to learn and understand about the practical and legal requirements of IEP development. I wondered how to break it down so that a student could understand it all. I did not want to overwhelm or scare Kathy away from the process. My first step was to assess what Kathy already knew about the IEP process and then help her fill in any gaps so that she could participate in the process and be successful. Kathy knew that an IEP was related to her educational goals in school. She lacked an understanding, however, of why the IEP was necessary, on what it should be based, and how that annual plan fit within the bigger picture of educational planning. I wanted this to be a process that Kathy could use to determine what she wanted and needed to know about her education and her dreams in life. Therefore, we moved forward by using the lesson plan (see Figure 3.4) to increase Kathy's understanding of the IEP process.

In order to assist in moving through the plan of action, Kathy and I used the Next Student Transition and Educational Planning Guide or Next S.T.E.P. curriculum (Halpern et al., 1997) as a way to get an understanding of her needs. The lessons and activities from the Next S.T.E.P curriculum provided a framework for working on identifying strengths, needs, goals, and present level of performance related to her personal life, dreams, educational needs, and transitional needs. This material proved to be really helpful as Kathy developed an understanding of why it was important to know more about herself and the IEP process. Something else occurred—the more she learned about herself, the more motivated she was to complete additional components of the Next S.T.E.P. process, set goals, and share stories

---

Carrying out your IEP meeting

Target group: *IEP students*
Target curriculum: *STEPS*

Objective/purpose:

The teacher will review with students how to conduct an IEP meeting. Students will listen for key words that are often heard during an IEP meeting. Students will learn the components of an effective IEP meeting and how student participation is important and necessary for communicating with IEP team members.

Materials:

* Guide for student participation in the IEP process
* Student-directed IEP video
* Computer to create student-directed PowerPoint
* Paper and writing material

Procedure:

1. Assess students' background, knowledge, and understanding of participation in the IEP meeting process by asking the following questions:
   * Who knows what an IEP is?
   * Who has gone to their IEP meeting before?
   * Would someone like to volunteer to explain the IEP process?
   * What does it mean to participate in your IEP meeting?

2. Show students the student-directed IEP video. Inform students that they will be watching a video of a student their own age who is participating and directing his or her own IEP meeting. Direct students to write down the members who introduce themselves during the IEP video and to write down "key terms" that they have heard discussed in the class or during their own IEP meeting.

3. Review and define for students key terms that are used in the meeting and key terms students have written.

4. Stop the video after 5-minute increments to discuss the sections of the meeting. Students will identify the greetings section of the IEP meeting, student presentation of their material/IEP, IEP team discussion, and the close of the IEP meeting.

5. After the student-directed IEP video, give students a copy of the Step-by-Step Student-Directed IEP Guide and break students into groups of four so that they can practice the IEP meeting process with each other.

Evaluation:

6. Ask student to create a PowerPoint guide using the key terms they have defined and the student-directed IEP guide. Ask them to reflect on the idea: "What if you were required to participate in your IEP? How would you conduct the IEP meeting?" Students will use the information from the video, what they have practiced, and the key terms to complete a 10-slide PowerPoint that will aide in guiding and participating in their IEP meeting. Slide topics may include introduction, review of information, strengths, weaknesses, current class performance, plans after high school, clubs/activities, community activities, supports needed, and closing.

Figure 3.4. Lesson plan for carrying out the individualized education program (IEP) meeting.

of her accomplishments. Guided by the original goals set through use of the Self-Determined Learning Model of Instruction, Kathy learned significantly more about herself and the steps and components of an IEP. She learned that the IEP was more than pieces of paper that outlined what she did in school; it also provided a way to help her set and achieve goals for her own life.

Student's Perspective

Setting the goal to learn about the IEP process and about myself was really fun and exciting. I cannot believe that I learned so much about myself. And once I knew so much about myself, I also knew that I had to be a part of the IEP process. I know I can be a leader and someone who can have a say in what it is I want to do.

Parent's Perspective

I knew that Kathy was learning more about the IEP process because she would come home and talk to me about it weekly. She would talk about who would be in the meeting and the significance of the meeting. It was almost as if she wanted to have the meeting right away. She told me that she would surprise me with how well she would be able to lead her meeting, so I knew as she learned more about the process, her confidence was growing.

Reflection on Kathy's Example

Figures 3.5 and 3.6 were developed by Mr. Scott to help Kathy learn more about the IEP process and her rights throughout all three phases (premeeting, meeting, and implementation/evaluation). He used activities typically used in the classroom, such as word searches, true/false questions, and open-ended questions, that can be adapted as needed. In the word search activity (see Figure 3.5), Kathy increased her familiarity with IEP terms. The activity was not only fun for Kathy, but also meaningful for the journey on which she was preparing to participate.

The second activity (see Figure 3.6) provided an opportunity for Kathy to identify individuals who were important to her (Question 3 in the example), which could help her identify key participants that she and Mr. Scott would invite to her IEP meeting. Kathy used this information to describe a general education classroom teacher whose teaching style was particularly conducive to Kathy's learning style. This teacher was therefore invited to the IEP meeting, even though she was not typically a person who would have been at the table. In addition, Kathy's answers to all the questions provided other information that was used to draft IEP goals that could be discussed during the IEP meeting. The information provided by the general education teacher and Kathy herself helped the team identify supports and services Kathy needed to help achieve her annual goals.

My Own IEP

```
L  R  S  P  S  I  S  R  Z  E  L  J  W  Y  C  S  L  Z  K  J
I  E  P  E  W  N  I  P  S  Y  V  A  Q  J  A  E  A  X  O  M
J  S  A  J  V  G  O  W  E  Z  E  N  G  C  S  T  I  D  Z  E
R  P  E  D  H  I  T  I  W  C  O  O  C  E  Y  F  T  I  Z  E
M  O  D  T  E  I  T  F  T  I  I  O  K  T  L  N  N  S  Z  T
F  N  S  Q  N  R  B  C  T  A  M  A  I  X  H  P  E  A  Y  I
E  S  V  G  O  F  S  A  E  M  C  L  L  H  D  E  D  B  E  N
Q  I  Z  L  M  H  C  H  O  J  I  I  O  H  V  O  I  I  N  G
M  B  A  E  F  U  U  D  I  B  B  F  F  A  H  Z  F  L  O  Y
O  I  Y  L  D  Q  A  N  I  P  K  O  L  I  O  A  N  I  I  K
V  L  Y  E  D  T  R  G  M  X  Q  U  W  Z  D  N  O  T  T  K
B  I  F  M  I  A  I  W  S  L  A  O  G  W  N  O  C  Y  I  T
D  T  B  O  W  L  Z  N  Y  T  Q  R  O  T  U  X  M  E  S  S
J  Y  N  R  E  S  T  R  I  C  T  I  V  E  Y  V  R  H  N  A
X  S  Z  F  U  D  G  O  A  D  V  O  C  A  C  Y  C  M  A  E
F  S  S  F  W  X  N  G  I  K  G  X  T  O  W  T  I  O  R  L
S  B  L  F  T  W  O  A  U  U  Z  F  S  Q  B  T  L  V  T  H
O  E  O  E  Q  V  C  S  U  L  A  U  D  I  V  I  D  N  I  E
S  W  J  F  B  X  J  C  T  B  J  T  D  E  K  C  F  Z  H  Q
H  W  J  J  D  I  K  N  O  I  T  A  N  I  M  R  E  T  E  D
```

ACCOMMODATIONS	ADVOCACY	CONFIDENTIAL	DETERMINATION
DISABILITY	EDUCATION	ELIGIBILITY	EVALUATION
GOALS	IEP	INDIVIDUAL	LEADERSHIP
LEAST RESTRICTIVE	LEGAL	MEETING	MODIFICATIONS
OBJECTIVES	RESPONSIBILITY	RESTRICTIVE	RIGHTS
SELF DETERMINATION	SPECIAL EDUCATION	TRANSITION	

Figure 3.5. Word search game to help familiarize individualized education program (IEP) terms. Two-word entries may appear on different lines.

 # Tips and Strategies

As discussed previously, not every student will be at Kathy's stage of the continuum and be able to direct and lead as much of the IEP process. The following are tips and strategies from teachers who work with students at all age levels and at all ability levels who have begun the process of helping students understand the IEP process and their rights within that process. Teachers speak about the need to begin early to teach students about their rights in the IEP process and identify ways that they want to be and are able to be involved. Students might not be able to understand all of their rights; the first step is to determine whether they are aware that they can have a say in the process.

Being aware of me…

1. I believe that I have strong skills in the following areas

   _____

2. I believe that my weaknesses are in

   _____

3. These are the people I believe may be able to help me the most

   _____

4. Here are things that help me perform well in school

   _____

5. If I had my choice, I would take the following classes

   _____

6. Here are things I most enjoy about school

   _____

7. I have been involved in an IEP meeting before.	**True**	**False**
8. I know what happens in an IEP meeting.	**True**	**False**
9. I know what my goals are in my IEP.	**True**	**False**
10. I have rights according to my IEP.	**True**	**False**
11. Only my parents have responsibilities for carrying out my IEP.	**True**	**False**
12. I have been invited to my IEP before.	**True**	**False**
13. I can name two people at my last IEP meeting.	**True**	**False**
14. I know exactly what to say at my IEP meeting.	**True**	**False**
15. I know what my disability is.	**True**	**False**

Figure 3.6. Self-awareness questionnaire.

- Start by helping students understand advocacy and/or self-advocacy. Even students with an understanding of advocacy might not feel comfortable being a self-advocate. Explain the range of options: self-advocacy, self-advocacy with support, joint advocacy, bringing in an advocate while still being present, or choosing an advocate while not being present.

- Help students understand their disability. There are many books that you can use that are tailored to different ages and reading levels and can help introduce the topic or help students gain a better understanding of their own disability. Picture books can be particularly useful for this process. The appendix at the end of this book includes some of the prepared curricula for self-determination, which have great lesson plans for helping students understand their disability and its affect on their education as well as postschool goals.

- Talk with the student to do an informal assessment of his or her understanding of the IEP process. Collect information from parents as well as past teachers to help paint a clearer picture of student knowledge of the IEP process. Although this is particularly important for students with limited communication ability, it is important to do this for all students. Self-reports are not typically completely accurate.

- Find a rationale that speaks to each student. Many students have a difficult time understanding long-range contingencies, so find ways to help them understand a reason to be involved in their IEP meeting that is more immediate. Students will still have that long-range benefit even if they cannot quite understand the implications. For example, a fifth-grade student would better understand the need for self-advocacy if the explanation is about how it will help him or her next year in middle school rather than when he or she is in college.

- Encourage students to share what they are learning with their parents and with other adults who are important in their lives. Sometimes parents are reluctant to come to IEP meetings or they are reluctant to have their son or daughter attend. Usually that is because they believe that the meetings will be run in the same way as the past. They quickly change their minds when they hear students talk enthusiastically about the meeting and their involvement in it.

Here are some suggestions for building awareness of the IEP process when students have significant support needs:

- Develop a set of picture cards to represent and teach key concepts of the IEP process

- Develop other instructional materials (crossword puzzles, games, worksheets, reading comprehension activities) to teach about main parts and key concepts of the IEP process

- Make student-specific adaptations as needed (e.g., high-contrast line drawings, raised letters)

- Make sure that teaching strategies and materials match students' communication and learning modes (e.g., object cue rather than a picture card for a student who is deafblind)

Here are some suggestions for assessment of knowledge about IEP/rights when students have significant support needs:

- If picture cards have been developed, then they can be used to assess student knowledge (e.g., have student place cards in sequence, match cards to correct step in the process)

- Use other instructional supports to assess student knowledge (e.g., place correct braille label under each textured picture, use sign language to explain what student learned when attending a friend's IEP meeting).

Conclusion

This chapter discussed students' rights and responsibilities pertaining to the IEP process. The student has a number of rights and responsibilities that should be carefully reviewed before and after the IEP meeting. It is also critical that all parties participating in the IEP process be aware of the rights and responsibilities of the student. Equally important, knowing and carrying out the roles and responsibilities of the participants at the IEP meeting is critical to not only sustain legal requirements but also provide needed support for the student during the meeting.

Students must be prepared to know their rights, responsibilities, and roles of the individuals attending their IEP meeting. Teachers may use various forms of instructional strategies to assess students' understanding of the IEP process. By following these suggestions, students will be better prepared to participate in their IEP meeting.

References

Agran, M., Alper, S., & Wehmeyer, M. (2002). Access to the general curriculum for students with significant disabilities. *Education and Training in Mental Retardation and Developmental Disabilities, 37,* 123–133.

Halpern, A., Herr, C., Wolf, N., Doren, B., Johnson, M., & Lawson, J. (1997). *The Next S.T.E.P. (Student Transition and Educational Planning) curriculum.* Austin, TX: PRO-ED.

Individuals with Disabilities Education Improvement Act (IDEA) 2004, PL 108-446, 20 U.S.C. §§ 1400 *et seq.*

Lehmann, J.P., Bassett, D.S., & Sands, D.J. (1999). Students' participation in transition-related actions: A qualitative study. *Remedial and Special Education, 20,* 160–169.

Lovitt, T.C., Cushing, S.S., & Stump, C.S. (1994). High school students rate their IEPs: Low opinions and lack of ownership. *Intervention in School and Clinic, 30,* 34–37.

McGahee, M., Mason, C., Wallace, T., & Jones, B. (2001). *Student-led IEPs: A guide for student involvement.* Arlington, VA: Council for Exceptional Children.

Morningstar, M.E., Turnbull, A.P., & Turnbull, H.R., III. (1995). What do students with disabilities tell us about the importance of family involvement in the transition from school to adult life? *Exceptional Children, 62,* 249–260.

Powers, L.E., Turner, A., Matuszewski, J., Wilson, R., & Loesch, C., (1999). A qualitative analysis of student involvement in transition planning. *Journal for Vocational Special Needs Education, 21,* 18–26.

Rockingham County Public Schools. (2008). *Special education handbook.* Harrisonburg, VA: Author.

Sweeney, M. (1996). Effectiveness of the self-directed IEP (Doctoral dissertation, Florida State University, 1996). *Dissertation Abstracts International, 58,* 03A.

Thoma, C.A., Bartholomew, C.C., & Scott, L.A. (2009). *Universal design for transition: A roadmap for planning and instruction.* Baltimore: Paul H. Brookes Publishing Co.

Thoma, C.A., & Getzel, E.E. (2005). Self-determination is what it's all about: What post-secondary students with disabilities tell us are important considerations for success. *Education and Training in Mental Retardation and Development Disabilities, 40,* 35–48.

Thoma, C.A., Rogan, P., & Baker, S. (2001). Student involvement in transition planning: Unheard voices. *Education and Training in Mental Retardation and Developmental Disabilities, 36*(1), 16–29.

U.S. Department of Education. (2000). *A guide to the individualized education program.* Retrieved September 1, 2008, from http://www.ed.gov/offices/OSERS

Wehmeyer, M.L., Palmer, S.B., Agran, M., Mithaug, D.E., & Martin, J. (2000). Promoting causal agency: The self-determined learning model of instruction. *Exceptional Children, 66,* 439–453.

4

....

Student Involvement in Assessment

Colleen A. Thoma, Christina C. Bartholomew, and Ronald Tamura

Effective individualized educational planning requires high-quality, targeted assessment of student strengths, skills, and needs, even when the education is linked to a common set of academic standards, such as the general education curriculum. Although each student will be learning the same academic information (more or less), he or she may do so in a number of different ways and demonstrate his or her knowledge and skills in a variety of ways. It is critical that teachers find ways to assess each student's knowledge and skills so that the teacher and other members of the individualized education program (IEP) team can build on strengths, remediate challenges, and determine growth over time.

For a student-directed IEP approach, assessment goes beyond informing the teacher's practice and decisions. Assessment should also provide an opportunity for students to understand their own strengths and needs to target their goals for the year, as well as have some way to analyze their progress (or lack thereof) over the past year. Students should have the opportunity to engage in multiple assessment practices and should be allowed to explore which options best support their preferences and abilities. Creating multiple assessment opportunities and allowing the student to have input in assessment options can help ensure that quality information is shared with the IEP team and, in turn, becomes the data used to make decisions. This chapter provides information about how to involve students in a number of assessment practices from identifying assessment questions and collecting data to using assessment data to make instructional/educational program decisions.

Assessment Options that Facilitate Student Choice

There are multiple assessment options available in different academic and transition domains, and different assessments should be used for different students based on what you already know about the student and what information you still need to gather in order to make wise decisions (Sax & Thoma, 2002). Involving students in the assessment process provides additional benefits—teachers can begin to understand how students effectively demonstrate their knowledge and their preferences for communication. This information is particularly important during the IEP process for team members who will have a broader understanding of how to collect information that accurately demonstrates a student's progress, abilities, and interests. You can involve students by helping them identify what they already know, what they want to know, and then the steps to discover that information (i.e., what assessment to choose).

There are three different types of assessment procedures that can be used to inform the IEP development process—formal, informal, and alternative (Sax & Thoma, 2001). This chapter provides a brief overview of these types and some examples of assessment practices that fit under each of these categories. If you need more detailed information about assessment, however, then you should seek additional information, as the IEPs you develop will only be as good as the information on which they are based. Some resources for this basic information about assessment are included in Table 4.1.

Formal Assessments

Formal assessments can provide the beginning framework for planning and instruction. Formal assessments are sometimes referred to as *standardized measures* and are usually either criterion or norm referenced. One example of a formal assessment is the Woodcock-Johnson Achievement Test (Woodcock, McGrew, & Mather, 2006), which measures areas such as cognitive abilities, oral language, academic achievement, and intellectual abilities.

These types of assessments can allow students to demonstrate their knowledge in a certain area or can provide information about how students compare with their peers in a certain domain. Information gained from these types of assessments can help the IEP team begin planning for cognitive and/or social supports, as well as for other assessments that may be needed. In addition, formal assessments can also help students understand how they perform when given specific directions and a formal format to follow. Information gained from formal assessments can be used as a starting point in planning and should be supplemented with additional information gained from other assessment options.

Table 4.1.   Assessment resources

Chandler, L.K., & Dahlquist, C.M. (2010). *Functional assessment: Strategies to prevent and remediate challenging behavior in school settings.* Upper Saddle River, NJ: Prentice Hall.

Herman, J.L., Aschbacher, P.R., & Winters, L. (1992). *A practical guide to alternative assessment.* Alexandria, VA: Association for Supervision and Curriculum Development.

McLoughlin, J.A., & Lewis, R.B. (2001). *Assessing students with special needs* (5th ed.). Upper Saddle River, NJ: Prentice Hall.

Overton, T. (2009). *Assessment in special education: An applied approach.* Upper Saddle River, NJ: Prentice Hall.

Sitlington, P.L., Neubert, D.A., Begun, W.H., Lombard, R.C., & Leconte, P.J. (2007). *Assess for success: A practitioner's handbook on transition assessment.* Thousand Oaks, CA: Corwin Press.

Thompson, S.J., Quenemoen, R.F., Thurlow, M.L., & Ysseldyke, J.E. (2001). *Alternative assessments for students with disabilities.* Thousand Oaks, CA: Corwin Press.

Trice, A.D. (2000). *A handbook of classroom assessment.* Boston: Addison Wesley.

Wiggins, G., & McTighe, J. (1998). *Understanding by design.* Alexandria, VA: Association for Supervision and Curriculum Development.

Informal Assessments

Informal assessments are designed to provide information about how a student is currently performing and/or his or her knowledge in a certain area. These types of assessments can be based not only on academic scores or current functioning, but also on documentation of progress. Informal assessments can include items such as teacher checklists, teacher observations, student checklists, tests (e.g., unit tests, quizzes) designed to measure student knowledge (not norm referenced), and interviews. These types of assessments can support the findings of formal assessments by providing a more detailed look into particular areas of a student's functioning. This supports the IEP team when creating the IEP plan because they gain an overall picture of functioning in multiple areas. By allowing multiple informal assessment opportunities, students can begin to understand their preferences and strengths in demonstrating their knowledge and interests. For example, some students will find that they prefer using technology when asked to provide information about themselves or their knowledge of certain academic content. Other students may find that they would rather express this information through a written essay format. Educators must allow students to provide information in a variety of ways so that students can gain an understanding of how they perform best. By understanding student preferences in assessment practices, the IEP team can collect information in ways that support these preferences, thus gaining information more efficiently. This can also support students as they begin to develop their career interests and begin planning for postsecondary options.

Alternative Assessments

Alternative assessments include methods such as portfolios, student journals, performance-based assessments, and oral defenses. They represent very diverse procedures, but the common thread is that they require that students "perform, create, produce or do something" (Herman, Aschbacher, & Winters, 1992, p. 6). In fact, they include strategies that teachers have used for years to guide their practice, but alternative assessment strategies make these practices explicit. They provide more than a snapshot of student abilities; when used appropriately, they should provide a record of student growth over time.

Portfolios are a collection of a student's work designed to demonstrate his or her progress, accomplishments, knowledge, and/or skills. Portfolios are alternative assessments that can focus on academics and/or functional abilities, as well as a student's progress in a certain area (e.g., employment experiences, social interactions, academic progress). Evidence for portfolios should be collected over time and can include items such as completed student work, photographs of group activities, teacher-made checklists that record multiple observations of a student's ability or knowledge, videotape or audio recordings of the student's performance, graphic organizers, pictures of the student's projects, and traditional tests and worksheets.

Alternative assessments can be used by the student to share information with the IEP team about his or her accomplishments, interests, and experiences. Allowing the students to have a choice in the types of evidence included in their portfolios encourages students to self-manage their assessments, provides opportunities for students to make decisions, and provides the teacher insight into the way students like to learn and the items that they feel are good examples of their abilities.

Steps Needed to Effectively and Efficiently Link Assessment to the IEP Process

The Individuals with Disabilities Education Improvement Act (IDEA) of 2004 (PL 108-446) requires that academic and transition decisions be addressed in the IEP. The quality of these decisions is dependent on the accuracy, depth, and breath of the information used by the members of the IEP team. Assessments are an integral part of this information gathering, and the importance of the quality of information collected through assessments cannot be underestimated.

IEP team members must be provided with accurate and relevant information in order to also demonstrate a clear picture of the student's interests and abilities. Assessments are a key factor in assuring that a student's voice is heard through the IEP process and that the information is relevant in relation to the student's strengths, needs, preferences, interests, and long-range goals. He or she must be given the opportunity to understand and reflect on his or her abilities and interests prior to an IEP meeting in order to effectively be involved. In addition, it is important to involve the student in planning the assessments to ensure that goals and objectives are written in accordance with his or her preferences. See Figure 4.1 for an example of helping students think about and summarize these interests and preferences. Time spent collecting assessment information can detract from time spent teaching new information, so it is important that wise decisions are made regarding what information is needed, what assessment strategies and procedures will provide that information, and how to combine assessment with instructional practices.

Step 1: Identify the Information You Want to Obtain from the Assessment

What do you want to accomplish with your assessment efforts? Is this a student whose behavior challenges have not been adequately addressed so you need to conduct a functional behavior analysis to determine why the behavior occurs? Is this is an older student who needs information to help make a decision about an employment goal? Is this a student who has not been included in general education classrooms, so you need information about what supports he or she would need to be successful in this new setting? Or, do you simply need information about academic progress to ensure that this student is making sufficient progress in school? The first step of identifying exactly what information is needed from the assessment will help guide your assessment process and prevent duplication of efforts.

Dwight did not know what he wanted to do after high school; he only communicated that he wanted to have "a job." He also did not have much prior work experience. He and his team identified that an assessment needed to be completed that would *identify Dwight's work interests and abilities.*

Figure 4.2 provides a framework you can use to highlight the information you already know about a student and target the questions that need answered by an assessment.

Individual interest inventory

For (name): _____   Date: _____

Assisted by: _____

- First, have your classmates list your likes and rank your top 10.
- Second, add or delete whatever you think is correct. Then, rank your top 10.
- Do the same for what you dislike. Use more paper if you need it.

Things I like	My top 10	Top 10 by others		Things I don't like	My top 10	Top 10 by others

Figure 4.1. Individual interest inventory. (Developed by Sandy Martin in conjunction with the Vermilion County Transition Planning Committee TOTAL Team. Reprinted by permission.)

(continued)

Figure 4.1. *(continued)*

Interest ideas

____ Taking a walk
____ Playing a ball game
____ Watching a ball game
____ Reading a book or magazine
____ Talking on the telephone
____ Swimming
____ Doing crafts
____ Making model cars, etc.
____ Playing card games
____ Playing board games
____ Baking
____ Hitting golf balls
____ Being a member of a club: _____
____ Listening to music
____ Dancing (kind): _____
____ Watching movies at the theatre
____ Hiking
____ Canoeing
____ Skateboarding
____ Rollerblading/skating
____ Shopping
____ Driving
____ Walking/playing with a pet: _____
____ Eating vegetables
____ Watching television
____ Playing a sport: _____
____ Listening to the radio
____ Boating
____ Fishing
____ Talking to people who are trustworthy
____ Eating Chinese food
____ Visiting friends/family
____ Visiting a theme park
____ Going camping
____ Going to a flea market
____ Playing a musical instrument: _____
____ Going to concerts
____ Going to sporting events: _____
____ Cheerleading
____ Eating Mexican food
____ Planning/working at dances/social events
____ Working on the school newspaper/yearbook
____ Being a leader
____ Eating fruits
____ Taking directions from others
____ Working by myself (independently)
____ Working in a team
____ Being alone

____ Riding a horse
____ Bicycling
____ Riding a motorcycle/ATV
____ Going on a vacation/traveling
____ Going to the city
____ Going to the beach/lake
____ Being around people who are generous
____ Eating in a restaurant
____ Going to the library
____ Eating at fast food places
____ Going to museums
____ Exploring caves
____ Hunting
____ Cooking meals
____ Cleaning things
____ Doing laundry
____ Making myself look good
____ Sewing
____ Trying new/unusual foods
____ Drawing
____ Painting
____ Playing video games
____ Eating my favorite food: _____
____ Surfing the Internet
____ Learning new computer programs
____ Writing letters
____ Sending e-mails
____ Meeting new people
____ Talking to people who are kind
____ Eating hamburgers and french fries
____ Eating pizza
____ Watching movies at home
____ Working to make spending money
____ Doing yoga
____ Exercising
____ Attending aerobics class
____ Gardening
____ Acting/drama
____ Giving a speech
____ Singing
____ Writing stories/poems
____ Being a member of a fan club
____ Being kind to others
____ Looking at fashion magazines
____ Volunteering to help others
____ Establishing a regular routine
____ Enjoying change/new things to do
____ Attending school/learning new things

What do we want to learn?	What do we already know?	What questions do we still have?	How will we answer those questions?
What job do I want to have after high school?	I worked in a fast-food restaurant and did not like it. I do not know what I might want to do.	What jobs match my preferences and interests?	Complete an interest inventory
	Inventory indicated jobs in data entry and/or computer science.	Are my computer/data entry skills sufficient? What other preferences are necessary to make a job choice?	Have three or more on-the-job experiences in computer/data entry positions. Collect data about work performance, supervisory evaluation of work, and reflect on preferred and non-preferred aspects of the jobs.
	A job in data entry or computers is a good match for me. My computer/data entry skills are sufficient for an entry-level position. I need a computer work station with some adaptations (alternative keyboard, word prediction, voice output). I also prefer to work independently with some occasional interactions with others. I prefer a supervisor who is direct and funny.	What other possibilities are there? What are the require-ments for post-secondary training in computers?	Complete an Internet search of computer jobs and their educational requirements. Visit three local postsecondary institutions with computer programs (university, community college, training program) and collect information about costs, admission requirements, and job outlook and placement, as well as program requirements.

Figure 4.2. Example of student direction of assessment.

Step 2: Choose the Appropriate
Assessment Strategy to Gather the Targeted Information

There are many assessment strategies, and each one has its own strengths and weaknesses. It is important to keep this in mind when making decisions about which assessments you will use. Some assessment choices are obvious—if you want to know about a student's academic progress, you do not use an interest inventory. Instead, you look at a curriculum-based measure that provides the most comprehensive information about what a student has learned. In order to gain knowledge of academic progress, you may choose to start gathering information by examining posttests in certain academic areas, interviewing the student with targeted questions and recording answers using a checklist, or building a portfolio collection of past work samples.

Once you choose the appropriate category of assessment (e.g., an assessment of reading, employment skills, or behavior), you need to choose which of the multiple assessment instruments you will need. In general, assessments that are standardized or paper-and-pencil based will provide information about what a student knows or believes and are good starting points particularly if you do not have much prior knowledge.

Dwight's team needed to pick assessment strategies that would *identify Dwight's work interests and abilities.* Dwight's teacher showed him how to use a web-based employment interest inventory.

This type of assessment can provide a great starting point for exploration into career fields and job experiences. Of course, a standardized interest inventory has some drawbacks. First, it is only as accurate as the answers that students provide. Dwight might not have sufficient experiences in his life to make some decisions about his preferences, or a preference might not be a determining factor in a good job match. Dwight might prefer to be alone, but given a job he enjoys, he might be fine with more interaction with others. That kind of in-depth information can only be assessed by more subjective, performance-based assessment processes that provide opportunities to try jobs out and reflect on the experiences. Dwight's ability to perform tasks on the job, as well as meet the social and interactional components of the work, would be gathered through observations of Dwight at work. Of course, this type of assessment provides additional complications in that it would take more time and coordination to implement than more traditional classroom-based assessments.

It is important to think creatively in the assessment process—Dwight's teacher worked with Dwight to identify a summer job and then arranged for both Dwight and his supervisor to collect some of the data necessary to bring back to the IEP team. For other students who needed similar performance-based assessments of work skills, the teacher used parents, job coaches, instructional assistants, and/or co-workers to help collect the on-the-job information. For others in school or in the classroom, jobs provided some baseline assessment information that could be used for educational planning purposes. The last column of Figure 4.2 provides a way to target the assessments that will best provide missing information necessary for IEP teams to make educational decisions and plans.

To target the assessment strategy that would best provide the information teams need, however, one must be familiar with available assessments and their strengths and weaknesses. There are so many options that it is probably unrealistic to expect that teachers would have sufficient comprehensive knowledge of the assessment strategies and instruments that are available. The National Secondary Transition Technical Assistance Center's (2009) web site provides a starting point for expanding your knowledge of assessment strategies and instruments. See the resources list in the appendix at the end of this book for more information.

Step 3: Conduct the Assessment and Evaluate the Data

The third step is to implement the assessment procedures that were chosen to specifically target the information you need to make educational decisions and transition plans. Collect and then analyze the data to determine 1) what you learned about this particular student and 2) if you learned what you needed to learn (or need to have additional assessments). It is important that you follow a few simple rules when you are evaluating the data collected during the assessment.

If your assessment was a formal assessment, then it is important that you follow the prescribed protocol for collecting and analyzing the data. In addition, you must be sure that the data is being used for the original intended purpose. An assessment of math achievement will provide fairly reliable information about what a student has learned in math. It will not provide information about whether that student will be able to be an accountant.

If your assessment is subjective, such as an observation, a portfolio, or a performance-based assessment, then you will want to take steps to double check the results. Having interrater reliability checks, in which another observer/evaluator conducts the assessment process simultaneously and results are compared, would be a preferred strategy to control for any possible bias in the results. Having two people available to conduct an assessment might not be possible; in those instances, you should seek other information to help either confirm or counter the results you obtained (e.g., conducting a similar assessment at a different time of day or in a different location, collecting other information to triangulate your results).

In Dwight's example, the purpose of the assessment was to *identify Dwight's work interests and abilities* through an interest inventory and a series of observations at different work sites based on the results of the interest inventory. A web-based interest inventory was used to identify a starting point for his work experiences, and it targeted work in the computer field. As a result, Dwight's teacher found two job shadowing experiences for him. Job shadowing is a common work assessment strategy that provides an opportunity to spend time at a specific job, working alongside an employee in your area of interest. It is typically short term, from 1 week to about 1 month in duration.

Dwight's job shadowing experiences included data entry and web design. Observational data was collected by the teacher, and Dwight kept a checklist of his work tasks and used a tape recorder to keep a verbal journal that chronicled his perceptions of the two jobs (what he liked, what he did not like, and what he thought about the work experience).

Dwight's teacher also created informal assessments to record Dwight's typing speed, his errors in data entry, the number of interactions with others, and length of time he could work without frustration. They also collected qualitative data about his preferences related to interacting with others and typing and entering data into the computer, as well as subjective ratings of his ability to interact with others, his confidence in his ability to learn the job, and his comfort in the overall experience of working in each setting. Once all the data was collected, Dwight and his teacher sat down to look at the data and discussed what they each thought it said about his ability to hold a job in data entry and/or web design. Both agreed that the data collected indicated that a job in data entry was a good option for him, matching both his skills and his preferences for work environment.

Step 4: Share the Information

It is essential to the IEP process that all team members have adequate information to make effective decisions regarding goals, objectives, academic placement, and transition services for the student. IEP team members must be able to share information with one another prior to, during, and after the IEP meeting. Consideration should be given to how colleagues can share information strategically and effectively. Once all the data is collected, you need some way to summarize it and share it with others so that it can be most effectively used to make educational decisions. Figure 4.3 is a comprehensive strengths/needs planning tool that supports team members as they plan universally for assessments during the transition planning process. This tool helps to document specific assessments given, their targeted purpose, and the information learned from the data collection and evaluation process. It further helps IEP team members share assessment information with one another and document the clarity and depth of the information gathered during the planning process (Thoma, Bartholomew, & Scott, 2009).

 Listening to the Experts

Teacher's Perspective

By getting Kathy involved in her IEP, essential steps of the process seem to have gotten easier. Collecting data to assess characteristics of Kathy's disability, educational needs, and transitional needs are basic requirements for accurately completing an IEP. By involving Kathy in collecting this information, I was able to do a better job of reviewing her strengths, weaknesses, and preferences. The IEP team was able to do a better job in creating meaningful academic and transition goals.

Formal assessments, such as psychological and achievement tests, are typically reviewed during the IEP process. Information about her performance on the state standardized academic tests for courses she completed (math, science, English, social studies), as well as her IQ tests, were shared in the IEP team meeting. That provided information to help with choosing courses for the coming year, as well as identifying the supports she might need when and if she goes to postsecondary education.

Student: _____   IEP date: _____

Academic assessments

Academic content	Grade-level performance	Standardized test performance	Accommodations/ modifications
Reading			
Math			
English			
Social studies			
Science			
Progress toward school requirements			

Other assessments required by IDEA 2004

Area	Current performance	Prior assessment	Current accommodations	Assessments needed
Behavior				
Assistive technology				
Time with peers without disabilities				
Participation in standardized assessments				

Getting the Most Out of IEPs: An Educator's Guide to the Student-Directed Approach by Colleen A. Thoma & Paul Wehman
Copyright © 2010 by Paul H. Brookes Publishing Co., Inc. All rights reserved.

Figure 4.3.   Individualized education program (IEP) assessment planning form.

(continued)

Figure 4.3. *(continued)*

Area	Current performance	Prior assessment	Current accommodations	Assessments needed
Communication				
Braille				

Self-determination/transition assessments

Area	Current level	Preferences	Summary of assessments	Assessments needed
Knowledge of self and disability				
Transition: Employment				
Transition: Post-secondary education				
Transition: Functional skills				
Transition: Independent living				
Transition: Adult services				
Progress toward graduation requirements				

Yet, that information was not sufficient to use in developing Kathy's transition IEP plan. Because Kathy, her mother, and I agreed to involve Kathy in the assessment process as we collected information about her community involvement skills and abilities, she identified that she wanted to learn to take a bus. A situational assessment was organized to help determine her ability to use the city bus to travel to work. Based on the assessment data, goals related to reading bus schedules, learning to understand street signs, and learning to handle emergency situations using a problem-solving approach were linked to academics and included in her IEP. Then, once they were implemented, Kathy completed simple checklists to measure her progress toward achieving those goals and shared that information at her next IEP meeting.

Student's Perspective

When I first began to collect information about myself, I did not understand it. But, after a while, I started noticing what areas I was strong in and where I was weak. When I noticed what my weaknesses were, I started to ask Mr. Scott if maybe they should be goals for me to work on.

Parent's Perspective

I have noticed an increase in Kathy's involvement in gathering information about herself. I think it's great. She is noticing more things about herself. This will help her not only in school but in life in general. There has definitely been a growth in the wealth of information that is included in determining Kathy's IEP, and I'm proud that she was a factor in collecting that wealth of information. I think overall it will make her a better person.

Reflection on Kathy's Example

There were a variety of ways that Mr. Scott involved Kathy in assessment as one of the ways they prepared for her student-directed IEP. First, he used a combination of assessments from commercially available student-led IEP curricula that helped Kathy succinctly describe her preferences, interests, strengths, and needs as she saw herself. Many of the assessments were from the Next S.T.E.P. curriculum (Halpern et al., 1997), and these were critical in helping Kathy identify her strengths and needs and eventually target additional assessments that would provide information beyond what she and her IEP team members already knew.

He then used the IEP assessment inventory (see Figure 4.3) to help Kathy summarize all the information so that she could share it with her IEP team. It made a significant difference in how her team viewed her strengths and needs. They each reported that they felt better prepared to participate in her educational planning process and felt that they could make more informed decisions about Kathy's educational goals.

Tips and Strategies

This book is not only about students who can easily assume more responsibility for directing their IEP process. It also helps IEP team members find ways to facilitate the involvement and direction of students with more significant support needs. The following tips and strategies will help you get started and/or help students with whom you work take another step forward in directing their IEP process.

- Focus assessment practices to measure individual steps within academic and functional tasks.

- Plan for assessments to be part of your instructional practices.

- Record information over time and across multiple settings.

- Focus on functional tasks as they relate to the academic objectives.

- Look beyond the standardized assessments.

- Investigate the multiple free or low-cost assessments that are available online. By themselves, they are not sufficient for educational planning, but they can provide useful information when used in concert with other assessments.

- Student involvement in assessment can begin with identifying preferences and interests through a self-report or interview and by observing students in multiple settings, doing a range of different activities.

- Provide opportunities for students to try different things to assess preferences and interests. Be creative and give students adequate time to determine if an activity or setting is a preferred one, especially if the student needs to learn a new skill to be successful in the new situation/setting.

- Link a preferred activity with a new one to increase/broaden students' experiences.

- Be aware of new opportunities to assess and people who can help. Parents, friends, and other adults in the community can provide useful information.

- Identify key times over the course of a student's academic career to conduct a comprehensive reassessment. For example, at the time of critical transitions (going to a new school, after a period of growth, after a significant change at home or in the community).

- When you are working with a new student, do not assume that the present level of performance is an adequate summary of a student's complete assessment information. Go back and read through past assessment reports, and conduct assessments that will give you information to determine the accuracy of past assessments.

- Even students who struggle with writing can provide information about their preferences and interests. You can have them point to pictures of things they like to do or would like to do. Having students complete a collage or presenting two options and having them point to the one they like can be effective strategies in which students will be more likely to participate.

- Do not forget to develop a record of preferences and interests that can survive beyond the IEP preparation process and can be modified as the student and educational team learn more.

- Remember to involve students in the functional behavior assessment process. Their perception of why they struggle with keeping their behavior under control and what might help is important. It might not solve the problem, but it can often lead to the right combination of supports, replacement behaviors, and/or environmental modifications.

- Consider collecting information about the adequacy of the adaptations, modifications, and/or accommodations, as well as a student's academic skills and needs.

- Look at a student's coping skills and/or stress management skills.

Conclusion

Assessments are an integral part of effective IEP planning. When choosing assessments, educators need to consider the information they need to gain, the types of assessments that will provide the needed information, the preferences and strengths of the student, and how they will record and share the information. Both formal and informal assessments should be considered to develop and record progress on goals and objectives. In addition, by providing multiple assessment opportunities, students gain an understanding of how they best perform as well as a more accurate picture of their current functioning. Effective and accurate assessment opportunities are essential in planning quality academic and transition outcomes.

References

Halpern, A., Herr, C., Wolf, N., Doren, B., Johnson, M., & Lawson, J. (1997). *The Next S.T.E.P. (Student Transition and Educational Planning) curriculum.* Austin, TX: PRO-ED.

Herman, J.L., Aschbacher, P.R., & Winters, L. (1992). *A practical guide to alternative assessment.* Alexandria, VA: Association for Supervision and Curriculum Development.

Individuals with Disabilities Education Improvement Act (IDEA) of 2004, PL 108-446, 20 U.S.C. §§ 1400 *et seq.*

National Secondary Transition Technical Assistance Center. (2009). *Age appropriate transition assessment guide.* Available online at http://www.nsttac.org/products_and_resources/tag.aspx

Sax, C.L., & Thoma, C.A. (2002). *Transition assessment: Wise practices for quality lives.* Baltimore: Paul H. Brookes Publishing Co.

Thoma, C.A., Bartholomew, C.C., & Scott, L.A. (2009). *Universal design for transition: A roadmap for planning and instruction.* Baltimore: Paul H. Brookes Publishing Co.

Woodcock, R.W., McGrew, K.S., & Mather, N. (2006). *Woodcock-Johnson III NU.* Rolling Meadows, IL: Riverside Publishing.

5

....

Student Involvement in Meeting Preparations

Mary Held, Patricia Rogan, and Mary Fisher

The Individuals with Disabilities Education Act Amendments (IDEA) of 1997 (PL 105-17) mandated student involvement in the individualized education program (IEP) process. Yet, student involvement in planning and conducting IEP meetings has been limited or nonexistent. This is the case despite the following: 1) the IEP meeting is a required annual event; 2) the student involvement mandate can be best accomplished by expecting and supporting active student participation and leadership of IEPs; 3) planning and assuming responsibility for their own IEPs gives students a way to learn or improve self-advocacy, decision making, self-evaluation, and goal-attainment skills; and 4) student involvement, including identifying strengths, interests, and preferences, increases their investment in the process and improves the likelihood that they will pursue their goals (Powers, Turner, Matuszewski, Wilson, & Phillips, 2001; Thoma, Held, & Thomas, 2004; Thoma, Rogan, & Baker, 2001). Typically, designated school personnel (usually special education teachers) set up IEP meetings with family members and other professionals. Attempts are made to contact the parent(s)/guardian(s) (hereafter *parents* will be used) and identify a suitable date, time, and location for the meeting. In a growing number of cases, teachers contact the parents in advance of the meeting to get their input and/or feedback about priorities or goals for the next school year. It is *not* yet common, however, for students to have an active role in preparing for their IEP meetings.

A growing number of schools have implemented student-led conferences as the norm for general education students. Student-led conferences hold advantages for all students (Condeman, Ikan, & Hatcher, 2000), and such conferences can be a means to increase parent participation and to empower students to be accountable for their learning (Goodman, 2008; Kinney, 2005; Shulkind, 2008). This is a valuable strategy for sharing student work with family members. It also involves students in self-evaluation and self-reflection; they select materials to represent their best work and areas targeted for improvement.

This chapter provides a step-by-step guide to assist teachers in maximizing student involvement in the tasks associated with preparing for an IEP meeting. The chapter focuses on the rationale for active student participation as a team member and delineating numerous ways they can participate in the logistics of organizing a meeting.

Underlying Assumptions

Before describing strategies for supporting student involvement in meeting preparation, it is important to describe several underlying assumptions that should guide the work of the IEP team.

- **Students can and should be active participants.**

Team members, including educators, parents, agency representatives, and students themselves, need to believe that it is both possible and appropriate for all students to be active participants in meeting preparation, even if it means that a student is supported to partially participate at the most basic level. This may require a shift in perspective for some or all team members. This shift includes moving from a professionally driven approach to a student-centered process that focuses on student and family empowerment and self-determination. Team members need to hold high expectations for students. The greatest impediment is when teams underestimate students' abilities and thus deny them opportunities for growth and development.

- **Student learning requires an investment by a team.**

It is important for team members to realize that this undertaking requires a commitment of time. Students need individualized and systematic instruction in order to acquire and practice needed skills. Many students are unfamiliar with IEPs and do not understand the purpose of annual case conference meetings. In addition, students may not understand their roles and responsibilities as an IEP team member (Allen, Smith, Test, Flowers, & Wood, 2001; Powers et al., 2001). Students need repeated opportunities to practice their skills with others in a supportive environment using the necessary accommodations and adaptations to maximize their participation. Students benefit from creative approaches including the use of audio, visual, and/or tactile modes of learning.

- **Individualized, student-centered, strengths-based approaches should be used.**

Activities need to be selected based on the particular skills, interests, and needs of the student in order to address the student as a valued individual and to promote student identity as a team member. An asset-based approach is more constructive than a deficit orientation, and an individualized approach underscores the fact that what worked well for one student may not be needed or desired by another. Using an individualized approach requires strong person-centered assessment and planning approaches and ongoing creativity.

Strategies for Involvement

A variety of strategies can be used to promote student involvement in meeting preparations, as described here. This listing is not meant to be exhaustive. Rather, it is intended to provide samples of the types of activities in which students have been involved. The section is divided into two parts. First, strategies for preparing students as informed and active participants in their IEP meeting are shared. Next, a discussion of the logistics and possible roles that students might assume in the orchestration of a meeting is provided.

Preparing Students for Their Meeting

The process for preparing students for their IEP meeting should be individualized and adapted to meet each student's needs. Obviously, the IEP meeting itself is just one part of a larger process aimed at discovering the gifts, interests, needs, and desires of a particular student and developing a plan for identifying priorities and proactively moving forward to implement the plan. Thus, there must be communication and planning prior to and after the meeting. In many ways, the meeting is symbolic of the effectiveness of the team to work together toward a common set of goals and outcomes.

Explain the IEP and IEP Process   Students need support to understand IEPs and IEP meetings. For some students, it will be helpful to show them an IEP form and discuss each section. Options and examples can be given regarding learning environments, goals, related services, transition services, accommodations, and so forth. A variety of strategies can be used to describe what takes place at a meeting, who might attend, where it might be held, and what the expectations are for student involvement. For example, students can attend all or part of a friend's IEP meeting, observe an IEP meeting, or be shown visuals (e.g., videotape, photos) depicting typical processes. Knowing one's rights is an important aspect of the IEP process and central to being a self-advocate.

Develop Self-Determination Skills   A student-directed IEP is a process that requires using knowledge, skills, and attitudes associated with self-determination. In order to prepare students for the tasks involved, regular, ongoing times to work on learning and practicing self-determination skills need to be scheduled during the school day and outside of school. Opportunities for practice should be infused into daily routines in meaningful contexts so students have many ways to practice throughout the school year. Hands-on, activity-based learning using various modalities will bring the material to life for most students. For example, a portfolio with sections representing each life domain (e.g., work, living, leisure, community involvement) may be an effective organizing tool. Videotapes and photos, discussions, role playing, and individual work can be used to teach self-determination skills. In addition, peers without disabilities can be involved as partners in this process. After all, many general education teachers understand that student-led conferences are a recommended strategy for sharing student work with families.

Assist Students to Understand the Impact of Their Disability   Students need assistance with 1) identifying their strengths and interests, 2) describing or representing the impact of their disability on daily life, 3) identifying necessary accommodations and supports, 4) learning to set goals, and 5) developing problem-solving skills. Such awareness develops over time through varied experiences and individualized supports. Teachers play an important role in encouraging student self-awareness. Adults with disabilities can be recruited as mentors who can also play an important role in this regard.

Help Students Explore Career Options and Other Meaningful Life Options   Experiential learning, including active involvement in setting the direction of their lives, is a core element of the IEP process for students. Students need to explore options for life after high school, including aspirations for employment and other life domains.

Students can discuss their dreams for the future as part of the person-centered planning process and can explore their interests as part of daily teaching and learning opportunities at home and at school. Once again, students typically benefit from representing their dreams or goals in concrete, visual ways and revisiting these on a regular basis.

Organizing a Meeting

Students can assume responsibility for various tasks in planning their IEP meeting.

- Scheduling the meeting time and place

- Deciding who to invite to the meeting

- Sending out invitations to participants

- Preparing refreshments, name tags, and other materials

- Setting up audiovisual (AV) or other equipment

- Escorting participants to the meeting room and/or to their seats

- Preparing a presentation for the meeting

- Preparing questions for participants

- Preparing answers to possible questions that might be asked by other team members

Schedule the Meeting:
Setting a Date, Time, and Place

This section describes the logistics of organizing a meeting and actively involving students in these preparations.

- Select a convenient day and time for the student and his or her family member(s). Be sure to inform the family that the meeting can be scheduled for more than the typical 1 hour, and it can be after school rather than during the school day.

- Select a comfortable location for the meeting. A setting outside of the school building can be selected, if desired. Visit the location prior to the meeting and decide where the student will sit.

Max wants to meet at a coffee shop that has art on the walls and a separate space for private meetings. Dwight wants to meet in the technology lab so he will have access to the computers and other technology he wants to use for the meeting. Susan and Alejandra prefer meeting at home after school. Kathy would like to meet in her classroom at school so that she will have the technology to support her involvement as well as friends who could more easily join the meeting in the day.

Decide Who to Invite to the IEP Meeting

- Provide a checklist for students that lists required attendees.

- Have students consider including a few close friends.

- Consider a balance between professionals and nonprofessionals.

- Consider including relevant paraeducators and support staff.

- Include outside experts and interagency partners.

- Invite select people who know the student well. Consider inviting a family advocate who may come from outside the school environment (e.g., minister, neighbor).

- Be sure to consider the size of the group. Some may prefer a smaller number of people at the meeting, whereas others prefer representation from those who are most closely involved in the student's life and education.

Kathy invited her mother; her friend, Teresa; her teacher, Mr. Scott; and three of her core subject area teachers to her meeting. Dwight invited his transition coordinator, his mother, his vocational rehabilitation counselor, his supervisor from work, and his paraeducator. Alejandra invited her cousins, aunts and uncles, and a few family friends. Max invited his technology teacher, and Susan wanted a family friend to join the meeting.

Send Out Invitations

- Students can choose the format of the invitation such as a letter, card, telephone call, or e-mail.

- Students can send out a reminder prior to the meeting.

Dwight and Max chose to send out e-mail invitations. Kathy sent out personal hand-made invitations and used a list to help her keep track of who was invited and who could make it. Alejandra and Susan delivered printed invitations within the school with the support of a peer.

Prepare Meeting Agenda, Presentation Materials, and Paperwork

It is important to prepare an agenda for the meeting that helps all participants understand topics for discussion and time lines. The agenda should also reflect the student's role in the meeting. For example, the agenda might state, "Welcome and introductions: Dwight" or "Presentation of strengths, accomplishments, and goals: Kathy."

In addition, meeting materials must be prepared and shared in advance. Attendees deserve the courtesy of being informed so they can be equal participants in meeting discussions. Considerations include the following:

- Sharing the agenda with attendees prior to the meeting so they know who will be attending, what will transpire, and their role and responsibilities

- Sending relevant forms and procedures to attendees in advance so they can review the information

- Providing written drafts of goals or other IEP components that have been developed prior to the meeting

Finally, students should choose how best to share information at the meeting. It has been helpful for students to organize the content of their materials around the components of daily life: home living, work, leisure time, community involvement, and relationships. If this organizing framework is used, then consider developing materials that depict the following elements:

- Strengths, skills, and interests

- Dreams, goals, and desired outcomes

- Experiences, achievements, and accomplishments

- Daily/weekly schedule

- Nature of and need for supports

Some students might choose from among samples of their work or from pictures, photos, or videotape clips when deciding what to put into the presentation.

It is also important to decide the format for presenting the information. Formats that have proven effective include PowerPoint, videotapes, and photographs accompanied by voice over and/or printed words. The following tips are offered when considering the format:

- Practice using technology to enhance student comfort and maximum involvement.

- Encourage students to be creative and to reflect their personality in their presentation. For example, students may choose their favorite music, select the icons and background, choose the photographs, and so forth.

- Consider ways that students with high support needs and/or limited physical movement can be meaningfully involved. For example, some students might learn to use a switch, mouse, or other technological device to activate the equipment.

Address Meeting Space Details

- Reserve a room or make arrangement for a meeting site.

- Reserve or acquire technology.

- Get refreshments, if desired.

Max arranged with the coffee shop to reserve their private meeting space and asked if the room had a power outlet. He plans to develop a PowerPoint presentation for use at his meeting. Kathy was able to confirm the meeting date, location, and time with all members of her team by telephone. Dwight set up his laptop and a projector to share a Word document that summarizes what he has done and what he plans to do next year, which includes using Inspiration to map his dreams and goals. Susan decided to make lemonade for her guests. With support, Alejandra developed an agenda for her meeting.

Listening to the Experts

Kathy became very involved in preparing the components of her IEP and her meeting. She created a PowerPoint presentation that she and the meeting participants could follow as she read through her IEP. Her PowerPoint presentation summarized the assessment information (from Chapter 4), her long-range goals for transition outcomes, and her ideas about goals she would like to see included in her annual IEP (see Figure 5.1). She used a template from a word processing program to make invitations to her meeting (see Figure 5.2). Of course, she first found a place, a day, and a time that worked for her, her mother, Mr. Scott, and whomever she decided to invite. Last, once the logistics for the meeting were arranged, Kathy and Mr. Scott discussed what would happen if she became nervous and could no longer conduct the meeting. If Kathy became nervous, then she and Mr. Scott prepared color-coded index cards that would sit next to them both. The green index card would sit between Kathy and Mr. Scott, and this meant that she was "green for go," whereas changing the index card to red would indicate that Kathy was ready to "stop and have Mr. Scott take over." This was their discreet way of communicating with one another. Fortunately for them both, Kathy did not have to use the red index card.

Teacher's Perspective   I was excited to guide Kathy through the logistics of organizing her IEP meeting. It can be difficult to arrange a meeting, including who will come and where to meet. Having Kathy involved in the process of setting a day and time, deciding whom to invite, as well as organizing the logistics of where and how the meeting would be conducted was my favorite part of this entire process.

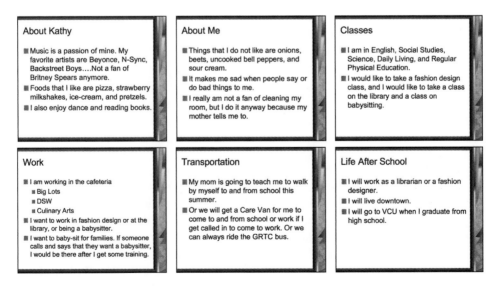

Figure 5.1. Kathy's PowerPoint presentation.

I need to plan my educational program for the coming year, as well as discuss my goals for life after high school, and I need your help. I hope you will be able to attend my IEP meeting:

* Tuesday, March 12th
* 2:00–3:30 pm
* Thoma High School, room 110
* RSVP to Mr. Scott at 666-1234

I hope to see you there!

Kathy

Come to my IEP!

Figure 5.2. Kathy's invitation to her individualized education program (IEP) meeting.

It did not take long to see that Kathy had gathered confidence in the steps preceding her IEP meeting. With some support, she decided that sending personal invitations to her guests would be the best option for securing meeting participants. I provided her with a form that kept track of who she would like to invite and whether her invitation was ultimately accepted or rejected by the participants. She was involved in every step of the invitation process. She made decisions on the design, whether she would deliver the invitations, whether they would be mailed, or whether I would be the one to send the invitation to a particular participant.

Even more involvement went into the rehearsal for the meeting. After rehearsing and reviewing the information that she wanted to present, Kathy and I made decisions on what she needed that would make her meeting flow and make the environment comfortable. Choosing the correct technology was essential in deciding on her needs. Kathy prepared a PowerPoint presentation about herself on her laptop. Other things we identified through our rehearsals were what snacks to have (popcorn), how many chairs to have at the table, where everyone would sit, and what system to use if Kathy needed to take a break.

Student's Perspective

I had a lot of ideas for my meeting. I wanted to feel happy. I wanted everyone to feel happy and see what I had prepared. I was glad that we practiced the meeting because I got to read everything and ask how to pronounce difficult words. It was also good to have cards I could pass to Mr. Scott, so if I got nervous he would know to take over. I think I made a good decision with the popcorn and beverages. Everyone seemed to like that choice and it made me feel like they enjoyed my meeting.

Parent's Perspective	I was amazed when I walked into the meeting and saw how prepared everything was. You can tell that a lot of thought and practice had gone into the meeting. Kathy really worked hard pulling everything together. The PowerPoint she made was my favorite. I had never seen those things pulled together in that way. She did an amazing job.

 # Tips and Strategies

Students cannot adequately participate in their meetings without some preparation. This preparation can include activities such as role playing the student's meeting so that he or she knows what to expect and feels more confident in his or her ability to be involved in the process. Other tips and strategies include the following:

- Even students with strong communication abilities and a clear understanding of the meeting and educational planning processes might need support to participate in the meeting itself. Talk with students about their comfort level in speaking to a group of adults, about the expectations in their family for disagreeing with parents (especially in public), and about their ability to answer questions that adults might have for them.

- If students are not comfortable, then talk about strategies that might make them feel more comfortable (e.g., having a friend there, recording some of the information through audio or videotape clips, having an outline of important information to share).

- Make sure that you help students consider a setting for the meeting that will help facilitate their involvement. Rooms can be too distracting, too quiet, too public, too small, or too large for student comfort. Deciding on the right location is key.

- Think about the impact of the scheduled day, date, and time on student involvement. If a student is more worried about missing a critical or preferred class than participating in the meeting, then you will be setting up a barrier rather than facilitating student involvement and comfort in the process. Also, plan for the time of day or day of the week when each student is at his or her best.

- Include meeting preparation activities in existing classes and activities, such as language arts (e.g., composition, spelling, writing), computer (e.g., keyboard, graphic design, e-mail), math (e.g., counting, one-to-one correspondence, buying stamps), and art (e.g., preparing invitations, organizing work portfolios, adding pictures and graphics to PowerPoint). This also provides opportunities for practicing other practical skills (e.g., locating addresses, mailing, tallying responses).

Conclusion

It is important that team members take time to prepare students for their IEP meeting through a variety of strategies. Even students who have strong self-advocacy skills in most typical situations can have difficulty with the complexity of the IEP meeting and the typically large number of unfamiliar adults at the table. This chapter described why it is important for students to be active participants and provided numerous suggestions for how students can be involved. Using approaches that help students feel comfortable and participate meaningfully can make all the difference.

References

Allen, S.K., Smith, A.C., Test, D.W., Flowers, C., & Wood, W.M. (2001). The effects of self-directed IEP on student participation in IEP meetings. *Career Development for Exceptional Individuals, 24,* 107–120.

Condeman, G., Ikan, P.A., & Hatcher, R. (2000). Student-led conferences in inclusive settings. *Intervention in School and Clinic, 36*(1), 22–26.

Goodman, A. (2008). Student-led teacher-supported conferences: Improving communication across an urban school district. *Middle School Journal, 39*(3), 48–54.

Individuals with Disabilities Education Act Amendments (IDEA) of 1997 (PL 105-17) 20 U.S.C. §§ 1400 *et seq.*

Kinney, P. (2005). Student-led conferences. *Principal Leadership, 6*(2), 33–36.

Powers, L.E., Turner, A., Matuszewski., J., Wilson, R., & Phillips, A. (2001). *TAKE CHARGE* for the future: A controlled field-test of a model to promote student involvement in transition planning. *Career Development for Exceptional Individuals, 24*(1), 89–103.

Shulkind, S.B. (2008). New conversations: Student-led conferences. *Principal Leadership, 9*(1), 54–58.

Thoma, C.A., Held, M.F., & Thomas, K. (2004). The John Jones Show: How one teacher pulled it all together to facilitate self-determined transition planning for a young man with autism. *Focus on Autism and Developmental Disabilities, 19*(3), 177–188.

Thoma, C.A., Rogan, P., & Baker, S. (2001). Self-determination in transition planning: Voices unheard. *Education and Training in Mental Retardation and Developmental Disabilities, 34,* 16–29.

||
....
The IEP Meeting

6

....

Student Involvement in IEP Meetings

Mary Held, Patricia Rogan, and Mary Fisher

Chapter 5 described how students can be involved in preparing for their individualized education program (IEP) meetings. This chapter focuses on the mechanics of the actual student-led meeting (i.e., how students can take leadership in beginning the meeting, setting the agenda, and managing the flow of the meeting itself). Specifically, the chapter addresses meeting logistics, conducting the meeting, and meeting follow up, with particular attention to examples of students with various levels of support needs. Examples of ways to maximize student involvement in their IEP meeting will also be shared in this chapter.

In a survey about student preparation for and involvement in their IEP meetings, few building-level special education administrators expected students to lead their own IEP meetings (Martin, Greene, & Borland, 2004). As indicated in the previous chapter, the first step in this process is establishing the expectation that students will be involved in leading their meetings and then investing in students' skill development and supports to do so. The beauty of this investment is that involvement in IEP meetings teaches students the skills that relate directly to their IEP, including 1) describing one's strengths, skills, interests, support needs/accommodations, and legal rights; 2) setting goals, working toward them, and evaluating one's progress; and 3) advocating for oneself. If we start at an early age and support students to gain these skills and experiences, then it is more likely that they will be stronger self-advocates and more responsible citizens in life (Konrad & Test, 2004). These skills will be helpful as students make the transition to postsecondary settings where they will need to advocate for their needs and seek appropriate accommodations and services.

Meeting Logistics

As team members plan ahead for an upcoming IEP meeting, it is important to consider the following questions:

- How can students be maximally involved in the meeting?

- What should be the structure and tone of the meeting?

- How can you prepare team members prior to the student-led meetings?

There are many possible responses to these questions based on the students' desires and needs, as well as the suggestions of key team members. Team members should consider the following issues, however (Thoma, Held, & Thomas, 2004):

- *Schedule longer meetings*—Traditional meetings, which are often scheduled for a mere 30–45 minutes, do not allow sufficient time for student presentations and team discussions. One hour to one and a half hours can be used as a guideline for scheduling meetings. Teams may need more than one meeting to fully discuss and plan an IEP.

- *Address students directly*—Participants should talk with, not about, students when they are present. With the student in attendance, professionals tend to speak in lay terms. This allows a more relaxed sharing of ideas rather than a formal reporting process.

- *Listen and learn*—Participants need to truly listen to students and provide appropriate wait time for them to respond to questions. They should not assume that they know what the student wants or needs.

- *Focus on the positive*—Team members should focus on students' strengths, interests, and support needs. Negative discussions that dwell on deficits should be avoided. When negative topics need to be addressed, they should be addressed privately prior to the meeting so as not to embarrass students. Consider developing and implementing meeting ground rules.

- *Obtain technology needs*—Arrangements need to be made to have the necessary technology on hand and in good working order. Back-up plans should be considered in case the technology malfunctions.

- *Use rooms conducive to open discussion*—Finding a room that is comfortable and conducive to having team members see and hear each other and the student's presentation is important.

- *Record information in a convenient format*—The IEP forms should not dictate the flow and dynamics of the meetings. School personnel responsible for recording information can bring a laptop and translate the information to required forms after the meeting or in discreet ways during the meeting.

Student-Led IEP Meetings

Kathy was nervous about her upcoming IEP meeting. Her teacher, Mr. Scott, reassured her by bringing her down to the meeting room an hour before the meeting was scheduled to start. Mr. Scott set up her PowerPoint equipment and calmly reminded her who would be there and how the meeting would flow. He pointed out her seat at the head of the table and helped her to rehearse her presentation. There was still time for Kathy to set out the agendas around the table and set up the refreshments before participants began to arrive. When they did, Kathy directed attendees to their seats.

Some students get nervous before and during IEP meetings. Some students have never attended their own meetings, whereas others have attended for a short time and then left. It is important to be sensitive to each student's needs prior to the actual meeting and provide as much support as necessary. Support can be provided by a teacher, parent, friend, or another trusted person selected by the student.

Tips for Student Participation in IEP Meetings

No two IEP meetings need to look exactly alike. There are common elements that should be addressed, however. For example, at a typical student-directed IEP meeting, the student may do the following:

- Introduce participants

- Highlight his or her accomplishments in the past year

- Present his or her interests, preferences, and desired transition outcomes

- Address what he or she does well and what help he or she needs

- Share goals and benchmarks for the next year

- Ask for feedback from team members

A commercially available program called the *Self-Directed IEP* mirrors the previous agenda. It consists of 11 steps students can follow to lead their own IEP meeting (see Table 6.1).

Table 6.1. Steps from *The Self-Directed IEP*

Step 1: Begin meeting by stating the purpose of the meeting. This involves students learning how to explicitly state the purpose of the meeting (e.g., review present goals and discuss plans for the next year).

Step 2: Introduce everyone. This involves students learning of who is required to be at an IEP meeting and who else they would like to invite, as well as practicing introducing these individuals.

Step 3: Review past goals and performance. This involves students stating their goals and learning which actions can be taken to help meet their goals.

Step 4: Ask for others' feedback. This involves students learning what feedback is and the different ways they can receive feedback on their goals.

Step 5: State and discuss your future school and transition goals. This involves students identifying their interests, skills, and needs and the goals they would like to achieve in school.

Step 6: Ask questions if you don't understand. This involves students learning how to ask questions for clarification.

Step 7: Deal with differences in opinion. This involves students learning the LUCK strategy (Listening to other person's opinion, Using a respectful tone of voice, Compromising or Changing your opinion if necessary, and Knowing and stating the reasons for your opinion).

Step 8: State the support you will need to reach your goal. This involves students learning about the supports that will help them in achieving their goals.

Step 9: Summarize your current goals. This involves students restating their goals, the actions they will take to meet those goals, and stating how they would receive feedback in meeting those goals.

Step 10: Close meeting by thanking everyone. This involves students learning how to bring closure to the meeting by using closing statements and thanking everyone for attending.

Step 11: Work on IEP goals all year. This involves students being reminded to work on their goals all year by taking actions, receiving feedback, and receiving support to accomplish these goals.

Source: Martin, Marshall, Maxon, & Jerman (1997).

Examples of Student Presentation Formats

There are many ways that students can present information at their IEP meetings. Many, if not most, students will benefit from visual and/or audio formats. Several student examples illustrate such formats and describe the flow and dynamics of their meetings.

Max wrote his script out on note cards and read them to his IEP team. Then, he showed a videotape that depicted what he had accomplished during the past year. After a round robin of reports by others at the table, Max began his presentation by telling the group about his interests and strengths. Finally, Max read his goals so the group could see what he desired (see Figure 6.1 for examples of slides one student used in his IEP meeting to share his interests and goals for the future).

By having Max lead the meeting, the entire dynamic changed. Rather than start the meeting with a teacher describing his "present level of performance," Max set a positive, strengths-based tone. Not all adults can easily adapt to this change, however. For example, during his meeting, one of the group members repeatedly brought up negative information about Max and began talking about him, rather than to him. Adults may need to be reminded about "ground rules" in order to avoid these problems. In addition, you can help students have a plan of action—things they will do if team members break the ground rules (e.g., giving them a phrase to use when that happens, having an advocate serve as a facilitator to bring the team back to their purpose, establishing a problem-solving process to use if the original process is not successful). Max's PowerPoint included a slide designed to solicit feedback from the others in the group (see Figure 6.2).

Interests and Preferences
- I like to watch WWE Raw.
- I like to watch the weather channel
- McDonalds is my favorite restaurant
- I like to swim and play basketball at the YMCA.
- I like to get videos and games from the Movie Gallery.
- I like to mow lawns.
- I like to make people laugh

Things I do well
- I'm friendly and work well with others.
- I read well.
- I use the computer.
- I am good at sports.
- I am good at throwing pots on the wheel.
- I keep my things tidy.
- I help customers well.

Need Help With...
- Deciding healthy things to eat.
- Talking with others.
- Making new friends.
- Managing my money.
- Reading better
- Making good choices.
- Telling people how I feel.
- Understanding about my disability.

Figure 6.1.   Slides one student used in his individualized education program (IEP) meeting to share his interests.

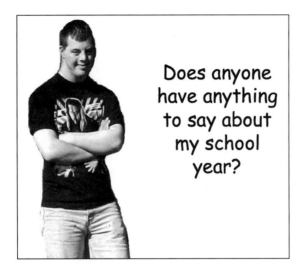

Figure 6.2. Slide designed to solicit feedback from the others in the group.

Dwight's teacher started by explaining that the purpose of the meeting was to talk with Dwight about what he had been doing over the past year and to support him in planning for the following year. She specifically mentioned, "We want this meeting to be positive. We do not want to look at what Dwight cannot do or what is wrong with him. No horror stories allowed."

Dwight asked the group to introduce themselves. People went around the table following his request. He put up his first set of PowerPoint slides about his interests and preferences. He talked about each point and was able to add comments. At the end of this section he said, "Does anyone have any responses?"

All eyes were at the front, either on Dwight and what he was saying or on his presentation. Any questions were directed to Dwight himself. There was brainstorming with him about his future. One of his slides said that he wanted to have a paid job in the community. The team became engaged in a conversation with Dwight about the kind of job he would like. Because he had said that he wanted to work outside, and he had stated that he loved hunting and fishing, ideas flowed about places that might be a good job match for him.

When Dwight left the room for a short time, however, the team returned to the "old way" of doing business. People began to talk about him, saying that they "didn't feel he could work full time when he graduated because of his stamina" and it was "too much to ask an employer to communicate with Dwight and his communication device." Others talked about his stated goal to attend a vocational school because they did not feel that the vocational school would accept him.

It is interesting to note that, without the student in the room, the tone of a meeting can change quickly from focusing on possibilities to focusing on barriers. In such cases, a team member can provide a gentle reminder about the purpose of the meeting.

At Susan's IEP meeting (the first she had ever attended), Susan helped pass out the materials to her team members, get the food ready, and set up the technology. Once it was set up, she sat in the chair at the head of the table and waited for team members to arrive. Her teacher practiced the presentation with her one last time. Susan had learned to click the mouse to advance the PowerPoint slides on her own with a physical cue (a touch to her hand). Susan used a yes/no communication board. Her teacher explained that, "These are her family's ideas. We all did a lot of brainstorming and asked her to say yes or no to what we had."

Susan clicked the first slide, and the Mozart music began to play. She smiled. Her teacher's voice in the presentation asked people to introduce themselves. Each team member gave their name and what their role was in Susan's life. Her team was quite large and included her mother, a case manager, the speech-language pathologist, an occupational therapist, and her teacher. Someone asked why Mozart had been chosen as background music and her teacher told the group, "She loves Mozart."

Susan looked at the computer screen and seemed to follow along with each new slide. She was sitting very still, which meant that she was listening carefully. The bell sound at the end of each slide not only helped her get feedback from the team, but it also served as a cue to her to change to the next slide. At the end of each slide, her teacher asked the team if they had anything they wanted to say to her.

On the fourth slide, the team had a surprise. Susan initiated the mouse click without a reminder or a physical prompt. She presented her support needs. "I like structure and routine." "I need my own space." "I need assistance moving from one floor type to another." She smiled again. After this slide, Susan looked at her teacher, and the teacher said, "You can do it." She initiated the mouse click on her own a second time. Team members seemed to be amazed at what they were witnessing. They had never seen her do anything like this before.

Susan's participation illustrates that student involvement is possible, even if students have high support needs and even if they do not communicate verbally. It just takes time and an investment in preparing students in advance. In Susan's case, when team members observed her involvement, it raised their expectations about her capabilities. A similar situation occurred for Max.

At the beginning of his IEP meeting, Max shared his current schedule and accomplishments from the past year. This helped the team focus on his strengths and build on them rather than focus on his deficits. (See Figure 6.3 for an example of similar slides.) Then, Max presented his goals for the future. Having these goals did not limit the team from addressing other goals that might be appropriate for this IEP, but they helped guide his team members to hold high expectations for his future, and to identify steps to help him achieve these goals. (See Figure 6.4 for examples of slides used to share one student's goals for the future.)

Tips for Success

The following tips are offered to better prepare team members for student-directed IEP meetings.

- Prior to the meeting, consider sending team members materials to review in advance. In this way, members will also be prepared ahead of time.

- Always clarify the purpose of the meeting—bringing team members up to date on student achievements made in the current year and using the information to set goals for the following year.

- Prep team members regarding how best to give feedback to each student. Feedback should be user friendly and able to be translated into action by the student.

At City Hall.

Waiting for the bus

Schedule

- <u>Mornings</u> – Work 9:00 am – 1:00pm
- <u>Afternoons</u>:
  - <u>Monday</u> –Class at the YMCA
  - <u>Tuesday</u> – Adult Ed Class
  - <u>Wednesday</u> – Class at the YMCA
  - <u>Thursday</u> – Adult Ed Class
  - <u>Friday</u> – Volunteer at City Hall

Accomplishments

- I moved into my own apartment.
- I do things like cooking, laundry, vacuuming, and mopping the floors by myself without anyone telling me.
- I can walk places like the library and City Hall by myself after work.
- I like my job and get great evaluations.
- I check my mail, my email and phone messages every day.

Figure 6.3. Slides showing one student's schedule and accomplishments.

- Some topics can be addressed prior to the meeting or throughout the year to maximize the meeting time when team members are present.

- Provide guidance regarding talking with the student rather than about the student and avoiding negative stories.

Follow Up After the Meeting

Student-led IEP meetings are just the start of the process. The goals and benchmarks that are set in the meeting are then used to guide curriculum and instruction. Team members need to partner with students to continually address targeted goals, set and revise action plans, and evaluate outcomes. In other words, the entire student-centered, student-led educational process should continue year round, not only when IEP meetings occur. More information about this part of the IEP process is provided in Section III of this book.

Listening to the Experts

Teacher's Perspective

When the guests began to arrive for the IEP meeting, you could tell by their reaction that they knew this meeting was going to be different, even for them. You heard sighs as the guests began

Figure 6.4. Slides of one student's goals for the future.

to walk in and sit where their names were strategically placed by Kathy. The smell of buttered popcorn and sight of other refreshments also captured their attention.

Because Kathy and I had rehearsed the meeting, we made several accommodations to help her prepare for any potential problems that might occur. We decided to use color-coded index cards that would be used to indicate Kathy's level of anxiety and provide direction to my actions. The color-coded index cards would be by her side, and if she became nervous or wanted me to take over the meeting for her, she would pass the red index card (red for *stop*) to me. The green card (green for *go*), which remained on the tabletop, indicated that she was fine with her place in the meeting. Because it was only she and I who knew what the cards were for, we were comfortable having them out. Fortunately, she never had to go to the red card, but we were prepared.

Kathy and I worked on creating an agenda for the meeting to give the guests an idea of what they were to expect throughout the meeting. Kathy was wonderful at reading the agenda and taking the initiative to let everyone introduce themselves. By following the agenda, Kathy arranged for everyone to say their name and explain what their role at her meeting would be.

Student's Perspective

I was excited about having the meeting but also nervous. This is what I was waiting for. It was a good thing that Mr. Scott and I got a chance to practice the meeting because I knew what to do. Having the colored index cards by my side also gave me some relief so if I got nervous or could not continue with the meeting, I would not be embarrassed. I am happy I did not have to use the cards.

Parent's Perspective

I was thrilled to see how prepared everything appeared when I got to the meeting. The only thing I had to do was come in and find where I would sit. I had a smile on my face, and so did everyone else. The setting was inviting and made me feel like this meeting was less about me and more about Kathy.

Reflections on Kathy's Example

Kathy and Mr. Scott developed a PowerPoint presentation that she could use to organize the information she wanted to share during her meeting. Each slide was tailored to highlight information required by national, state, and local policies, as well as the information that best summarized Kathy's preferences and interests. Because Kathy is in high school, her slides also include a summary of the long-range goals that she envisions for her adult life (see Kathy's PowerPoint example in Figure 5.1 in the previous chapter). She also had the opportunity to add background colors, pictures, and sounds that reflected her personality, preferences, and interests.

Of course, these slides should be tailored for each student individually. For older students who might be taking a computer class, this can be accomplished as a class project. Younger students might work with a teacher, a parent, or with a volunteer who understands how to keep the student's information confidential. Figure 6.5 shows slides tailored for a much younger student.

Some things I like...

- I love to swim.
- I like to visit family in Florida
- I like to play with my cousins.
- I like "telling" people what I want.
- I like things to be the same.
- I like to draw pictures
- I love my dog.

Goals and Objectives: some ideas...

- I want to use my communication board better
- I want to increase the pictures on my communication board
- I want to learn to use money to make purchases
- I want to learn to organize my work

Accomplishments

- I love my family and my dog
- I like elementary school
- I joined a brownie scout troop
- We traveled to Florida to visit my aunt and uncle and my cousins
- I use my picture communication board
- I learned to ride a bike

Some things I need help with...

- Riding the bus.
- Paying attention in class.
- Trying new things.
- Letting people know what is making me unhappy.
- Writing
- Math

- IEP Transition Planning Conference
  - February 9

Some things I do well...

- I am happy.
- I am a good friend
- I try hard.
- I work hard at using my communication board.
- I let people know how I feel.

Figure 6.5. Slides tailored for a younger student.

 **Tips and Strategies**

The following tips and strategies can help students lead and participate in their IEP meetings.

- Find a way to share 1) the student's accomplishments from the past year; 2) a summary of his or her present levels of performance; and 3) his or her preferences, interests, strengths, and needs. The student can represent this information in a variety of ways, including a portfolio, videotape or audio clips, a scrapbook, a poster, a collage, or a summary booklet. Preparing these materials can be part of a computer/technology class, an art class, or an English/writing class or the material can come from information already collected for an alternative assessment.

- Refer to and review the student's IEP goals, accommodations, and progress on a regular, ongoing basis. To the extent possible, involve students in monitoring, recording, and/or assessing their performance over time so that they will be familiar with these items when they attend their IEP meetings.

- After the meeting, talk about what worked and what did not work. Let the student help determine any changes needed for the future. Such student involvement lays the groundwork for recognizing and advocating for appropriate accommodations.

- Involve students in discussions about reconvening the IEP team to revise the IEP.

Conclusion

In summary, this chapter focused on the student-led IEP meeting. By having students take leadership roles in conducting their meetings, the entire tone and dynamic can be changed. A variety of ways to maximize student involvement in their IEP meeting were shared in relation to meeting logistics, conducting the meeting, and meeting follow-up.

References

Konrad, M., & Test, D.W. (2004). Teaching middle-school students with disabilities to use an IEP template. *Career Development for Exceptional Individuals, 27,* 101–124.

Martin, J., Greene, B., & Borland, B. (2004). Secondary students' involvement in their IEP meetings: Administrator's perspectives. *Career Development for Exceptional Individuals, 27*(2), 177–188.

Martin, J., Marshall, L., Maxon, L., & Jerman, P. (1997). *Choicemaker instructional series: Self-directed IEP* (2nd ed.). Longmont, CO: Sopris West.

Martin, J.E., Van Dycke, J.L., Christensen, W.R., Greene, B.A., Gardner, J.E., & Lovett, D.L. (2006). Increasing student participation in their transition IEP meetings: Establishing the self-directed IEP as an evidenced-based practice. *Exceptional Children, 72*(3), 299–316.

Thoma, C.A., Held, M.F., & Thomas, K. (2004). The John Jones Show: How one teacher pulled it all together to facilitate self-determined transition planning for a young man with autism. *Focus on Autism and Developmental Disabilities, 19*(3), 177–188.

7

....

Quality Educational Outcomes and Annual Goals

Carol Schall and Colleen A. Thoma

This chapter focuses on developing annual goals for a student and takes a different twist by helping you think through the development of annual goals based on larger educational outcomes. This chapter also helps you develop annual goals through a process that increases and enhances student direction of and participation in this process.

In special education, your work with a particular student is usually planned year by year because of the legal requirements of the Individuals with Disabilities Education Improvement Act (IDEA) of 2004 (PL 108-446). Meeting yearly to rewrite the individualized education program (IEP) is a sound approach for tracking progress and making timely adjustments, but it does not serve students well when considering achieving quality educational outcomes if no long-term goal or plan is also established.

If the focus for a student's IEP shifts year by year without an overall plan guiding that student's education, then the student may complete his or her education with a collection of skills that do not result in any particular outcome. The IEP itself should be a part of a larger plan that results in identified and desired outcomes. Most students want more than a diploma after they complete their education. They want to be able to work in a job they like, live in a supportive community, and have enriching relationships with others. In short, the general outcome of a quality education is to live *inter*dependently. Each person is then left with the task of identifying the specifics for him- or herself. In fact, from the perspective of self-determination and self-direction, this is really where most of the work occurs: at the level of long-term planning.

Importance of Long-Term Goals in Education Planning

Many of us remember our days in school when we had to take classes that did not interest us or we performed at a lower level in a particular class. One of the motivating factors in getting through such classes was the long-term vision or outcome for which we hoped. Likewise, for a student with disabilities, having a long-term vision significantly affects that student's motivation to make it through school and assists him or her in participating actively in problem solving, even when he or she is not able to meet the requirement for the desired outcome.

It is important for the student to be able to prepare and identify goals for him- or herself. When considering outcome-based educational planning in light of student self-direction, this is the critical point. Instead of writing an IEP that is full of what others think a student should study, the team members should strive to write an IEP that the student leads and results in desired outcomes. Quality educational outcomes are dependent on these self-identified goals. After framing each student's education in the context of a desired outcome or self-identified goal, the student and his or her team can write the IEP to include yearly goals, objectives, and plans that 1) lead the student to his or her desired outcome, 2) are developed by the student in collaboration with the adults on his or her team, and 3) assist the student in determining the goodness of fit between his or her own abilities and desires and his or her identified desired outcome.

Kathy has important life goals and priorities. She wants to have a say in her life, not just in next year's school schedule and IEP. In other words, the frame and focus of her junior and senior school year will be on getting *to* the next stage in her life and not on just getting *through* the next school year.

This is exactly what is meant by having the IEP be the yearly implementation of a larger, outcome-based transition plan. After discussing the way to get into a career, the various jobs available in that industry, and the educational requirements for those jobs, Kathy will be able to make an informed decision about her future in school and her IEP for the coming year. She can select from viable alternatives, rather than being present for a meeting where people make decisions on her behalf. The process of planning for quality educational outcomes requires members of the team to assist the student in identifying his or her long-term vision. That vision guides the development of yearly goals and becomes the focus of the IEP for the next year. When IEP teams listen to the student, they are able to consider the student's vision. Then, they ask themselves important questions about how to help the student get a step closer to that vision.

Legal Requirements for Long-Term Educational Planning

This section discusses the legal requirements in IDEA 2004 and the No Child Left Behind (NCLB) Act of 2001 (PL 107-110) related to planning for desired student outcomes. It also reviews the literature related to this topic and discusses how to involve students with disabilities in identifying the outcomes they desire related to their education.

IDEA 2004 and Quality Educational Outcomes

There are clear indications that IDEA 2004 requires that educational planning for students with disabilities address quality educational outcomes, especially for youth with disabilities who are 16 years or older. First, the law requires that schools provide transition services, which are designed to assist the student in moving from school to adult life.

These services must be provided "within a results oriented process that is focused on improving the academic and functional achievement…to facilitate the [student's] movement from school to post school activities" (34 C.F.R. 300.43[a]) (20 U.S.C. 1401[34]). These activities include higher education, vocational training, employment, adult education, adult services, independent living, and community participation. In addition, there is a clear requirement that high school students with disabilities who have IEPs must also have transition plans. A *transition plan* is a long-term plan that the IEP team develops to address a student's desired outcomes after he or she leaves public school and enters adulthood. Teams must include this plan in a student's IEP for the school year when the student turns 16 years old.

Teams can and should begin providing instruction in these postschool skills (e.g., choice making, decision making, problem solving, developing and implementing a plan) well before the age of 16. In fact, these skills are critical to the process of self-direction and self-determination (Wehmeyer & Powers, 2007). For example, with these skills, students with disabilities will be able to direct the planning for both their IEPs and their future. Thus, teachers need to provide instruction in self-determination early on in a student's educational career.

Self-Determination as a Best Practice for Increasing Student Decision Making, Planning, and Problem-Solving Skills

Self-determination is a set of skills that result in an individual's ability to make life decisions and solve problems related to his or her life goals (Wehmeyer & Powers, 2007). A person can be described as "self-determined" when he or she can make his or her own choices and decisions, solve life problems, set goals, and implement actions to achieve those goals (Martin & Marshall, 1995). Thus, the link between teaching self-determination skills, encouraging student-directed IEPs, and developing outcome-based IEPs is clear. In order for an IEP to be outcome based, students must frame their IEPs around their long-term goals. In order for students to direct their own IEPs, they must be able to make choices and decisions, set life goals, and take actions to achieve those goals. In order for students to make choices and decisions and set life goals, they must have these skills that allow for self-determination. Figure 7.1 demonstrates the interrelationship between these three important aspects of student-directed educational planning.

Beyond this connection between self-determination and outcome-based educational planning, there are impressive research findings developing around the topic of self-determination for students and adults with disabilities (Martin, Dycke, D'Ottavio, & Nickerson, 2007; Thoma, Williams, & Davis, 2005). This literature indicates that students and adults with disabilities who receive education and training in self-determination have higher academic productivity, better employment outcomes, and better problem-solving skills (Goldberg, Higgins, Raskind, & Herman, 2003; Konrad, Fowler, Walker, Test, & Wood, 2007; Wehmeyer & Powers, 2007). These findings demonstrate the importance of teaching the component skills that result in self-determination to students with disabilities (Wehmeyer, Gragoudas, & Shogren, 2006). Without self-determination, students are not

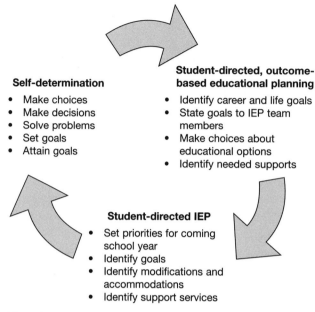

Self-determination

- Make choices
- Make decisions
- Solve problems
- Set goals
- Attain goals

Student-directed, outcome-based educational planning

- Identify career and life goals
- State goals to IEP team members
- Make choices about educational options
- Identify needed supports

Student-directed IEP

- Set priorities for coming school year
- Identify goals
- Identify modifications and accommodations
- Identify support services

Figure 7.1. Interrelationship between student-directed educational planning, student-directed individualized education programs (IEPs), and self-determination.

likely to be able to direct the IEP effectively, speak for themselves, or share their personal vision for their future.

Transition Planning: From Vision to Action

The transition plan requires that teams include measurable long-term goals on the following postsecondary school domains.

- Postsecondary school vocational training and/or higher education

- Employment

- Independent living skills (where appropriate)

- Transition services needed to assist the student in reaching those goals

In essence, this transition plan requirement provides long-term planning for students with disabilities and defines what a quality educational outcome should be for each student in the context of his or her IEP. As with all other IEP-related documents, IEP teams must consider the transition plan from the student-directed frame. That is, rather than filling in the transition plan form on behalf of the student with general information, IEP teams should use tools and methods to discover and encourage the student to identify his or her own goals and desired outcomes. That type of meeting requires that the student trust the adults in his or her life to honor those goals.

Imagine a similar experience for yourself. What would it be like to meet with your teacher and other adults and discuss your most personal goals and dreams? It is likely that this type of meeting would be difficult, even in the best of situations. It is likely that you might withhold some information from the team for fear that they might ridicule your dreams. Maybe you might fear that this group of adults might tell you all the reasons why your dreams are impossible. Maybe you fear that you cannot accomplish your dreams. All of these feelings might act as a barrier to sharing this important information with your parents, teachers, and other adults in your life.

Identifying the Student's Vision Through Person-Centered Planning

Person-centered planning describes a set of values and derived processes that make every effort to include people with disabilities in life planning to mitigate the barriers discussed previously. Person-centered planning strives to assist individuals with disabilities in planning processes that lead to self-directed lives. Unlike IEP meetings, person-centered planning meetings do not have a predetermined agenda or legally required paperwork. In fact, one of the goals of person-centered planning is to include the person with disabilities as a partner in planning his or her own supports and services (Sax, 2002). The values of person-centered planning are as follows.

- Services and supports are based on the person's dreams, interests, preferences, strengths, and capacities.

- The person and those important to the person have the opportunity to make informed decisions, exercise control, and be included in planning the person's life.

- The person is provided with experiences and meaningful choices.

- Natural and community-based supports are preferable to paid services.

- The focus of services and supports is to increase relationships, inclusion, dignity, and respect.

- Planning and implementation are flexible.

- People should have varied personalized opportunities and experiences.

- Planning is collaborative and not agency/school based only.

- Personal satisfaction, not mastery of curriculum, is the desired outcome.

Person-centered planning is more than just individualized planning. *Individualized planning* is the act of meeting to make an individual plan but does not necessarily include the aspects of person-centered planning described previously. Consider the difference between an individualized meal and a personalized meal. An individualized meal could be a frozen dinner. The food is apportioned in individualized servings. Each person gets his or her individualized meal in the freezer-to-microwave tray. Individuals have a choice of meals, but they cannot choose specific components such as medium rare Salisbury steak or creamed corn. A personalized meal, however, could be one served at a sit-down restaurant. The waiter wants to know if you want soup, a garden salad, or a Caesar salad. He wants to know how you like your steak cooked, what side dishes you prefer, and what dessert you desire. You may order a porterhouse steak, like 10 other people in the same restaurant, but your meal will be personalized to your tastes while also being individualized for you on your own plate. Thus, it is possible to be individualized and personalized at the same time.

Like ordering a meal in a restaurant, Kathy must "order" an educational plan that will be personalized to her current learning needs and her long-term vision. Her team uses person-centered planning to allow her to define her long-term goals, then assists Kathy in leading her IEP meeting to ensure that her educational plan takes her closer to those goals.

This analogy falls short in one important way, though. When you choose your meal, you are only making a decision that will affect you for the next hour or so. When you develop a transition plan, you are making decisions that will affect you for the next year and possibly beyond. If a person with a disability ends up with an individualized, but not person-centered, educational program, then he or she may not have the opportunity to make a new choice tomorrow.

The difference between individualizing and personalizing educational plans is critical. An individualized program is likely to be similar to others with the same types of disabilities. In such a plan, all people in the same program travel together to the same places and have the same experiences. Decisions are based on convenience for the staff or program. This is why person-centered planning emphasizes flexibility. It is only through flexibility and creative problem solving that programs can meet students' needs in a personalized way. An individualized program might engineer job experiences at a local fast-food restaurant where everyone in the high school class gets the same job tasks. A personalized program might creatively look for a larger establishment such as a mall where students could have different job experiences based on their vision for themselves. Kathy could work in the ready-to-wear women's clothing store if she is interested in a career in fashion design, whereas another student who is interested in a career with pets could work in the pet department. This would represent a creative way to solve the problem of meeting the personalized needs of each student, while not favoring one person's needs over another's needs.

Creatively addressing the barriers mentioned previously is another aspect of person-centered planning. It is unlikely that any 12- to 18-year-old will open up and share his or her personal vision in a conference room full of people in professional clothing gathered around a big table. The venue should be a person-friendly meeting place. If the student has difficulty in school, then meeting in school may not foster openness among the participants. Frequently, teams select venues such as church meeting halls or private rooms in favorite restaurants. In addition, the list of invitees might be unique and distinct from IEP meeting invitees. If the student does not feel comfortable around his or her math teacher, then he or she may decide not to invite the math teacher. The list of invitees is determined by the student and his or her family. Person-centered plan team members typically participate based on their knowledge of the student or expertise in the student's interest areas. Also, the way information is presented in a person-centered plan is unique: participants frequently use chart paper and draw pictures of ideas. Music, food, and room arrangement also can enhance a creative atmosphere that lends itself to dreaming and imagining. An important aspect of person-centered planning is having a facilitator for the process who is neutral and who can engage the whole team. Finally, specific person-centered processes lead the person-centered team through a specific series of questions to identify the student's vision for his or her future and develop a sound action plan to move closer to that vision. Some of these processes are as follows.

- Planning Alternative Tomorrows with Hope (PATH; Pearpoint, O'Brien, & Forest, 1993)

- Making Action Plans (MAPS; Forest & Pearpoint, 1992)

- Personal futures planning (Mount, 2000)

- Personal lifestyle planning (Smull, 2005)

Research Outcomes with Person-Centered Planning

Researching outcomes related to person-centered planning is limited and difficult to collect. Because this is a personalized process, everyone is likely to have different outcomes (Holburn, 2002; Michaels & Ferrara, 2005). Nevertheless, the research literature has documented some positive outcomes related to using person-centered planning for students with disabilities. Specifically, in two studies from the United Kingdom, person-centered planning has been associated with increased benefits in social networks, community involvement, quality day services, contact with friends, contact with family, and increased choice (Robertson et al., 2006, 2007). Although these benefits are moderate and variable, when compared with no person-centered planning, individuals who receive the opportunity to participate fully in person-centered planning report improvements in their quality of life.

At the same time, not all people who participate in a person-centered planning process receive all of those benefits. Robertson et al. (2006) found that there were personal, contextual, and process variables associated with receiving the highest rate of benefit from person-centered planning. Specifically, they found that individuals with fewer health or behavior problems were more likely to have a person-centered plan and experience increased community involvement, choice, and contact with family and friends. In this study, women seemed to benefit more from increased community involvement and increased social networks, whereas men seemed to benefit from increased time in productive activities. These gender-specific findings could be a byproduct of general gender differences. These differences could also be opposite of each other. That is, if one person desires increased community and social involvement, then that person will not have as much opportunity for increased time in productive activities and vice versa. Other findings support this theory (Robertson et al., 2006, 2007). In fact, under the category of "contextual factors," Robertson et al. (2007) found that individuals who increased their time in productive activity had decreased benefits related to increased social network. This is important to consider when supporting students to make choices and direct their own IEPs. According to this research, other contextual factors associated with positive outcomes from person-centered planning include having a case manager, an individualized plan before participating in a person-centered plan, and stable staff. Finally, and perhaps most important, the process variables associated with improved outcomes in person-centered planning included having a plan facilitator who is committed to the process. It is also important to have a facilitator whose job is to facilitate person-centered plans rather than to facilitate that person's staff (Robertson et al., 2007).

Interestingly, there is another link between person-centered planning and student-directed IEP processes. Test et al. (2004) found that participating in person-centered planning was associated with increased student participation in the IEP. Thus, in addition to resulting in increased positive outcomes and a better understanding of the student's long-term vision, participating in person-centered planning processes can provide important experiences in self-direction.

Finally, it is possible to be person centered without being self-directed. Being person centered requires that teams consider planning from the perspective of the person's desires and strengths. It does not require the courage that empowers a student to be self-directed. Although these two concepts are not mutually exclusive, they also are not mutually inclusive either.

For example, in Kathy's past experience, her team was person centered but did not encourage self-direction. The teacher led the meeting and drove the IEP. Nevertheless, person-centered planning provides an excellent opportunity to develop a long-term, specific transition plan that is directed by the student.

Considering the requirements of IDEA 2004 related to long-term educational planning, it is clear that learning how to be self-determined and using person-centered planning tools provide the best opportunities to encourage student direction in educational planning, increased achievement of desired outcomes, and increased quality of life.

No Child Left Behind Act of 2001 and Quality Educational Outcomes

The next section explores the impact of NCLB on long-term educational planning and student-directed IEPs. NCLB requires that states develop an accountability system for every public school based on a set of state standards. For all public school students, this results in a multilevel testing system to measure the effectiveness of schools and school divisions in the curriculum areas of reading, science, and math. Although NCLB only requires assessing reading, science, and math skills, many states expand accountability criteria to include social studies and other core educational content domains. This act, although mostly a measure of schools and school divisions' effectiveness, affects every student in public school through repeated standardized assessment. For students with disabilities, this act does allow for five possible options related to state testing (Shriner & Ganguly, 2007; Wakeman, Browder, Meier, & McColl, 2007). Table 7.1 shows the different assessment options for students with disabilities and the students who would qualify for each.

In other words, all students in public school, regardless of disability, regularly take standardized assessments to verify that they have mastered the state standards and to document their school's success in teaching those standards to their students. Good outcomes for every grade and course are defined by a predetermined set of standards that are the same for every student in the state. Although this type of assessment does not necessarily relate to long-term outcomes, it does have a strong impact on design of educational programs.

Table 7.1. Five types of state standard testing alternatives for students with disabilities

Type of testing	Description	Students eligible for testing
General standardized assessment, no accommodations	Standardized assessment of state standards administered with exact format as given for students without disabilities	Any student who is on grade level and does not require accommodations to the testing format
General standardized assessment with accommodations based on state guidelines	Standardized assessment of state standards administered with accommodations such as allowing extra time, permitting students to record answers in test booklet instead of on answer sheet, and letting students take test in a quiet area	Any student who is on grade level but requires testing accommodations; individualized education program (IEP) team identifies types of accommodations needed
Alternate assessment on grade-level standards	Portfolio assessment or testing on grade-level standards across the school year outside of standardized format	Any student who is able to complete grade-level work but cannot demonstrate learning on yearly standardized assessment because of his or her disability
Alternate assessment on modified academic achievement standards	New assessment that allows flexibility in identifying standards relevant to students and testing procedures; still in development in many states	Any student who is below grade level and progresses at a slower rate than students on grade level but does not fall within the 1% of students who have significant intellectual disabilities; best suited for students who are not on grade level but who do not qualify for the alternate assessment described next; limited to only 2% of students in a school, school division, and state
Alternate assessment on alternate academic achievement standards	Various assessments (can be a formal test or portfolio) based on an alternate set of standards for students with significant intellectual disabilities	Students with significant intellectual disabilities who are not on grade level and are not expected to achieve grade level at any point in their education; limited to only 1% of students in a school, school division, and state

For most of this chapter, we have defined a *quality educational outcome* as one that results in a student's personalized desired outcome in adulthood. We will also call this a *functional education*—an education that allows a student to function beyond school into adulthood. Due to the emphasis on yearly standardized testing and accountability in reading, science, and math to state academic standards, it appears that NCLB would define a quality educational outcome as an outcome in which students learn the knowledge, skills, and abilities detailed in the state standards and pass standardized tests. We will call this a *standardized academic education*—an education that results in acquiring knowledge, skills, and abilities as defined by state academic standards. NCLB mandates testing and accountability in reading, science, and math to assess the effectiveness of a standardized academic education, but does not have any such similar mandate to measure the effectiveness of a functional education.

This may present a barrier to Kathy, who wants to have an educational plan that leads to her desired outcome. How can her educational team teach her to pass her yearly test if it seems irrelevant to her desired career? Is there time in the day for her school team to teach her all of the academic standards and teach her about her desired future career? Is it possible to have a functional education *and* a standardized academic education?

To answer these questions, first consider the desired outcome for students without disabilities who all receive a standardized academic education. In fact, the goal of education for students without disabilities is to prepare them with the knowledge, skills, and abilities they will need to be successful in their own future. As students without disabilities advance through their education, they have increasing responsibility to select coursework that will prepare them for their post–high school future. Generally speaking, students without disabilities begin to choose electives around the sixth grade. In high school, their choices expand to core coursework. Some students take advanced math, whereas others enroll in vocational programs. These choices are related to their own desired outcomes. Presumably, a student who chooses a vocational program in landscaping and plant management is planning to use that coursework in his or her future. Likewise, a student who chooses calculus is planning to use that course in his or her future. From this perspective, for students without disabilities, a standardized academic curriculum is the same as a functional curriculum.

Next, consider whether the academic needs of students with disabilities are somehow so different from students without disabilities to demand an entirely different curriculum, especially in reading, science, and math. To address this question, we have to differentiate curriculum from method. There is no doubt that students with disabilities may require specialized instruction using scientifically based teaching methods to acquire reading, science, and math skills. Most students without disabilities learn to read using a combination of sight word memorization and phonetics, with extensive exposure to written materials. By definition, many students with disabilities do not acquire the same abilities using this method of reading education and require a higher intensity of phonetics or a higher intensity of exposure to written material. In addition, some students with disabilities may require modification of materials to include written materials of particular interest to the student. Despite these methodological differences, students with disabilities are learning the same words and reading them in the same way as students without disabilities. Thus, the reading *curriculum* is not dramatically different, but the *methods* used to teach students with disabilities are different. In addition, the pace at which a student with a disability learns the material, or the depth with which such a student studies a curriculum area, may be different. Again, these differences do not suggest that there is a different curriculum; rather, these differences suggest modifications to the standard curriculum. Snell and Brown (2006) identified four different ways that students with disabilities might access the reading and math curriculum. Table 7.2 presents these four ways and identifies which of the five types of state assessments students with disabilities may take.

Students with intellectual disabilities may require a different curriculum; therefore, NCLB allows states to create an alternate set of standards. Nevertheless, the goal for all students, regardless of disability, is to achieve independent functioning in reading, science, and math. Thus, the methodology, pace, and depth of access varies based on the student's need. In essence then, the standardized academic curriculum in reading, science, and math is a functional curriculum for students with disabilities as well.

Table 7.2. Four ways students gain access to the educational curriculum and the type of assessment accountability

Access to curriculum	State assessment
General education curriculum based on state standards without accommodations	General standardized assessment with no accommodations
General education curriculum based on state standards with accommodations	General standardized assessment with accommodations based on state guidelines
	Alternate assessment on grade-level standards
Basic literacy in reading and math but below grade level with focus on linking literacy to functional skills	Alternate assessment on modified academic achievement standards
Basic literacy in reading and math achieved through picture and matching systems with focus on independence where possible	Alternate assessment on alternate academic achievement standards

The question remains, however: How can a student achieve a personalized self-determined outcome when states define success as receiving a passing grade on a standardized test? The answer to this question is in the teaching method.

All state standards require some level of proficiency in reading, science, and math as a quality educational outcome. Yet, these standards do not define where and when those reading, science, and math skills must be mastered. Teachers can embed those standards in the context of functional and life skill activities that advance the student's personal goals and desired outcomes (Schall, 2009). Thus, Lowrey, Drasgow, Renzaglia, and Chezan noted

> Both [IDEA and NCLB] make provision for students who may need a different approach. Whereas both laws require that curriculum be aligned with the state standards and that students with severe disabilities be given access to the general education curriculum, neither law mandates a curriculum for students with severe disabilities that is a replication of general education standards. (2007, p. 247)

Although Kathy is designing an IEP that will result in employment, the team can also embed reading and math literacy skills in her functional coursework. For example, while in a community-based job internship, Kathy can also learn the reading skills associated with that job and, thereby, meet the state standards. In short, even within the context of a functional, community-referenced education based on personalized desired outcomes, teachers can develop an educational plan that meets state standards. Thus, when teams design educational programs that will result in the educational outcomes that students desire, they will also be readily able to meet the state standards within planned functional activities. Such an educational program meets IDEA's requirement that this program is based on strengths, interests, and preferences with a measurable identified outcome and NCLB's requirement that students be proficient in the reading and math general education curriculum. Figure 7.2 demonstrates how these elements interact to result in such a program.

When all of the identified elements in Figure 7.2 are at work, the student's desired outcome is the focus of the IEP, not the state-identified standards. Instead, the state standards evolve from the student's self-directed IEP goals. To achieve this level of

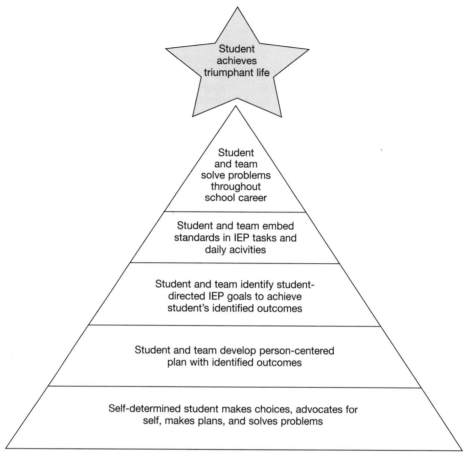

Figure 7.2. Essential elements from the Individuals with Disabilities Education Improvement Act of 2004 (PL 108-446) and No Child Left Behind Act of 2001 (PL 107-110) that result in a sound student-directed educational plan. (*Key:* IEP, individualized education program.)

self-direction with state standards embedded into functional learning activities, students must have the skills to be self-determined, IEP teams must have access to person-centered planning facilitation, and teachers must have the skills to embed state standards into functional activities. Finally, teachers who teach students with limited communication abilities must be able to coordinate closely with the student's family to identify preferences and extrapolate those preferences to potential career and age-referenced recreation/leisure activities. Each of these issues are explored in the next section.

Tips for Increasing Self-Determination in Educational Planning

Moving from theory to practice is sometimes difficult. Thus, this section focuses on specific tips to assist teachers, parents, and administrators in teaching self-determination, providing school- and community-based experiences, developing person-centered plans, and embedding state standards into IEP goals and activities.

Teach Self-Determination Across the Age Range

Figure 7.2 demonstrates that self-determination is the key building block for students to meaningfully identify their desired personalized educational outcomes. Early on in their education, many students experience school as a place where they must do whatever the teacher tells them. Then, as if by magic, they enter high school, where they are expected to suddenly make choices and identify personalized career, living, transportation, and recreation/leisure goals. In other words, with no previous experience in making plans or setting goals, students suddenly have to direct a complex process in which they have to make a long-term plan for their own lives. It seems a bit much to ask students to move from total compliance to full self-determination simply by virtue of changing school buildings. Instead, we have to teach the component skills of self-determination throughout the student's school career.

At each age, the student will have more opportunities to make choices, make plans, implement plans, solve problems, and advocate for him- or herself. Across the age range, from elementary through high school, students need multiple daily experiences to acquire the skills that result in self-determination. Table 7.3 demonstrates how teachers can offer students frequent opportunities in everyday tasks across the age range to learn the component skills that result in self-determination. Without daily practice in the component skills that result in self-determination, students may not be able to make good decisions regarding their life plans.

Table 7.3. Tips and activities for teaching self-determination skills to students of all ages and ability levels

Offer choices of pencils or crayons (for younger students) when writing, locations to complete independent work, snack, recess activities, order of seatwork, and so forth.

When students make a nonpreferred choice by accident, allow them to problem-solve to make a new choice.

Begin by offering choices between two preferred items or activities, then gradually offer choices between less desired preferences.

Begin with two options and gradually increase number of options presented.

Honor student choices even when the teacher knows the student prefers a different option.

For students with limited verbal communication skills, choice making can also result in an increase in communication skills.

Assign small projects that require students to construct everyday items from common home and school supplies (e.g., construct a car out of toilet paper rolls, construction paper, and pencils).

Have students list the pros and cons of playing outside versus inside during recess.

Have students decide how to organize their daily schedules.

Have students decide how long to engage in a school or play task.

When students make a poor decision, help them identify why it was a poor decision and what they could do differently the next time.

Talk through your own decisions to model decision making for students.

Have students talk about their decisions and how their plan worked out for them.

Develop a picture sequence to show how to make a decision, and practice this sequence many times a day.

(continued)

Table 7.3. *(continued)*

Set up problems by withholding items, hiding items, or locking items away that students need to complete projects.

Ask for help from your students when solving your own problems in the classroom.

Allow students to experience problems when making choices and decisions, then guide them through the problem-solving steps.

Set simple daily and weekly goals with students and the class as a whole, develop a plan to meet goals, and review progress toward the goals.

Allow students to try new things and reinforce them for taking the risk.

Teach students about risks and safety regarding risks.

Give students tasks where they can lead other students (e.g., keeping track of playground items, completing the lunch count and taking it to the office).

When students succeed, point out the skills they have and the actions they took that led to their success.

Help students identify their strengths and preferences.

Provide many opportunities to complete meaningful tasks for the school and community.

Let students develop their own learning targets and modules.

Show each student his or her individualized education program (IEP) and explain it.

Involve younger students in IEP decisions by offering choices of skills they want to learn.

Prior to the IEP meeting, ask students to identify three to five personal strengths to share at the meeting.

Provide School- and Community-Based Experiences to Identify Student Preferences

This chapter has detailed the importance of students with disabilities having a long-term vision to guide the development of their IEP and transition plan. Students cannot formulate that vision if they have not had life experiences. For example, if a student has never worked, then that student may not know where he or she wants to work. Thus, another practical aspect of long-term educational planning is providing a rich variety of experiences to students of all ages (e.g., completing jobs; engaging in daily living skills, such as cooking, cleaning, and personal hygiene; engaging in leisure; interacting with others who share their interests).

This is a relatively simple task for students who are able to talk and be fully engaged. The teacher has to set up school- and community-based experiences, teach students how to complete those experiences using structured teaching methods, and assist the students in evaluating their experiences. For students who do not use verbal language to communicate or who have more significant disabilities, however, this can be more difficult. In this case, teachers must observe their students to identify sensations, activities, and tasks that the students seek out.

For example, Alejandra's teacher wants to make sure that she offers her choices to encourage the development of self-determination, but she is stuck because Alejandra seems to like very few activities in her classroom. In fact, the only activities that she appears to like are smelling things and playing in the water when she washes her hands. Her teacher wonders what work and leisure tasks she could do from such limited activities. The first task that comes to mind is washing dishes. The dish soap usually smells good. Also, there is a lot of time to put your hands in the water to find the dishes, rub them off, and rinse them. A leisure activity that Alejandra might like is swimming.

Table 7.4. Translating student preferences into meaningful activities

Preference	Possible activities	Possible worksite	Possible recreation/ leisure site
Being outdoors, moving things, and motion	Gardening Landscaping Boat rides Horseback riding	Garden center Dock Farm	Garden center Home Farm Park
Water, baths, and smells	Swimming Laundry Dishwashing	Hotel Restaurant Candle store	Pool
Vibrations	Baking/cooking Vacuuming Bike riding Amusement park rides	Hotel restaurant Bike store Amusement park	Amusement park Bike trail
Moving things, pushing things, and people	Shopping Cleaning Delivering things Pushing a stroller Rowing machine	Mall Grocery store Child care Post office	Gym Mall

Reprinted by permission from Barb Purvis.

Alejandra's teacher might consider trying to find a community-based work experience for her at a hotel or health club where she could wash dishes or laundry. At the end of her work shift, she could swim in the club or hotel pool. Table 7.4 provides more examples of how teachers can move from such limited preferences to meaningful activities, job sites, and leisure sites.

Given the fact that Alejandra takes a long time to adjust to and learn skills, she will have to go to these environments often. She may be unaccustomed to the lighting, the noises around her may be new, and she may not be used to the people walking in and out of her area. Her teacher will have to teach her to cope with these differences and give her an opportunity to really experience the job before trying another job. In fact, although 12 years old might sound early to start job experiences, this is not too early for a student like Alejandra. It will likely take her time to learn about these new experiences. Because we do not want to prescribe a job for Alejandra, we want her to have many experiences so that when the time comes for her to express a preference for her life, she will have had many community-based work and leisure experiences to guide her. As she works in a variety of community-based experiences, her teachers will observe her performance and affect while completing these jobs. Then, they will discuss their observations with her team. From this discussion of combined observations at home, in school, and in the community, her IEP team will be directed by Alejandra's preferences instead of making decisions for her.

Develop a Person-Centered Plan to Frame the Quality Educational Outcome

Person-centered plans are ideal for identifying a student's vision for his or her own future. Unlike an IEP that is completed yearly, person-centered plans are usually completed once and then the information is updated as needed. If a student's personal vision for his or her future changes dramatically, then a team might repeat the process. For the most part though, once students identify their life dreams, the team will meet yearly to make and remake action plans to achieve that dream. Making Action Plans (MAPS; Forest & Pearpoint, 1992) is exemplary of this creative process and requires a team chosen by the student or his or her family, a facilitator, and a graphic recorder. Graphic recording (drawing instead of taking notes or just talking) is essential to the process. The graphic facilitator will need chart paper on the wall and an array of colorful markers, crayons, and other drawing media. In a MAP, the student and his or her chosen team brainstorm, discuss, and illuminate the answers to eight questions.

1. *What is a MAP?* The facilitator explains the meaning of a literal map, then makes the figurative connection to a map for the student's life.

2. *What is the student's story/history?* The student and his or her team tells the student's story, emphasizing important details that indicate growth and change over time.

3. *What is the student's dream?* The student and his or her team brainstorm a positive and possible future that is not limited by resources, disability, or "nay saying." Instead, team members are asked to listen respectfully, not make judgments, and contribute their own creativity to the process.

4. *What is the student's nightmare?* The team gets a sense of the fears that the student and his or her family have about the future. This becomes a compelling way to engage team members to work toward the dream while avoiding the nightmare.

5. *Who is the student?* For many professionals, it is tempting to rely on test report phrases to describe the student. Yet, the point of defining the student in this question is to leave the labels that constrain a student behind. Instead, team members are asked to describe how they experience the student in real terms that everyone understands.

6. *What is the student good at?* What are his or her strengths and gifts? Team members are asked to speak from their heart and to avoid educational diagnostics. When talking to a friend, people without disabilities hardly ever report their IQ score or reading level. Instead, they report the unique skills and interests about which they are passionate. The goal is the same for this question. Teams should talk about those skills, gifts, and interests that make the student unique.

7. *What are the student's needs?* What would this student's perfect day be like? What do we need to do to meet these needs and make more days like the perfect day? Team members begin the problem-solving process and begin to think about the person from a new perspective.

8. *What is the plan of action to avoid the nightmare and make the dream come true?* The student and his or her team consider how to move from a grand and triumphant dream to the reality of the present. The team must be specific in this plan. These specifics should include detailed steps and identify team member responsibilities and due dates.

Table 7.5.   Using MAPS for individualized education program (IEP) planning

Step 1: Determine needs.

Ask, "What needs to happen to achieve the student's dreams?" "How can we overcome the fears (or barriers) of the student, family, and team?"

List the needs; then, discuss and clarify them.

Transfer needs to the planning grid.

Step 2: Prioritize needs.

Look for common themes.

Prioritize needs important to all and/or critical to the student.

Step 3: Develop goals.

Create goals in education, employment, independent living, and community participation.

Use goals from each area for the IEP.

Step 4: Discuss next steps.

Share resources and strategies.

Generate ideas collectively.

Problem-solve collaboratively.

Step 5: Action plan.

Determine when to meet again and whether any subgroups need to be formed.

Include strategies for sharing information with others.

Identify someone to monitor the plan.

List tasks, assign role and responsibilities, and include time line.

Reprinted by permission from Barb Purvis.

Despite the creativity and energy generated when completing a MAP, teachers may not know how to translate the dream and action plan into an IEP. Table 7.5 demonstrates how to translate ideas from the MAP into annual goals for the IEP.

It is critical that teams harness the energy that results from creating the MAP and use that to inform the IEP. Figure 7.3 graphically demonstrates how a person's dreams are translated into the IEP along with preferences, strengths, interests, and needs.

Embed State Standards into Student-Directed Annual Goals

The focus of the IEP is not the state standards; however, state standards also have to be addressed. The teacher and student have to decide where they can best meet the state standards within the context of their identified IEP goals by finding natural matches between state standard and IEP goals.

For example, if Kathy wants to work at a library or in a clothing store, she can address many of her reading, science, and math standards at these job sites. The teacher needs to track her achievement of these literacy skills so that she can demonstrate them through one of the five different state standards testing methods detailed in Table 7.1.

Second, the teacher has to match instruction within the context of the annual goal and to the type of assessment for that student. Imagine that Kathy is able to submit a portfolio of her work in achieving the state standards in reading, science, and math. Kathy's teacher might have a videotape of Kathy placing price tags on clothing during one month. In another month, she might save a worksheet in which Kathy calculates the state

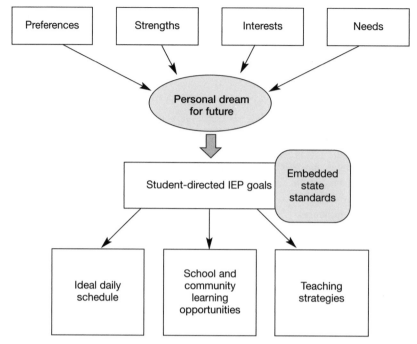

Figure 7.3. Interaction between dreams, preferences, strengths, interests, and needs to the individualized education program (IEP) and educational activities revision. (Reprinted by permission from Barb Purvis.)

sales tax for different items from the store. Another month, while she is working in the library, the teacher might save a copy of the Dewey Decimal "cheat sheet" that Kathy made for herself to demonstrate her ability to sequence complex alpha-numeric codes. These pieces of evidence that show Kathy has mastered many of the state math standards are saved in a portfolio for review at a later time in the school year.

Third, the teacher must ensure that the requirements for the assessment are met. It is possible that Kathy may not be able to address all of the required standards through the functional, community-based experiences in which she engages. Imagine that Kathy had to demonstrate an understanding of the impact of heat on elements for science. Because this is a task that would not easily fit into her workday, Kathy could learn to bake a cake while documenting the impact of heat on the cake batter. This task would result in a functional life skill, a skill that can also result in greater self-determination, while satisfying that state standard requirement.

The final step is to submit the evidence to the state examiners for review. In Kathy's case, each piece of evidence that demonstrates that she accomplished the state standard needs to be submitted for evaluation as a part of her overall portfolio.

 # Listening to the Experts

In addition to teaching Kathy to work in a clothing store or library, the IEP team that encourages her self-determination through developing skills provides her with unlimited lifelong opportunities.

Teacher's Perspective

Ultimately, one of my main goals is to set a course for Kathy that will lead her to a successful life during school, but also to have a triumphant life once she has graduated. As Kathy's teacher, I can say that if I did not go through this process with her, I would not have learned as much detailed information about her that helped with preparing her for life after high school. It's so easy to develop IEPs that lead to a life you think a student wants for herself. This process assured that the plan targeted Kathy's dreams for her adult life and the goals on which she wanted to work.

Kathy and I reviewed her strengths and weaknesses and used that information to make a plan of action for improvement. Kathy had some weaknesses in work skills, daily living skills, and academic skills. Those were the areas that were targeted for annual goals. I was so proud of her ability to identify those goals and communicate not only with me, but also with her entire IEP team.

Student's Perspective

Making the goals was easy and hard. Although I knew some of the things I wanted to work on, I did not know how to write it in the IEP. Mr. Scott had to make some changes to make the goals be clear, but I was happy I got to choose what I really wanted to work on this year. I got to understand that the goals that I work on were to benefit me for my future. One day I want to work in a library or at a clothing store, so I wanted some goals that would help me get to those places.

Parent's Perspective

I absolutely want Kathy to be successful in school and once she graduates. I liked the goals that she chose for herself, and I think they will begin to get her what she wants out of life. The most important thing is that she is happy and will be given the opportunity to prepare herself for her dreams.

Reflections on Kathy's Example

Kathy's plans obviously stemmed far beyond just the IEP meeting. Kathy kept documents of her plans for her education as well as her transition. She noted where she currently stood in regards to completing her life goals and where she needed to be. Kathy, her mother, and Mr. Scott all recognized the journey ahead of her, and this example helped IEP participants remain focused on the long-term goals and plans for Kathy.

Tips and Strategies

The following tips and strategies help students remember the purpose of the IEP meeting and communicate that with team members:

- When identifying adaptations, accommodations, or modifications, remember to help the student think about the adaptations, accommodations, or modifications he or she might need to participate in statewide/district testing. In addition, be sure that you know the "allowable" adaptations for standardized assessments.

- Sometimes it is difficult for students to understand long-range goals; you might need to use short-term contingencies/motivations. For example, a 16-year-old student might not be able to think about what he or she wants to do for a career or job as an adult, but he or she might be able to make a choice about two part-time jobs that he or she might hold on weekends.

- Although it is critical to develop annual goals that reflect a student's desired adult outcomes during the high school transition ages, it is important to help students think about employment and other adult outcomes early so that they can explore options and have enough information to make decisions later.

- Helping the student choose short-term behavior goals or one or more educational goals can be a good place to start when involving students in their IEP process.

- Have the student and his or her team members create a Personal Preferences Chart (from a MAPS process) as a first step in identifying educational goals.

- Have students cut out pictures from magazines that reflect their goals for an adult life. Alternatively, have the student find pictures on the Internet or point to pictures in a book, in a magazine, or online.

Conclusion

The four components of teaching self-determination across the life span, providing a variety of school- and community-based experiences, completing person-centered plans, and embedding state standards into the student directed IEP goals are critical and necessary to ensure that students are able to direct their plans for a quality educational outcome while also meeting state and federal requirements. If any of these essential components is missing, then the plan for a quality educational outcome will be weakened.

Although IEP teams are required to develop IEPs based on a long-term educational plan only when a student enters high school, the skills required for students to meaningfully direct the development of that plan must be learned and practiced throughout their entire school career. In addition to the specific academic skills required to be a successful adult, the greatest gift a teacher can give a student is to be self-determined. People who are self-determined are able to change course, solve problems, and cope with setbacks with greater confidence in themselves and confidence in their abilities to address difficulties and seek assistance from others.

References

Forest, M., & Pearpoint, J.C. (1992). Putting all kids on the MAP. *Educational Leadership, 50,* 26–31.

Goldberg, R.J., Higgins, E.L., Raskind, M.H., & Herman, K.L. (2003). Predictors of success in individuals with learning disabilities: A qualitative analysis of a 20-year longitudinal study. *Learning Disabilities Research and Practice, 18,* 222–236.

Holburn, S. (2002). How science can evaluate and enhance person-centered planning. *Research and Practice for Persons with Severe Disabilities, 27,* 250–260.

Individuals with Disabilities Education Improvement Act (IDEA) of 2004, PL 108-446, 20 U.S.C. §§ 1400 *et seq.*

Konrad, M., Fowler, C.H., Walker, A.R., Test, D.W., & Wood, W.M. (2007). Effects of self-determination interventions on the academic skills of students with learning disabilities. *Learning Disabilities Quarterly, 30,* 89–113.

Lowrey, K.A., Drasgow, E., Renzaglia, A., & Chezan, L. (2007). Impact of alternate assessment on curricula for students with severe disabilities: Purpose driven or process driven? *Assessment for Effective Intervention, 32,* 244–253.

Martin, J.E., Dycke, J.V., D'Ottavio, M., & Nickerson, K. (2007). The student directed summary of performance: Increasing student and family involvement in the transition planning process. *Career Development for Exceptional Individuals, 30,* 13–26.

Martin, J.E., & Marshall, L.H. (1995). ChoiceMaker: A comprehensive self-determination transition program. *Intervention in School and Clinic, 30,* 147–156.

Michaels, C.A., & Ferrara, D.L. (2005). Promoting post school success for all: The role of collaboration in person-centered transition planning. *Journal of Educational and Psychological Consultation, 16,* 287–313.

Mount, B. (2000). *Person-centered planning: Finding directions for change using personal futures planning.* New York: Capacity Works.

No Child Left Behind Act of 2001, PL 107-110, 115 Stat. 1425, 20 U.S.C. §§ 6301 *et seq.*

Pearpoint, J., O'Brien, J., & Forest, M. (1993). *PATH: Planning possible, positive futures.* Toronto: Inclusion Press.

Robertson, A., Emerson, E., Hatton, C., Elliot, J., McIntosh, B., Swift, P., et al. (2006). Longitudinal analysis of the impact and cost of person-centered planning for people with intellectual disabilities in England. *American Journal on Mental Retardation, 111,* 400–416.

Robertson, A., Emerson, E., Hatton, C., Elliot, J., McIntosh, B., Swift, P., et al. (2007). Person-centered planning: Factors associated with successful outcomes for people with developmental disabilities. *Journal of Intellectual Disability Research, 51,* 232–243.

Sax, C.L. (2002). Person-centered planning: More than a strategy. In C.L. Sax & C.A. Thoma (Eds.), *Transition assessment: Wise practices for quality lives* (pp. 13–24). Baltimore: Paul H. Brookes Publishing Co.

Schall, C. (2009). Educational and transition planning. In P. Wehman, M.D. Smith, & C. Schall, *Autism and the transition to adulthood: Success beyond the classroom* (pp. 39–77). Baltimore: Paul H. Brookes Publishing Co.

Shriner, J.G., & Ganguly, R. (2007). Assessment and accommodation issues under the No Child Left Behind Act and the Individuals with Disabilities Improvement Act: Information for IEP teams. *Assessment for Effective Intervention, 32,* 231–243.

Smull, M. (2005). *Essential lifestyle planning for everyone.* Annapolis, MD: The Learning Co.

Snell, M.E., & Brown, F. (2006). Designing and implementing instructional programs. In M.E. Snell & F. Brown (Eds.), *Instruction of students with severe disabilities* (6th ed., pp. 111–169). Upper Saddle River, NJ: Prentice Hall.

Test, D.W., Mason, C., Hughes, C., Konrad, M., Neale, M., & Wood, W.M. (2004). Student involvement in individualized education program meetings. *Exceptional Children, 70,* 391–412.

Thoma, C.A., Williams, J.M., & Davis, N.J. (2005). Teaching self determination to students with disabilities: Will the literature help? *Career Development for Exceptional Individuals, 28,* 104–115.

Wakeman, S.Y., Browder, D.M., Meier, I., & McColl, A. (2007). Implications of No Child Left Behind for students with developmental disabilities. *Mental Retardation and Developmental Disabilities Research Reviews, 13,* 143–150.

Wehmeyer, M.L., Gragoudas, S., & Shogren, K. (2006). Self-determination, student involvement, and leadership development. In P. Wehman, *Life beyond the classroom: Transition strategies for young people with disabilities* (4th ed., pp. 41–69). Baltimore: Paul H. Brookes Publishing Co.

Wehmeyer, M.L., & Powers, L.E. (2007). Self determination. *Exceptionality, 15,* 1–2.

8

....

Present Level of Academic Achievement and Functional Performance

Renee Z. Bullano and Katherine M. Wittig

Susan is a third-grade student in a rural school division. She has a moderate hearing loss and is legally blind. She recently made an arduous transition to a public elementary school. Her previous school was attended by deafblind students; this setting provided opportunities and supports for Susan's participation in a self-determination project. Susan used her skills and assistive technology to communicate on a daily basis. Susan and her parents recently asked for permission to share with her teachers and administrators salient facts about her learning style, interests, and dislikes. They have asked to be included as the individualized education program (IEP) team develops her present level of educational achievement and functional performance.

This chapter provides guidance for educators, students, and parents as they create a student-directed present level of academic achievement and functional performance. Examples provide a framework for the development of this important section of a student's IEP. Kathy, Max, and Susan will illuminate specific strategies that promote student involvement and input that drives the elementary and secondary (transition) IEP process.

What Is a Student-Directed Present Level of Performance?

The present level of performance is part of a student's IEP. This section of the IEP summarizes academic achievement and functional performance, emphasizing needs that affect the student's goals. The present level documents assessments that identify the student's strengths, interests, and preferences. At the secondary level, age-appropriate transi-

---

The present level of academic achievement and functional performance will be referenced in this chapter as the present level of performance.

tion assessment results are described. In a student-directed IEP, the student develops and possibly discusses this section prior to and during the IEP meeting. This narrative component of the IEP offers a glimpse of the student.

Historically, developing a present level began by focusing on the educational challenges, wants, and needs of the student (Wehman, 2002). In the past, the sections of an IEP were developed by a teacher as a solitary activity without input from others, least of all the student (Wittig, 2009). The landscape has changed dramatically. The Individuals with Disabilities Education Improvement Act (IDEA) of 2004 (PL 108-446) stresses student involvement in IEPs, encouraging students' interests and preferences to drive decisions (Mason, Field, & Sawilowsky, 2004). Student participation in IEP meetings is beneficial for children and youth at any educational level (Konrad & Test, 2004; Wehmeyer & Field, 2007). A student-centered planning approach, starting in elementary school, may provide the tools to start this IEP process. The student-directed IEP's present level is shaped differently and driven by the student first.

Steps to Guide a Student Through the Development of a Present Level of Performance

Teachers and families may wish to use commercial products to guide students through the process of developing a present level of performance. Wehmeyer and Field (2007) provided a list of student involvement materials for use by classroom teachers. Although there are many commercial items available for purchase, teachers might research recommendations from the field instead of purchasing products. For example, Wehmeyer (2007) suggested a series of well-planned steps teachers can use to guide students in developing their own present level of performance.

1. Identify each student's interests and skills at home, at school, or in the community.

2. Identify what life might look like after high school.

3. Name courses to prepare for the future.

4. Identify student strengths and areas for improvement.

5. Identify what needs to be learned to achieve postschool goals.

At the elementary level, simple discussions, activities, or commercial assessments will assist with this process. During middle and high school, formal and informal age-appropriate transition assessment sources may measure interests and preferences, achievement, learning styles, learning strategies, and adaptive behavior. Also included might be behavior/social skills, self-determination skill sets, work readiness, work samples, aptitude, and situational assessment.

How Does IDEA 2004 Guide the Development of the Present Level of Academic and Functional Performance?

The Individuals with Disabilities Education Act Amendments (IDEA) of 1997 (PL 105-17) required that the present level of performance include educational performance measures. There were fundamental changes in IDEA 2004; the IEP must now reflect academic achievement and functional performance. The statute reads:

> The term "individualized education program" or IEP means a written statement for each child with a disability that is developed, reviewed, and revised in accordance with this section and that includes
>
> (I)   a statement of the child's present levels of academic achievement and functional performance, including
>
>   (aa)   how the child's disability affects the child's involvement and progress in the general education curriculum. (34 C.F.R. 300.43 [a])

Gibb and Dyches (2007) explained the purpose for the insertion of the term *functional performance* in the statute. In short, this change embraces students' needs for instruction not only in academic areas, but also in the day-to-day activities we all experience. Some students with intellectual disabilities, autism, or multiple disabilities might require a stronger focus on functional skill development.

How Does IDEA 2004 Guide the Development of the Present Level of Performance?

At the secondary level, the transition IEP's present level of performance reflects each student's needed services. The student's strengths, preferences, interests, and needs drive this section of the IEP. According to IDEA 2004, the term *transition services* means a coordinated set of activities for a student with a disability that

> (A)   is designed to be within a results-oriented process, that is focused on improving the academic and functional achievement of the student with a disability to facilitate the student's movement from school to post school activities, including
> - Postsecondary education,
> - Vocational education,
> - Integrated employment (including supported employment),
> - Continuing and adult education,
> - Adult services,
> - Independent living, or community participation;
> (B)   is based upon the individual student's needs, taking into account the student's strengths, preferences and interests; and includes instruction, related services, community experiences, the development of employment and other post school adult living objectives, and, if appropriate, acquisition of daily living skills and functional vocational evaluation. (34 C.F.R. 300.43[a])

The statute has opened the door for specific transition planning to occur within an IEP. Specifically, the present level of performance outlines the student's desired postsecondary goals as measured by age-appropriate transition assessments. This sets the stage for a student to determine annual goals and transition services to support the attainment of his or her desired postsecondary goals. This process should begin at the elementary level, tying each section of the IEP to the other, all driven by students' strengths, interests, and preferences.

Sample Present Level of Performance Statement from an Elementary-Level IEP

My name is Susan and I am in the third grade at George Washington Elementary School. I have a moderate hearing loss and am legally blind. This means that I need help with some things and that I learn differently. In my other school, I had lots of friends; I am making some new friends now. I am on the YMCA swimming team. I like to use a computer. My new teacher, Mrs. Sanders, is starting to help me with my work. I like my assistant, Mrs. Pierce. I want to like my new school.

Susan did not walk into her IEP meeting unprepared; she learned a well-planned set of strategies through a self-determination project offered in her previous school. She had been systematically instructed to understand her disability and the supports she needs for academic and functional success. As she progresses through school, she will build on those skills.

At the secondary level, the use of age-appropriate transition assessments is mandated by IDEA 2004. This information is then incorporated in the present level of educational performance. Many states (Delaware, Michigan, Virginia, North Dakota) now reference a secondary IEP as a transition IEP. Figure 8.1 shows the steps to integrating the present level into a transition IEP process.

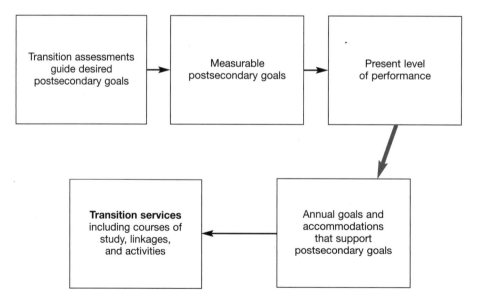

Figure 8.1. Transition individualized education program process. *Note.* From "Setting Transition IEP Goals: How It All Fits Together," by K. M. Wittig, 2009, *Transition IEPs: A Curriculum Guide for Teachers and Transition Practitioners, 3rd Ed.,* p. 34, P. Wehman and K. M. Wittig (Eds.), 2009, Austin, TX: PRO-ED. Copyright 2009 by PRO-ED, Inc. Reprinted with permission.

Sample Present Level of Performance Statement from a Transition IEP

My name is Max. I am a 9th-grade student at Benjamin Hooker High School. I have depression, and sometimes when I get upset, the teachers say that I act out. This all began when I was 11 years old. I also have a learning disability in math. I missed a lot of school this year because I had to get my medications straight and because sometimes my mom can't get me to school. I could have kept up with some help, maybe with a tutor. I want people to know that I can do the same work as everyone else. I just need my meds, my space, and some extra help sometimes.

I took some career tests last month and I scored high on computer skills. I didn't do too well with the math part, but I'm not into math. Being alone with a computer suits me just fine. I want to graduate on time and then go to Mid Coast Community College to learn the computer technician program.

Max shared with the IEP team his strengths and preferences based on recent data, as well as his mental health challenges. His work with the district's self-determination program provided him the skills needed to plan and chair his transition IEP meeting. He appears poised to move forward toward eventually achieving his postsecondary goals.

How Can Educators Encourage Student Involvement in Developing the Present Level of Performance?

For a young adolescent who craves independence, creating a present level of performance statement in preparation for a student-led IEP provides an opportunity for the student to be in control of his or her life. Educators interested in implementing this concept will benefit from providing direct instruction in the areas of choice making, decision making, goal setting, self-awareness, self-advocacy, and leadership. This preparation is necessary prior to the collaborative creation of a student's present level of performance statement.

In planning for a student-created present level of performance, it is essential that the student be involved in a discussion of his or her dreams and goals. It is helpful to pose the following questions to prepare the student for this task:

1. Who am I?

2. Where am I going?

3. Where am I now?

4. How can I get to where I want to go?

Participation in age-appropriate transition assessments will help students sort through the possible answers to the previous questions. Self-awareness will be advanced through administering informal measures, such as interest inventories and learning styles inventories. Career awareness and exploration activities will answer the question, "Where am I going?" It is crucial that a student be able to accurately describe his or her disability and how this disability affects his or her performance in both academic and functional areas in relation to school and life. Learning to interpret transition assessment results in order to identify needs, strengths, preferences, and interests in preparation for adult roles helps students to answer the question, "Where am I now?"

Comparing current performance to performance needs for stated postsecondary goals will assist in answering the question, "How can I get to where I want to go?" Others in the field have found creative ways to assist students in compiling information to be used in writing the present level of performance (e.g., peer and/or family interviews). Figure 8.2. shows an example of a questionnaire created by a classroom teacher to learn more information necessary for creating a present level of performance.

Reviewing the previous year's present level of performance will familiarize the student with his or her unique learning needs as they relate to his or her disability. The aforementioned discussions become part of the "premeeting" or "planning" component of student-directed IEPs. Only after much discussion, thought, and practice is a student prepared to present his or her present level of performance in the IEP meeting.

Teachers wishing to get their students involved in creating a present level of performance should begin with a structure to organize student work. A personalized notebook or portfolio is a helpful way to spark a feeling of ownership and encourage active participation. Educators can suggest various sections for the student's notebook, such as the following:

1. Definition of disability

2. Pertinent rights and laws

3. Current present level of performance

4. Transition information

5. Assessment information (state evaluation scores, transcripts, interest inventories, student surveys, vocational assessments, and informal and formal educational tests)

6. Work experience

7. Glossary and resources (e.g., web sites)

Students mastering the core components of self-determination and understanding the results of various transition assessments should better understand the purpose of their education as it relates to what they want in life. Only then are they prepared to begin writing their present level of performance.

How to Create a Present Level of Performance

Teachers might advise a student to begin with a history statement, written in the first person. The student should start with his or her name, grade level, and a definition of his or her disability. Then, the student proceeds to describe past school experiences. Next, the student describes life aspirations and what steps he or she needs to take to reach his or her goals. Finally, the student requests accommodations that are preferred and work for him or her. When the required information is complete, the student is given a choice of ways to

Student-led IEPs present level of performance

Name _____

1. Using complete sentences, describe some of your interests and hobbies. What do you enjoy doing on a weekend? Do you read, play sports, hunt or fish? Do you enjoy hanging out with your friends or spending time with your family? Try to be specific and write at least three sentences about your interests.

    _____

    _____

    _____

2. What types of responsibilities do you have at home? Where have you worked? At what kinds of jobs would you be most successful? Is there a type of work you enjoy?

    _____

    _____

    _____

3. Look back over what you've written above. Identify any skills you already possess that will help you in a future work position. What skills do you need to acquire, or what areas of your life can you improve in relation to job skills?

    _____

    _____

    _____

4. What are some areas that you feel are strengths in your academics or behavior? Identify at least three or four of your strongest areas and use complete sentences to describe them.

    _____

    _____

    _____

5. What are some things that you have a difficult time doing? What are some subjects that are frustrating to you at times? Are there behaviors that you know you have a hard time controlling, or areas that you need to improve? Again, identify three or four of your weakest areas and use complete sentences to describe them.

    _____

    _____

    _____

6. Look back over what you've written above. Was it more difficult to identify your strengths or your weaknesses? What things would you like to change? Identify a few areas you would like to improve. This will help you in writing your IEP goals.

    _____

    _____

    _____

Figure 8.2. Student-led IEPs present level of performance. (Reprinted by permission from Cheri Greenfield, Rockingham County Public Schools.)

present this information in the IEP meeting. Many students choose to create a PowerPoint slide show or use another type of presentation software. A template can be used to build a presentation of the present level of performance for the upcoming IEP meeting. Some students might choose to create a poster, whereas others may prefer to read the document aloud to participants.

Once the present level of performance is created, holding a mock meeting is beneficial to prepare the student for his or her actual meeting. Practicing in front of other students or a video camera will help to lesson anxiety on the day of the meeting. Instruction surrounding social skills in the IEP and strong teacher support contribute to the success of this process and lead to more self-determined students. Figure 8.3 is an example of an instructional PowerPoint in the area of social skills.

Kathy has an intellectual/developmental disability. Her mother tries to support her in strengthening her self-determination skills, and she has had the opportunity to participate in a series of modules designed to prepare her for taking an active role in her IEP development and meeting. This instruction took place during the after-lunch remediation time at her high school. Her teacher created products designed to instruct Kathy and her classmates in understanding their disabilities as well as in choice-making, decision-making, and goal-setting skills. Kathy and her classmates were provided with a notebook to organize their work. Because Kathy is receiving transition services as a high school student, her notebook also includes tabs for transition-related documents such as Kathy's résumé, a copy of her picture identification card, and work samples. The present level of performance tab contained Kathy's history, interest inventory, strengths/needs form, learning styles inventory, and postsecondary goal development form. The module on present level of performance creation took 3 weeks to complete. Using the above-mentioned resources, Kathy drafted her present level of performance in first person. Following the initial draft of Kathy's present level of performance, she began building a PowerPoint presentation to facilitate presentation in her upcoming IEP meeting. When the module was completed, Kathy was confident that she could deliver her PowerPoint presentation to the IEP team at her meeting. This presentation incorporated the main points of her present level of performance as illustrated in Figure 8.3.

Kathy had opportunities in school to explore, express, and feel good about her needs, interests, and abilities. She was thrilled to use her own words in her IEP meeting as she presented her present level of performance. All adults present at her meeting were proud of Kathy and the growth she displayed from last year's meeting. Kathy is well on her way to becoming the person she dreams she can be.

 # Listening to the Experts

Teacher's Perspective

Gathering information on Kathy regarding her present level of performance was important for bringing together the IEP. With putting together the PLOP [present level of performance], there were many items we considered about her in order to accurately present her current abilities. The items Kathy and I considered focused around recent evaluations, strengths, weaknesses, parental concerns, how her disability affects her in the classroom and community, interests, postsecondary goals, transition

Welcome to My IEP Meeting

Kathy
May 10

I invited these people...

- Robby Smith, Dad
- Bonnie Smith, Mom
- Mrs. Dreamer, Case Manager
- Ms. Burston, Guidance Counselor
- Mrs. Gordon, CTE teacher
- Mr. Scott

I'm here because...

- I want to learn more about my IEP.
- I want to learn more about myself.
- I need help reaching some of my goals.

I have an intellectual/ developmental disability.

This means...

➤ I have difficulty doing math other than addition and subtraction.
➤ It's hard for me to read the books that some of my peers are reading.

My strengths include...

- Making choices.
- Writing stories
- Hanging out with friends and going places.
- My terrific family!

My limitations are...

- I can't sit still for very long.
- Sometimes I blurt things out and distract others.
- Sometimes I try to do too much at once.

Figure 8.3. Kathy's PowerPoint presentation.

(continued)

Figure 8.3. *(continued)*

You can help me by...

✓ Allowing me to use a calculator.
✓ Prompting me when I forget a word.
✓ Providing audio books for me.
✓ Pair me with a strong lab partner so I can share a copy of his/her notes.

My education goals are...

- To take keyboarding and marketing.
- To learn how to keep myself focused and politely ask for help when I need it.
- To get involved in the student organization, DECA.

I'm glad you came!

Thanks!

My plans for the future...

➤ I want to graduate from high school with good grades.
➤ I want to work at a store as a fitting room attendant.

My Learning Style

- I learn best in a quiet, structured classroom.
- I am a visual learner and like hands on activities.
- I may need prompts to help me read aloud.
- I feel great when I get positive comments from my teachers.

services, learning style, and adaptive behaviors. All of this information was essential for accurately sharing with her IEP readers, what Kathy was all about.

I got Kathy involved with putting together the PLOP by having her gather all of the information she had collected about herself. We decided to synthesize only a small portion of what we saw as necessary to include on her IEP. Kathy was active in communicating what she thought she would like to have summarized on her IEP. She and I both sat down and composed the PLOP. I wanted her input, and I believed that she deserved to have much input in writing the document because she decided that she would read it during the meeting. Because she wanted to read it during her meeting, some of the information was decoded to simplify the language and understanding for Kathy, such as the formal assessment data.

Student's Perspective

I liked when we were able to sit down and start writing the PLOP. At first I was nervous about reading it, but because I helped write it and we practiced the reading, I knew that I could do it during the meeting. One of the fun things about helping write the IEP was going through my papers that I collected and helping to make a story about it. I did feel like I could not do it at first, but when I talked it through and wrote about me, it became easier.

Parent's Perspective

I think Kathy did a good job. She read through the paragraphs in the IEP with no problems. You can tell that she had input in writing it and that she had practiced the reading. The document really gave everyone at the meeting an understanding of where Kathy was in her education and where she wanted to be once she graduated from high school.

Reflection on Kathy's Example

In this example, Kathy was able to create sections that will go directly into her IEP by completing the document on how she currently sees her present level of academic and functional performance. Kathy was given this assignment to complete for Mr. Scott, and after the two of them reviewed the document, they decided to use many of Kathy's own words from this document in her IEP.

 **Tips and Strategies**

- Get to know the student before attending the meeting. Although most teachers do not need this advice, those who are responsible for a large number of students who are in general education classrooms for the majority of the day might not have a great deal of independent knowledge of each student. If that is your situation, then take the time to get to know the students before the meetings.

- Find ways to help students organize information and share it during the meeting.

- Develop rubrics to help interpret present levels of performance and to help students understand where they are in relation to others' expectations.

- For younger students, break it down to what they like to do, what they think they are good at, and where they need help.

- For students with more significant disabilities, you must use various assessment strategies to adequately determine what they can do and what they need help with, particularly with academic skills. If a student struggles with writing, then you might not have a comprehensive assessment of his or her reading skills if your only assessment consists of written answers (e.g., a reading log). Look for ways to triangulate your assessments.

Conclusion

This chapter provided guidance for educators and parents as they direct a student through the creation of their own present level of performance. Examples painted a mental picture for all involved in developing this important section of a student's IEP. Susan, Max, and Kathy were the benefactors of strategies that promoted student involvement in the IEP process. This sets the stage for a student to determine annual goals and transition services to support the attainment of his or her desired postsecondary goals. This process can begin at the elementary level, tying each section of the IEP to the other, and be driven by students' strengths, interests, and preferences.

References

Gibb, G.S., & Dyches, T.T. (2007). Describe the student's present levels of academic achievement and functional performance. In G.S. Gibb & T.T. Dyches (Eds.), *Writing quality individualized education programs* (pp. 39–44). Boston: Allyn & Bacon.

Individuals with Disabilities Education Act Amendments (IDEA) or 1997, PL 105-17, 20 U.S.C. §§ 1400 *et seq.*

Individuals with Disabilities Education Improvement Act (IDEA) of 2004, PL 108-446, 20 U.S.C. §§ 1400 *et seq.*

Konrad, K., & Test, D. (2004). Teaching middle-school students with disabilities to use an IEP template. *Career Development for Exceptional Individuals, 27,* 101–110.

Mason, C., Field, S., & Sawilowsky, S. (2004). Implementation of self-determination activities and student participation in IEPs. *Exceptional Children, 70,* 441–451.

Noonan, P., Morningstar, M., & Clark, G. (2003). *Transition assessment: The big picture.* Retrieved August 28, 2008, from http://www.transitioncoalition.org

Sitlington, P.L., Neubert, D.A., Begun, W.H., Lombard, R.C., & Leconte, P.J. (2007). *Assess for success: A practitioner's handbook on transition assessment.* Thousand Oaks, CA: Corwin Press.

Wehman, P. (2002). *Individual transition plans* (2nd ed.). Austin, TX: PRO-ED.

Wehmeyer, M.L. (2007). Student involvement. In M.L. Wehmeyer, *Promoting self determination in students with developmental disabilities* (pp. 157–174). New York: Guilford Press.

Wehmeyer, M.L., & Field, S.L. (2007). *Self determination: What is it and why is it important?* Thousand Oaks, CA: Corwin Press.

Wittig, K. (2009). Setting transition IEP goals: How it all fits together. In P. Wehman & K.M. Wittig (Eds.), *Transition IEPs: A curriculum guide for teachers* (pp. 29–33). Austin, TX: PRO-ED.

9

....

Assistive Technology

Shannon McManus, Frances Smith, and Sharon Jones

Since the 1970s, the growth and widespread acceptance of assistive technology (AT) has helped to expand the range of support options available to students with disabilities across a variety of settings (National Center for Technology Innovation, 2006). Still, educators often have limited knowledge of the AT tools and legal mandates for accommodating students with disabilities. The problem is not simply a technical one; it often involves negotiating the accommodations and AT with a range of people variously concerned about the well-being of students with disabilities and the resources that will be required. When matched appropriately and with the right supports, however, AT can help students perform tasks and reach goals, such as reading textbooks, spelling words correctly, turning on computers, and communicating with peers (Reed & Lahm, 2005). AT can also support the learning or academic achievement of students with disabilities, enable these students to be more independent, enhance their satisfaction with school, and even increase their self-esteem and confidence. For example, a portable word processor can provide a student with handwriting challenges a successful way to take notes or type journal entries, which could make a difference in the student's desire to try harder in difficult classes, complete a school project, or even stay in school.

As a member of the individualized education program (IEP) team, you share the responsibility for ensuring that students with disabilities have access to appropriate AT and services. Therefore, it is essential that you and other members of the IEP team have knowledge of AT in order to make informed decisions regarding the technological needs of students with disabilities. Encouraging the students themselves to be as involved as possible in the process of selecting AT will help your team make the most informed decisions. This chapter provides information, ideas, and resources about AT to meet the learning needs of students with disabilities, with an emphasis on secondary students as they make the transition into the community. The chapter focuses on essential areas needed by IEP teams working with students with disabilities, including defining AT, understanding the types of technology that are available, understanding relevant legislation associated with AT, understanding universal design strategies and how those relate to AT, identifying and selecting AT for students, ensuring student involvement in identifying and selecting AT, and understanding potential sources of funding AT for students with disabilities.

Defining Assistive Technology

The Individuals with Disabilities Education Improvement Act (IDEA) of 2004 (PL 108-446) defined AT as "any item, piece of equipment or product system, whether acquired commercially off the shelf, modified, or customized, that is used to increase, maintain, or improve the functional capabilities of children with disabilities" (§1401[1][A]). This term includes items that are homemade, such as communication boards; products that can be purchased, such as hardware and software; and AT services, such as AT evaluations, repairs to the technology, and instruction on using the device (Dell, Newton, & Petroff, 2008; Reed & Lahm, 2005).

There is a variety of AT available to help students compensate for their disabilities, perform tasks, and achieve more independence (Georgia Project for Assistive Technology, 2000). Often, AT is viewed with the misperception that technology is costly and requires a computer for optimal success. In actuality, AT ranges in cost and complexity from low tech to high tech. It is important that you consider the range of technologies available in order to make the best match for students with disabilities (Dell et al., 2008; Massachusetts Department of Education, 2002; National Assistive Technology Research Institute, 2001). Low-tech devices, such as a highlighter or pencil grips, are considered to be less complex, nonelectronic, less expensive, and readily available. They require little training. With more manufacturers producing products that consider the needs of a wider range of consumers, including those with disabilities, low-tech devices can be less stigmatizing for students with disabilities as they may see their peers using the same products (Tibbs, 2002). Mid-tech devices, such as calculators, digital recorders, and talking dictionaries, are often reasonably priced and portable and require some training (Dell et al., 2008; Massachusetts Department of Education, 2002). High-tech devices, such as text-to-speech software or word prediction software, are usually more costly, complex, and sophisticated. They may require extensive training and generally involve using a computer.

AT can also be classified based on the kind of activity it assists with: reading, writing, math, studying, communication, vision, hearing, mobility, computer access, recreation and leisure, daily living aids, and vocational (Reed & Lahm, 2005; Wisconsin Assistive Technology Initiative [WATI], 2004). For example, AT may include but is not limited to the following:

- *Reading*—color overlays, highlighters, large-print books, handheld talking dictionary, text-to-speech software, portable text reader

- *Writing*—pencil grips, slant boards, handheld speller with voice output, portable word processors, speech-to-text software, graphic organization software

- *Math*—graph paper, talking calculator, math processing software

- *Studying*—color-coded index cards, highlighters/tape, earplugs, portable digital assistants, graphic organization software

More information about additional examples is available in the appendix at the end of the book.

Legislation Supporting Assistive Technology

AT has its roots in several pieces of legislation that cross over rehabilitation, education, and technology. A number of laws pertain to the issues of educational access, AT, information technology, and the rights of individuals with disabilities.

- Section 504 of the Rehabilitation Act of 1973 (PL 93-112)

- Technology-Related Assistance for Individuals with Disabilities Act of 1988 (PL 100-407)

- Americans with Disabilities Act of 1990 (PL 101-336)

- Section 508 of the Rehabilitation Act Amendments of 1998 (PL 105-220)

- Individuals with Disabilities Education Act Amendments of 1997 (PL 105-17)

- IDEA 2004 (PL 108-446)

- No Child Left Behind (NCLB) Act of 2001 (PL 107-110)

Each of these laws either defines or highlights the importance of AT (National Assistive Technology Research Institute, 2007).

The Education for All Handicapped Children Act of 1975 (PL 94-142) set provisions for the importance of IEPs for students with disabilities. The reauthorization of this law, the Individuals with Disabilities Education Act of 1990 (PL 101-476), emphasized including students with disabilities in general education classrooms and "accommodating their special needs" (Council for Exceptional Children, 2005, p. 15). Subsequent legislation through NCLB has further strengthened the importance of AT as the progress of students with disabilities is included in the adequate yearly progress reports of school divisions and "access to the general curriculum" for these students is paramount (Council for Exceptional Children, 2005). Legislation and amendments within IDEA 2004 and President Bush's New Freedom Initiative (White House, 2005) strengthen the importance of AT and appropriate access by further articulating language that defines universally designed access for all.

Universal Design

Since the 1990s, there has been a growing interest in applying the principles of universal design to education, instruction, and learning. *Universal design* refers to "the design of products and environments to be usable by all people, to the greatest extent possible, without the need for adaptation or specialized design" (Mace, Hardie, & Place, 2007, p. 2). Applying the idea of universal design to the general education curriculum means that the widest possible range of students is able to gain meaningful access to essential content and skills. Implementing a universal design approach in the classroom with regard to AT can be beneficial in several ways. Because these technologies are available to all students, students with disabilities will feel more comfortable using a piece of technology that compensates for a disability. In addition, typically developing students may find the technology helpful. For example, text-to-speech software may be particularly beneficial and necessary for some students with disabilities, but all students can use it to proofread papers.

Rose and Meyer (2002) described how digital text and technology tools have the potential to benefit a classroom of diverse students. Traditionally, a classroom containing printed textbooks presents one-size-fits-all materials that exclude some students and lack challenge for others. Yet, a classroom using digital text can easily benefit English language learners, students who struggle with the content, students with advanced skills, and others. For example, students can manipulate instructional materials that are in digital formats to enlarge, color-code, or restyle text; read passages aloud with a speech synthesizer; and hyperlink text to supporting materials. By including curriculum enhancements, such as digital text transformations and graphic organizers, teachers can provide flexible representations of content to match different learning styles.

Assistive Technology and the IEP

The IEP team has the ultimate responsibility for ensuring that students with disabilities have access to appropriate AT and making sure that the AT is used effectively. According to IDEA 2004, school-based IEP teams have the responsibility to *consider* whether students with disabilities receive the necessary AT devices and services to support an appropriate education and achieve school success.

The process for considering AT and the results must be documented in students' IEPs, including a rationale for the decision and supporting evidence. At a minimum, the question to be answered is, "Does the student need AT devices and services?" The intent of the law, however, is that the IEP team carefully and thoughtfully considers students' strengths and needs and whether AT will provide them with the needed supports to make educational progress. In other words, will AT increase, maintain, or improve the functional capacity of the student?

Because IEP team members are empowered to make these decisions, they must know what the law says about AT, which AT devices are available, how a range of AT devices and services can benefit students with disabilities, and how to make data-driven decisions when selecting and continuing to use specific devices. IEP teams that do not have the required AT knowledge need to conduct a formal assessment (Dell et al., 2008). Many school systems have not focused their efforts on developing policies and procedures related to AT. It is important for school systems to have AT policies and procedures in their operating guidelines, including a process for considering AT for (and with) the student and a process for documenting this decision in the IEP.

Making Assistive Technology Decisions

A number of resources are available to support IEP teams in making AT decisions. AT consideration checklists, such as the WATI Assistive Technology Consideration Guide (WATI, 2004), prompt IEP teams to consider the task the student needs to do; document if AT is currently being used; and decide if AT would help the student perform a skill more easily, efficiently, or with less assistance from others. In addition, WATI (2004) suggested a nine-step process in making decisions about AT (see Table 9.1).

Table 9.1. WATI assistive technology assessment: Directions/procedures guide

Step 1: Gather information
Step 2: Schedule a meeting
Step 3: Complete problem identification portion of assistive technology planning guide at the meeting
Step 4: Prioritize the list of tasks for solution
Step 5: Generate solutions
Step 6: Select solutions
Step 7: Implement plan
Step 8: Implement planned trials
Step 9: Follow up on planned date

From Wisconsin Assistive Technology Initiative. (2004). *WATI assistive technology consideration guide.* Retrieved August 9, 2007, from http://www.wati.org/Products/pdf/Assessment_Forms_only.pdf; reprinted with permission.

The Student, Environment, Tasks, and Tools (SETT) framework (Zabala, 1995) is another widely accepted guide for AT consideration. The framework represents the four critical areas in AT assessment:

1. *Student's* strengths and needs

2. *Environments* and situations where help is needed

3. *Tasks* for the student to accomplish to meet IEP goals

4. *Tools* that might be useful to address the identified tasks

IEP teams can use the SETT framework as a guide to encourage communication and collaboration among team members throughout the process of AT consideration, assessment, service delivery, and evaluation. Furthermore, when students with disabilities are involved in this collaborative process, they can use this framework throughout their lives to help guide personal decisions about AT (Zabala, 2002).

Decisions about the effectiveness of specific AT should be data based and part of thoughtful conversations among team members. When the IEP team members determine that new AT materials are needed, they should develop a plan for trial use that includes careful documentation of successes, failures, and needed adaptations. Team members should collect data frequently on the student's performance with and without the use of the device to provide a comparison of the results (Parette, Peterson-Karlan, Wojcik, & Bardi, 2007). It is important to record the data over a period of time in order to make effective decisions about the technology and to account for the student's learning how to use the AT. If the AT device is determined to be appropriate for meeting the student's educational needs, then it needs to be written into the IEP.

Writing Assistive Technology into the IEP

AT can be written into the IEP in several areas, including present level of performance, annual goals and short-term objectives, related services, supplemental aids or service, and transition plans. The present level of educational performance should describe what specific AT is currently used, what purpose and for what tasks, and how often it is used. For example, the present level of educational performance might say, "Susan independently uses a dynamic display speech output communication device 90% of the day to communicate wants, needs, and ideas with adults and peers and uses this communication device to respond to questions and make comments in academic subjects."

When including AT in annual goals and objectives, be specific about the type of AT, its function related to the task, and the environment in which it will be used. The focus is on the outcome for the student, not the use of the specific AT device. Instead of naming a specific device, label its function (e.g., "word prediction software" rather than "Co:Writer"). This allows the school more flexibility in providing AT materials and meeting the needs of the student as the student's needs change. An example of a short-term goal is, "Dwight will use a page turner to turn pages independently 80% of the time with his reading books in order to participate in silent reading during language arts." As with all goals and objectives, it is important to develop measurable outcomes so decisions about AT are based on data collected.

AT is included as related services when the student would benefit from training on the use of the device prior to integrating the device into an educational setting (Zabala & Reed, 2000). Powered wheelchairs, some positioning devices, some communication devices, and hearing aids are examples of AT equipment that may require training prior to their use in academic environments.

AT is frequently listed on the IEP as a supplemental aid and service whenever the AT device or service is used to facilitate access and more independence in the general education setting or least restrictive environment. For example, "Dwight will use a portable digital text reader 80% of the time to read literature selections and respond to written questions in order to participate in discussion activities in English class." School divisions also have the responsibility of allowing the use of school-funded AT at home when it is required for student participation in school activities.

Assistive Technology and Transition

The need for AT follows students throughout their education and when they make the transition into the community. Specific AT needs change as students with disabilities learn increasingly difficult skills, change environments, and develop their own interests and preferences. This makes it imperative for IEP teams to exercise careful thought and involve students with disabilities in transition planning as it relates to AT. IDEA 2004 includes the following language:

> The public agency must invite a child with a disability to attend the child's IEP Team meeting if a purpose of the meeting will be the consideration of the postsecondary goals for the child and the transition services needed to assist the child in reaching those goals. (34 C.F.R. 300.321[a][7] under 34 C.F.R. 300.320[b])

It is especially important for students with disabilities to be involved in transition planning, particularly for their AT needs, because new considerations will arise once they exit secondary education. For example, who will support the student in obtaining and using AT in the home or work environment? If the AT breaks, who will repair it? Who will fund new AT? Who will provide training to young adults as they use AT in new environments?

Considering where AT fits in the transition programming for a student is often part of the transition or vocational assessment process (Canfield & Reed, 2001). Understanding how the AT is used by a student is important when considering traditional and community-based assessments as well as the future postsecondary transition opportunities (Sitlington, Neubert, Begun, Lombard, & Leconte, 2007). The following is an example of how this might be considered: "Dwight independently uses a screen-reading software program 80% of the day to communicate thoughts and ideas with adults and peers and uses this communication device to respond to questions and make comments in academic subjects. During the vocational assessment, he used this software to successfully master work tasks and activities. Future career training opportunities would be recommended in areas where this software could be used to maximize his work success."

Student Involvement in Selecting Assistive Technology

Student involvement in selecting AT is critical in matching the appropriate tool to students because they are the most knowledgeable about the technology they prefer and will use to complete specific tasks (Burgstahler, 2005; Dell et al., 2008; Moore, Duff, & Keefe, 2006). Unfortunately, students are often not consulted during this process (Moore et al., 2006). It is critical for students with disabilities to have a say in the selection of a device or it may never come out of the backpack and be used. For students with disabilities to use the AT that is best for them, they must be involved in the process of evaluating their own learning styles, strengths, goals, and needs for AT as related to different environments and tasks. Including the student in the AT selection process can potentially reduce the risk of technology abandonment and unnecessarily spending money on a piece of technology and can increase student satisfaction (Massachusetts Department of Education, 2002; Riemer-Reiss, & Wacker, 2000; Thoma & Wehmeyer, 2005).

Student involvement in selecting appropriate technology is critical in a number of ways, and perhaps one of the more significant reasons is developing a set of skills that will enable students with disabilities to make decisions and choices based on their own self-awareness of their strengths, needs, and preferences. These self-determination skills are critical for success in school, the transition from school to the community, work, and higher education. These skills are defined as "being able to advocate for what you need, understanding your disability and how it affects your learning, having self-confidence, being independent, and adjusting your schedule to make sure things get done" (Getzel & Thoma, 2008).

Funding for Assistive Technology

Although many wonderful AT products are available in the marketplace, they often come with hefty price tags and can be difficult to fund. This presents a challenge to both schools and families who are seeking to prioritize and identify appropriate low- to high-tech tools and cost-effective solutions.

The public school's special education system is a primary source for funding AT devices and services when a student requires AT to benefit from the public school's educational program (National Assistive Technology Advocacy Project, 2003). IEP teams need to work with administrators to identify available funding sources within the school division or program. Sometimes there is pressure to keep the funding of AT to a minimum, and this may affect the types of AT recommended by the IEP team and often forces schools to look only at AT that directly affects educational activities.

Families may turn to private insurance to cover the cost of AT, particularly related to mobility and communication-related expenses. Private corporations, grants, and foundations are other sources of funds that are becoming more readily available. Some grants will provide funds to a larger project under which individual technology needs can be addressed. For example, a grant that funds the design of an environment that meets the principles of universal design for learning may cover funds needed for text-to-speech software programs. Because there is a broad shortage of research to support the use of individual AT products, manufacturers may be interested in donating equipment in exchange for data collected on the AT tools and usage.

When typical funding sources are not accessible, available funds may be found through service clubs and organizations, such as the Lions Club, Shriners, the Rotary Club, neighborhood groups, and churches. Some of these groups are known for supporting specific disabilities, and others assist individuals with a range of disabilities. Frequently, it may be impossible to identify a single source to fund a higher priced device, so it may be necessary to pool resources together to purchase a product. In any case, it is important to collect data and relevant information to help funding sources understand the individual's need for AT, how and where it will be used, how the particular device will help the student make educational progress, and the cost of the AT.

Creativity is the key when trying to locate funding sources and understand the potential resources within the local community. This, of course, takes extra time, dedication, and effort from both the IEP team and the student's family. Finally, availing yourself to the latest Internet resources can provide endless funding opportunities.

 Listening to the Experts

Teacher's Perspective

AT has become a major component in considering the needs of students with disabilities. This major component of the IEP was also a factor that was carefully reflected upon by Kathy and the members of the IEP team. AT was considered in two areas in regards to assuring a successful meeting. One of those areas included choosing the appropriate AT that Kathy would need to conduct her IEP meeting. The second consideration focused on what AT she would need access to for services in school.

In choosing the correct AT that Kathy would need to conduct her meeting, it helped that we rehearsed and discussed her needs prior to conducting the meeting. Because we had narrowed down the location, one of the first evaluations Kathy and I did was to take inventory of what resources we could use in the room. In our evaluation, we considered using the television monitor located in the classroom. Kathy has had practice connecting her laptop to a television. Also, because she had her own laptop and was using her laptop to create a PowerPoint for the meeting, it would be easy for her to link the two. She was so used to using the television and laptop in her classes, this immediately jumped out to her as the option she wanted to use to present her material to the meeting participants.

Next, Kathy was involved in discussing her options for AT that could support her in the school day. There is a very exiting tool called the Assistive Technology Wheel that she and I flipped through to assess options regarding potential avenues of AT that we may not have considered. The Assistive Technology Wheel, although a great tool, did not answer some of the questions we had. For example, Kathy and her mother's greatest concerns centered on increasing Kathy's typing skills and abilities. So, in collaboration with her occupational therapist, during the IEP meeting the idea to format her laptop with typing web sites and programs that would allow her to work on her typing needs was introduced and accepted by the team.

Student's Perspective

I am pretty good with technology and computers. I like my laptop a lot, and I like to use it throughout the school day. I wanted to get better and faster at typing. I like that I'll have typing programs put on my laptop because I use it all of the time. I can use the typing programs at home, or in school, and whenever I feel like it. This is good for me.

Parent's Perspective

Kathy has issues with her handwriting, but I also know that she likes to use her laptop. I think by practicing her typing skills, she will improve her speed and comprehension of the computer. This is a skill that will also help her as she gets older and once she graduates into the working world.

Tips and Strategies

In order for students to develop self-determination skills and be actively involved in the AT selection process, you should encourage students to do the following:

- *Develop self-awareness.* To become self-determined and to find the technology that best meets the students' needs, students should explore their learning style, strengths and challenges, interests, long- and short-term goals, and strategies that help them compensate for their disability. Students should also consider their experiences and preferences with technology. Figure 9.1 provides an example of a form that you can use to help prompt discussion and develop future goals around AT and self-determination.

- *Become knowledgeable about AT.* Students should be introduced to the role that technology plays in all of our lives and given general information regarding AT. This information should include students' rights under the law, how AT may help students accomplish tasks that are difficult, and the types of tools that are available. In addition, you can discuss the benefits of student involvement in selecting AT.

- *Invite relevant participants to the IEP meeting.* As part of student-directed IEP meetings, you should encourage students to invite relevant people to the IEP meeting, including experts in AT when appropriate (Burgstahler, 2005).

- *Discuss feelings about using AT.* While you and the student are brainstorming and selecting AT solutions to explore, it is important that you consider the student's feelings about using a specialized piece of technology (Massachusetts Department of Education, 2002). This is important because if the student is embarrassed by the technology, then he or she may not use it. You should encourage students to explore feelings about the technology and, when appropriate, talk with peers who use AT, watch videotapes of students using AT, or invite an individual with a disability to the classroom to talk about technology. Social acceptance in adolescence often depends on how one looks and what is carried in a backpack—so AT must be age appropriate and acceptable to the student and his or her peer group.

- *Explore AT.* Students should take an active role during the trial period by exploring the devices that have been selected as potential solutions. If possible, this should be done before the device(s) has been purchased. This will help match students to the technology that meets their needs and preferences.

- *Collect evaluation information on the tools explored.* In order to make informed decisions about the selection of AT, teachers, technology specialists, and/or others should collect data on the various tools that have been explored (Parette et al., 2007). This data can be paired with the student's evaluation of the technology (Figure 9.2), giving the team the information they need to decide on which tool(s) will best help reach the student's goals.

- *Organize AT information.* Organizing the AT information will help students maintain the information as well as assist in developing organizational skills. You can help students develop a portfolio or notebook with the suggested components in Table 9.2. These components should be modified to meet each student's specific needs. If the student decides to pursue postsecondary education, then this notebook will be particularly helpful when meeting the staff member responsible for accommodations at the postsecondary level.

Things I need to know about myself and assistive tehchnology

This is a planning guide to help you think about your learning preferences and what types of assistive technology meet your needs. It is also intended to help you be a better advocate for yourself in the area of AT. Answer each question below with brief sentences. You may want to share this with your teachers and family.

Name: _____ Date: _____

Part I

Questions I need to answer	Yes ☑	I can answer that and the answer is...	No ☑	I don't know. Here is my plan to find the answer.	This is who I need help from.	This is when I will do this.
Questions about me and my learning style						
Do I know what classes are easiest for me?						
Do I know why I like these classes?						
Do I know what my strengths are in my classes?						
Do I know what classes are most difficult for me?						
Do I know why I have difficulty with these classes?						
Do I know what my weaknesses are in school?						

Figure 9.1. Form to help prompt discussion and develop future goals around assistive technology and self-determination. (*Key:* IEP, individualized education program.) (Copyright © 2008 by S. Jones & S. McManus, Virginia Commonwealth University; reprinted by permission.)

(continued)

Figure 9.1. *(continued)*

More questions I need to answer	Yes ☑	I can answer that and the answer is...	No ☑	I don't know. Here is my plan to find the answer.	This is who I need help from.	This is when I will do this.
Do I know my preferred learning style(s) and what learning environments work best for me?						
Can I explain my learning style to others?						
Can I explain my disability to others?						
Do I have long-term goals?						
Do I have short-term goals?						
Am I completing the goals on my IEP?						
Is there something I would like to improve or accomplish in school or work?						

Part 2

More questions I need to answer	Yes ☑	I can answer that and the answer is...	No ☑	I don't know. Here is my plan to find the answer.	This is who I need help from.	This is when I will do this.
Questions about the technology I use now						
Do I have any favorite pieces of technology and why?						
If I've used technology, do I know what type is most helpful to me in **reading?**						
If I've used technology, do I know what type is most helpful to me in **writing?**						
If I've used technology, do I know what type is most helpful to me in **studying and staying organized?**						
If I've used technology, do I know what type is most helpful to me in **math?**						
Do I have other AT needs in other school areas?						

(continued)

151

Figure 9.1. *(continued)*

More questions I need to answer	Yes ☑	I can answer that and the answer is…	No ☑	I don't know. Here is my plan to find the answer.	This is who I need help from.	This is when I will do this.
Have I thought about what AT I will need to meet my postsecondary education and/or career goals?						
Do I know how to find out more about this technology?						
Making the most of AT						
Do I know my rights related to AT?						
Can I explain why I need AT and when I need AT to my teachers, peers, family, and employers?						
Do I know who to contact to get the AT I need?						
Do I know how I will pay for it?						
What should I do if my AT breaks? Do I have a back-up plan?						
How will I get my AT repaired, cleaned, or maintained when needed?						
What is my plan for learning about new technology advances?						
Do I have a plan for organizing all of this information?						

Student assistive technology (AT) form

After trying an AT, answer the question, "Do I want to use this AT tool?" and then answer the questions in the corresponding column. Do not worry about spelling or grammar. This form is a guide to help you, your teacher, AT specialist, or others find the right AT tool to meet your needs and help you accomplish your goals.

Student name: _____   Date: _____

Goal(s)/task to accomplish: _____

Environment/setting: _____   AT tool to evaluate: _____

Do I want to use this AT tool?

Yes	No
⬇	⬇
Did the AT help me reach my goals?	**Did the AT help me reach my goals?**
Yes No Somewhat	Yes No Somewhat
⬇	⬇
What did I like about the AT tool?	**Why didn't I like this AT tool?**
⬇	⬇
Are there any changes needed to make it work better for me?	**What would make me like using it more?**
⬇	⬇
What questions do I have?	**What other tools would I like to explore?**

Figure 9.2. Student assistive technology evaluation form.

Table 9.2.   Assistive technology portfolio/notebook components

Student information: learning style survey, interest survey, relevant work samples, Things I Need to
    Know About Myself and Assistive Technology form (see Figure 9.1)
Documentation: individualized education program, documentation of disability, assistive technology
    evaluation
Technology: warranties, manuals, purchasing information, vendors for maintenance and repairs

Source: Canfield & Reed (2001).

- *Consider AT with regard to transition.* Not only is AT beneficial in secondary education, but it is also a tool that can help as students make the transition into postsecondary education or employment. In postsecondary education, many students are unaware of the technology that can help them compensate for their disability (Getzel, 2008; McManus, Getzel, & Briel, 2003). Access to technology that leads to increased success in higher education has the likelihood to improve career outcomes for individuals with disabilities (Burgstahler, 2005; Fichten et al., 2001; Kim-Rupnow & Burgstahler, 2004). Furthermore, technology is frequently used by adults with disabilities when trying to complete on-the-job tasks (Briel & Getzel, 2005). Students with disabilities should consider AT as they think about their future transition goals because AT may increase their academic success in postsecondary education, allow them to perform job-related duties, and improve their career outcomes.

Aside from the previous tips for working with individual students, teachers suggest the following general considerations and strategies:

- Remember to consider AT for all students. Too often, students with significant support needs and students with physical or sensory disabilities receive AT and those whose abilities are in between do not. There are many low-cost options that can help most students.

- Student preferences are critical to consider when recommending an assistive device or service. If a student does not feel comfortable using the device, then it will not be used. The SETT framework and Matching Person with Technology approaches can help assure that students are involved in the AT assessment and recommendation processes.

- Using augmentative and alternative communication devices during IEP planning sessions and meetings provides students the opportunity to actively participate as well as to demonstrate preferred methods of communication. Repeated opportunities allow students to practice advocating for appropriate AT.

Conclusion

This chapter provided an overview of AT and its use to enhance the learning opportunities for students with disabilities. The information, resources, and AT forms will enable you and other members of the IEP team to discuss, analyze, and determine the AT needs of students with disabilities as they move through their secondary educational experiences and make the transition into the community. It is important that all members of the IEP team participate in considering AT for students. The materials and information will provide you with ideas and strategies to ensure that students with disabilities are an integral part in selecting AT. A student's voice in the process of determining and selecting the appropriate AT is critical not only to ensure an appropriate match of AT with the student but also to create opportunities for students to strengthen their self-determination skills as active members of the IEP team.

References

Americans with Disabilities Act (ADA) of 1990, PL 101-336, 42 U.S.C. §§ 12101 *et seq.*

Briel, L.W., & Getzel, E.E. (2005). Internships and field experiences. In E.E. Getzel & P. Wehman (Eds.), *Going to college: Expanding opportunities for people with disabilities* (pp. 271–290). Baltimore: Paul H. Brookes Publishing Co.

Burgstahler, S. (2005). The role of technology in preparing for college and careers. In E.E. Getzel & P. Wehman (Eds.), *Going to college: Expanding opportunities for people with disabilities* (pp. 179–198). Baltimore: Paul H. Brookes Publishing Co.

Canfield, T., & Reed, P. (2001). *Assistive technology and transition.* Retrieved August 28, 2007, from http://www.wati.org/Curriculum/pdf/attransitionpacket.pdf

Council for Exceptional Children. (2005). *Universal design for learning: A guide for teachers and education professionals.* Upper Saddle River, NJ: Pearson Custom Publishing.

Dell, A.G., Newton, D.A., & Petroff, J.G. (2008). *Assistive technology in the classroom: Enhancing the school experiences of students with disabilities.* Upper Saddle River, NJ: Prentice Hall.

Education for All Handicapped Children Act of 1975, PL 94-142, 20 U.S.C. §§ 1400 *et seq.*

Fichten, C.S., Asuncion, J.V., Barile, M., Fossey, M.E., Robillard, C., & Wolforth, J. (2001). Computer technologies for postsecondary students with disabilities II: Resources and recommendations for postsecondary service providers. *Journal of Postsecondary Education and Disability, 15*(1), 59–83.

Georgia Project for Assistive Technology. (2000). *Introduction to assistive technology.* Retrieved March 8, 2008, from http://www.sweb.uky.edu/~jszaba0/GPAT%20Intro%20to%20AT.PDF

Getzel, E.E. (2008). Addressing the persistence and retention of students with disabilities in higher education: Incorporating key strategies and supports on campus. *Exceptionality, 16*(4), 207–219.

Getzel, E.E., & Thoma, C.A. (2008). Experiences of college students with disabilities and the importance of self-determination in higher education. *Career Development for Exceptional Individuals, 31*(2), 77–84.

Individuals with Disabilities Education Act Amendments (IDEA) of 1997, PL 105-17, 20 U.S.C. §§ 1400 *et seq.*

Individuals with Disabilities Education Act (IDEA) of 1990, PL 101-476, 20 U.S.C. §§ 1400 *et seq.*

Individuals with Disabilities Education Improvement Act (IDEA) of 2004, PL 108-446, 20 U.S.C. §§ 1400 *et seq.*

Kim-Rupnow, W.S., & Burgstahler, S. (2004). Perceptions of students with disabilities regarding the value of technology-based support activities on postsecondary education and employment. *Journal of Special Education Technology, 19*(2), 43–56.

Mace, R., Hardie, G.J., & Place, J.P. (2007). *Accessible environments: Toward universal design.* Raleigh, NC: Center for Universal Design.

Martin, J., Greene, B., & Borland, B. (2004). Secondary students' involvement in their IEP meetings: Administrator's perspectives. *Career Development for Exceptional Individuals, 27*(2), 177–188.

Martin, J.E., Van Dycke, J.L., Christensen, W.R., Greene, B.A., Gardner, J.E., & Lovett, D.L. (2006). Increasing student participation in their transition IEP meetings: Establishing the self-directed IEP as an evidenced-based practice. *Exceptional Children, 72*(3), 299–316.

Massachusetts Department of Education. (2002). *Assistive technology guide for Massachusetts's schools.* Retrieved March 8, 2008, from http://www.doe.mass.edu/edtech/assistive/ATguide.pdf

McManus, S., Getzel, E.E., & Briel, L.W. (2003). Providing intensive education supports at Virginia Commonwealth University. *Impact, 16*(3), 24–25.

Moore, V.M., Duff, F.R., & Keefe, E.B. (2006). The importance of student preference, human rights, and dignity. *Closing the Gap, 25*(4), 1, 12.

National Assistive Technology Advocacy Project. (2003). *The public school's special education system as an assistive technology funding source: The cutting edge.* Retrieved August 28, 2007, from http://www.nls.org/specedat.htm

National Assistive Technology Research Institute. (2001). *What is assistive technology?* Retrieved January 18, 2008, from http://natri.uky.edu/resources/fundamentals/defined.html

National Assistive Technology Research Institute. (2007). *Assistive technology legal mandates.* Retrieved August 9, 2007, from http://natri.uky.edu/index.html

National Center for Technology Innovation. (2006). *Moving towards solutions: Assistive and learning technology for all students.* Retrieved July 28, 2007, from http://www.nationaltechcenter.org/documents/MovingTowardSolutions.pdf

No Child Left Behind Act of 2001, PL 107-110, 115 Stat. 1425, 20 U.S.C. §§ 6301 *et seq.*

Parette, H.P., Peterson-Karlan, G.R., Wojcik, B.W., & Bardi, N. (2007). Monitor that progress! Interpreting data trends for assistive technology decision making. *Council for Exceptional Children, 40*(1), 22–29.

Reed, P.R., & Lahm, E.A. (2005). *A resource guide for teachers and administrators about assistive technology* (general ed.). Retrieved March 8, 2008, from http://www.wati.org/Products/pdf/resource%20guide%20-%20general.pdf

Rehabilitation Act Amendments of 1998, PL 105-220, 29 U.S.C. §§ 701 *et seq.*

Rehabilitation Act of 1973, PL 93-112, 29 U.S.C. §§ 701 *et seq.*

Riemer-Reiss, M., & Wacker, R. (2000). Factors associated with assistive technology discontinuance among individuals with disabilities. *Journal of Rehabilitation, 66*(3), 44–50.

Rose, D.H., & Meyer, A. (2002). *Teaching every student in the digital age.* Alexandria, VA: Association for Supervision and Curriculum Development.

Sitlington, P.L., Neubert, D.A., Begun, W.H., Lombard, R.C., & Leconte, P.J. (2007). *Assess for success: A practitioner's handbook on transition assessment* (2nd ed.). Thousand Oaks, CA: Corwin Press.

Technology-Related Assistance for Individuals with Disabilities Act of 1988, PL 100-407, 29 U.S.C. §§ 2201 *et seq.*

Thoma, C.A., & Wehmeyer, M.L. (2005). Self-determination and the transition to postsecondary education. In E.E. Getzel & P. Wehman (Eds.), *Going to college: Expanding opportunities for people with disabilities* (pp. 49–68). Baltimore: Paul H. Brookes Publishing Co.

Tibbs, S. (2002). *Low-tech assistive technology: Changing roles and paradigms in rehabilitation.* Retrieved March 8, 2008, from http://www.heath.gwu.edu/node/205

White House. (2005). *Fulfilling America's promise to Americans with disabilities.* Retrieved December 7, 2005, from http://www.whitehouse.gov/news/freedominitiative/freedominiative.html

Wisconsin Assistive Technology Initiative. (2004). *WATI assistive technology consideration guide.* Retrieved August 9, 2007, from http://www.wati.org/Products/pdf/Assessment_Forms_only.pdf

Zabala, J. (1995). *The SETT framework: Critical areas to consider when making informed assistive technology decisions.* Retrieved August 28, 2007, from http://sweb.uky.edu/~jszaba0/JoySETT.html

Zabala, J. (2002). *The SETT framework revisited.* Retrieved August 28, 2007, from http://sweb.uky.edu/~jszaba0/JoySETT.html

Zabala, J., & Reed, P. (2000). *Assessing AT student need.* Retrieved August 11, 2008, from http://atto.buffalo.edu/registered/ATBasics/Foundation/Assessment/index.php

10

....

Related Services

Pamela S. Targett and Paul Wehman

Related services, along with special education and supplementary aids and services, help children with disabilities benefit from their special education by providing extra help and support in needed areas. Under the Individuals with Disabilities Education Improvement Act (IDEA) of 2004 (PL 108-446), *related services* means

> Transportation, and such developmental, corrective, and other supportive services (including speech-language pathology and audiology services, interpreting services, psychological services, physical and occupational therapy, recreation, including therapeutic recreation, social work services, school nurse services designed to enable a child with a disability to receive a free appropriate public education as described in the individualized education program of the child, counseling services, including rehabilitation counseling, orientation and mobility services, and medical services, except that such medical services shall be for diagnostic and evaluation purposes only) as may be required to assist a child with a disability to benefit from special education, and includes the early identification and assessment of disabling conditions in children.

Typically, students with disabilities and their parents have depended on the schools to provide information about services and ultimately to arrange for services and supports as part of the individualized education program (IEP).

A special report related to the National Transitional Longitudinal Study-2 (NLTS-2; Levine, Marder, & Wagner, 2004) reported that 81% of parents learn about services from their child's school. Reportedly, a lack of information about services and the unavailability of a particular service are the barriers parents encounter most often in their efforts to obtain services for youth with disabilities. Approximately one fourth of youth had parents who reported these barriers to meeting their children's service needs. Notably, when asked about ease of locating services, 60% of parents of students with disabilities reported that it took only "a little effort" or "almost no effort." Although the research relates to the parent's experience, it would seem likely that students who are advocating for services would also be faced with this type of barrier. The study also found that schools provide service coordination for 4–6 times as many youth with disabilities as do other professionals or family members.

In more recent years, however, promoting and enhancing the self-determination of students with disabilities has led to more active student involvement in educational planning and decision making. This has led to multiple, parallel activities focused on teaching skills related to self-determined behavior, such as goal setting, choice making, problem solving, decision making, self-regulation, self-advocacy, and self-awareness. There are ample opportunities for students to learn these skills within the context of the educational planning process, including learning about and advocating for various related services. For example, to be an effective self-advocate, students have to learn how to advocate and what to advocate. When teaching self-advocacy, the teacher may focus on skills associated with assertiveness, effective communication, negotiations, and compromise.

The topic will vary when teaching what to advocate. Student rights and responsibilities under IDEA 2004, including related services, are topics that must be taught. Students are likely to need help thinking about the possible related services that could help meet their needs and learning to advocate for their rights in the process. This means teachers will have to understand the content to be able to teach students about the options and help them learn to make choices and decisions on related services.

This chapter provides a brief overview of related services, followed by definitions of some of the services. Understanding the various options available should better position educators to help students make choices and decisions about related services. The reader must note that the list is not all inclusive. In addition, a case study that illustrates how one student was supported in choosing related services is included. The appendix at the end of the book includes a list of resources where additional information about various related services can be found.[1]

Overview of Related Services

According to IDEA 2004, related services are necessary to help a child benefit from special education (§300.24[a]). A school is not required to provide services necessary to maximize a child's potential, however. Instead, schools are merely required to ensure a student can benefit from special education (see *Board of Education of Hendrick Hudson Central School District v. Rowley,* 1982). "Benefiting from special education" generally means making meaningful progress toward meeting IEP goals and objectives (see *County of San Diego v. California Special Education Hearing Office,* 1996; *Taylor v. Honig,* 1990).

Under the law, an initial evaluation of a child is required before any special education and related services can be provided. The purpose is to learn if the child has a disability, gather information that will help determine the child's educational needs, and guide decision making about appropriate educational programming for the child.

Under IDEA 2004, it is inappropriate and unacceptable to base any eligibility decision on the results of only one procedure. Instead, data about a student's strengths and weaknesses should be collected using a variety of assessment tools and strategies (e.g., observations, interviews, tests, curriculum-based assessment) and from a variety of sources (e.g., parents, teachers, specialists, the child). The school must use valid and reliable instruments and processes. In addition, the assessment should be tailored to examine a

---

[1]In addition to other resources, the information presented draws from copyright free resources from publications of the National Dissemination Center for Children with Disabilities.

student's specific needs, such as reading or math, rather than a general intelligence quotient. The information gathered through assessment is used to determine whether the child has a disability under IDEA 2004, the specific nature of the child's special needs, and whether the child needs special education and related services. If the child needs these services, the information can be used to design an appropriate program.

When the IEP is developed, it should state the service or services needed to meet a student's educational needs. Each IEP is individualized, and some students may require more related services than others. For example, Susan requires a range of related services to benefit from her educational experience. Susan receives speech-language and occupational therapies as well as orientation and mobility and assistive technology services. A special report related to the NLTS-2 said that 72% of secondary school students with disabilities received at least one of the related services, whereas 60% received one or more related services from school sources.

In addition to special education and related services, the student's IEP must also contain a statement of the supplementary aids and services to be provided to the child or on behalf of the child. Susan's visual challenges require that classroom furniture be adapted so she can move around the classroom unattended. She also uses a magnification device to enlarge words in text.

Part of developing the IEP also includes program modifications or supports that will be provided so that the child can advance appropriately toward attaining annual goals, be involved and progress in the general curriculum, participate in extracurricular and other nonacademic activities, and be educated and participate with other children in the classroom. Kathy, whose intellectual disability causes her to process information more slowly than a typically developing student, receives additional time to complete certain assignments.

The IEP should state how services will be delivered to meet the student's educational needs. Schools can provide services directly or can contract for their provision from other agencies, although the school is responsible for ensuring the services are provided. The IEP should indicate when services will begin and end.

When the IEP team has determined that a student needs a related service, school districts are responsible for paying for these services. If a child is eligible for Medicaid, then state Medicaid agencies are responsible for the cost of related services if the service is covered under the state's Medicaid plan. Parents or guardians cannot be charged for the costs associated with related services that have been included in the student's IEP.

The school district usually decides how the services listed in the IEP are delivered to the student. For example, if a student needs community-based vocational education program services, then these services may be provided by in-house personnel or purchased from an outside vocational service provider, if needed. There has been a push for related services to be provided in natural environments and to have services provided throughout the day rather than during a pull-out therapy session. Susan benefits when everyone knows how to orient her to her environment, and Max's behavior improves when everyone interacts consistently with him. Services and therapies that are provided throughout the day in multiple environments are more likely to be effective.

A variety of professionals may be involved in the delivery of related services, depending on the situation. For instance, to smooth Susan's transition to her new school, it is important for related services providers, such as a teacher of students with visual impairments, a teacher of students who are deaf or hard of hearing, or a deafblind specialist, to observe Susan in her new setting, provide services in the various environments, and consult with all of Susan's current teachers regarding her unique sensory learning needs. The IEP might also indicate the need for services from an orientation and mobility specialist, a speech-language pathologist (SLP), and an assistive technology (AT) professional. It is important that professionals who provide related services coordinate with special education staff. In general, related services are more beneficial when integrated across the student's academic day, as opposed to being provided in isolation. It is also important for the IEP team and related services providers to be able to communicate to make sure that services are delivered as specified in the IEP and that the student is making progress under these services. When progress is not indicated, the program may need to be adjusted or changed. Changes can be made by holding an IEP meeting or, if there is no overall change in the amount of services listed in the student's IEP, the parent and the school may agree not to convene a meeting and instead develop written documents to amend or modify the current IEP.

IDEA 2004 specifically notes that related services are to be considered in identifying comprehensive transition services. For example, an occupational therapist may be able to help identify types of AT or other supports to promote work in a community-based setting. Rather than clinical outcomes, professionals providing related services for transition planning should focus on accomplishing the student's transition goals.

The NLTS-2 (U.S. Department of Education, 2002) reported that 70% of secondary students with intellectual disabilities were supported by a variety of related services, including behavior or personal counseling (42%), speech communication services (38%), adaptive physical education (30%), transportation (29%), therapeutic services (16%), AT services and devices (14%), and health services (11%). Notably, 89% of the students with lower functioning and 78% of the students with moderate functioning received some type of related services, compared with only 51% of students with higher functioning.

A case worker is assigned to some students to ensure related services are coordinated into the student's overall education program. In some schools, this may be the special education teacher. In other schools, a supervisor within the school personnel may assume the responsibility.

A special topic report on NLTS-2 (Levine et al., 2004) provided details on using related services across disability groups. Some of the findings are highlighted next.

- Students with orthopedic impairments, multiple disabilities, deafblindness, or visual impairments are most likely to use specialized transportation, AT services or devices, and orientation and mobility services.

- Audiology services or classroom readers or interpreters are received predominantly by students with hearing impairments (76% and 40%, respectively) or deafblindness (70% and 31%, respectively). Notably, less than 10% of students in other disability categories are reported to use these services.

- Sixty-nine percent of students with emotional disturbances receive mental health services. Services also are received by 38%–46% of students with autism, other health impairments, traumatic brain injuries, or multiple disabilities, and by about one fourth of students in other disability categories.

- Most students with speech-language impairments (71%) receive speech-related services. The service is also provided to 62%–72% of students with autism, multiple disabilities, hearing impairments, or deafblindness, and by 44% of students with intellectual disabilities.

- Eleven percent of students with disabilities are reported to receive occupational therapy, and 4% receive physical therapy.

Related Services Definitions

There are a number of possible related services that can be used to help a student. The federal definitions of the related services in IDEA 2004 are offered at the beginning of this section. An example of a student who would need each type of service is presented after each explanation.

Artistic/Cultural Programs

Artistic/cultural programs (e.g., art, music) are developmental, corrective, or supportive services that a child needs to participate in special education.

Romano, a child with autism, participates in music therapy. The therapy has helped stimulate and develop the communicative use of his voice. He also has increased tolerance of sound that has led to positive behavior in the classroom setting.

Audiology Services

Audiology is the study of hearing, hearing disorders, and rehabilitation. It is intended to serve children with known or suspected hearing or listening disorders and/or those with speech-language delays. A child must be assessed as hearing impaired to receive audiology as a related service. Specific age-appropriate tests and developmental assessments are available. Also, parent and professional observations may be used in the assessment process.

Audiology involves identifying children with hearing loss; determining the range, nature, and degree of hearing loss; providing habilitative activities (e.g., language habilitation, auditory training, speech- or lipreading, hearing evaluation, speech conservation); creating and administering programs for prevention of hearing loss; counseling and guiding children, parents, and teachers regarding hearing loss; determining children's needs for group and individual amplification; selecting and fitting an appropriate aid; and evaluating the effectiveness of amplification.

Audiology is provided by an audiologist and an SLP. State law may define who is considered an audiologist. In general, audiologists have earned a master's or doctoral degree that makes them uniquely qualified to provide audiological services. Support personnel may also assist audiologists in the delivery of services. The roles of support personnel are assigned by the supervising audiologists. State law may have specific recommendations for use of support staff.

For the multidisciplinary team evaluation, the audiologist provides a report to document hearing loss. If the student uses an amplification device or hearing instrument, then that device or instrument is also assessed. If the student does not use amplification, then an audiologist will evaluate whether the student can benefit from amplification. Other tests may be performed to assess and monitor the student's speech-language, communication, and listening skills.

Service delivery may be direct, integrated, or consultative. The IEP should specify the approach. Direct involves one-to-one or small-group interaction. Consultative service delivery occurs when the audiologist serves as a consultant about student needs but does not provide direct therapy. This may include monitoring only and occasional direct contact. Integrated service delivery is a combination of the direct and consultative methods. The amount of service delivered will depend on each student's needs.

Jackie cannot hear. She has been fitted with a hearing amplification device but also requires training in speechreading. The SLP meets with Jackie to provide training on lipreading. In addition, the audiologist will evaluate the effectiveness of her aid on a scheduled basis.

Counseling Services

Counseling services are provided by qualified social workers, psychologists, guidance counselors, or other qualified personnel. Psychological services include counseling and psychotherapy. The difference between the two is determined by the qualifications of the provider. Counseling often focuses on school-related issues (e.g., behavior, grades). Psychotherapy focuses on the child's emotional status and feelings toward self, peers, and family. It can help children and families understand and resolve problems, modify behavior, and make positive changes in their lives.

Max is a student diagnosed with emotional and behavior disorders. He receives cognitive behavior therapy to help him manage his moods and anxiety and examine confused or distorted patterns of thinking. In addition, his teachers consult with a behavior specialist who helps them develop a comprehensive positive behavior support plan that provides direction for teaching alternative behaviors.

There are several types of psychotherapy that involve different approaches, techniques, and interventions. At times, a combination of different psychotherapy approaches may be helpful. In some cases, a combination of medication with psychotherapy may be more effective. It is also important to note that counseling services also include vocational rehabilitation counseling to assist students with career-related issues.

Medical Services

Medical services refer to "services provided by a licensed physician to determine a child's medically related disability that results in the child's need for special education and related services" (§300.24[b][4]). The physician is responsible for providing medical information during the evaluation and assessment process for the child. Services may also be needed if a question arises about a child's medical diagnosis and its impact on the IEP for a child who is already qualified for special education services. The school district's multidisciplinary evaluation team evaluates a child's eligibility for special education and related services once a child has been referred. During this process, medical services are to be provided for any diagnostic or evaluation purposes. The method of assessment must be tailored to the child. Required documentation varies from state to state. Medical services may be provided by a licensed physician, physician's assistant, or a registered nurse practitioner. Qualifications are determined by the state. It is important to note that a medical diagnosis does not automatically qualify a child for special education or related services if it does not affect the child's ability at school. The provision of medical diagnostic services can be provided either in a consultation or in a multidisciplinary team setting. Medical services can be provided on an ongoing basis (e.g., student who requires insulin injections on a daily basis to control her blood sugar levels) or can be more time limited (e.g., student who needs to have bandages changed until wounds from an accident heal).

Occupational Therapy Services

Occupational therapy services include

> Improving, developing, or restoring functions impaired or lost through illness, injury, or deprivation; improving [a child's] ability to perform tasks for independent functioning if functions are impaired or lost; and preventing, through early intervention, initial or further impairment or loss of function. (§300.24[b][5])

Occupational therapy is intended to serve children 3–21 years of age who have a verified disability. Federal law mandates that occupational therapy be *educationally relevant*, which means it should be used if a child has issues that are interfering with his or her educational performance. Feeding, self-help skills, fine and visual motor skills, visual processing, sensory processing, and positioning are examples of areas that may be addressed with occupational therapy. For example, Rochelle has trouble zipping up her coat, feeding herself lunch, and writing with a pen or pencil. She receives occupational therapy services to help her learn to perform these activities.

To qualify for occupational therapy, the team has to determine if the child's issue interferes with the child's ability to participate in his or her educational program and if occupational therapy can address this issue and promote a positive change. Various methods can be used to assess a child's needs for occupational services as related services. Assessments should include observations made in both academic and nonacademic environments. Assessments should also build on past assessment and should be age appropriate to the child.

Occupational therapy must be provided by a registered and licensed occupational therapist. An occupational therapist is a graduate from an accredited education program who has successfully passed a national certification examination. Sometimes services are provided by a certified occupational therapy assistant or by an occupational therapy aide. The type and frequency of services are determined by the IEP team based on the student's educational needs. Ongoing monitoring of student performance is needed to determine the appropriate amount of service.

Orientation and Mobility Services

Orientation and mobility services are defined as "services provided to blind or visually impaired students by qualified personnel to enable those students to attain systematic orientation to and safe movement within their environments in school, home, and community" (§300.24[b][6][i]). Orientation and mobility services are intended for students who are blind or visually impaired and have difficulty orienting themselves and traveling in school and community environments. A comprehensive assessment may evaluate the student's level of vision, use of travel tools, and level of independence across various environments. The assessment should include input from family members and other interested people. Services are provided by a certified orientation and mobility specialist who has specialized training in providing orientation and mobility instruction. A state may or may not have licensure or certification requirements. Service delivery varies depending on the student's needs and is determined by the IEP team.

A student such as Susan needs help with getting around a classroom, her home, and her community activity settings. An orientation and mobility specialist can teach Susan how to use the skills she learned in her specialized school in her new school, including learning travel routes within the classroom and throughout the school. An orientation and mobility instructor can demonstrate to teachers and peers appropriate strategies for supporting Susan in her new school environments and out in the community (e.g., field trips).

Parent Counseling and Training Services

Parent counseling and training services include "assisting parents in understanding the special needs of their child; providing parents with information about child development; and helping parents to acquire the necessary skills that will allow them to support the implementation of their child's IEP or IFSP [individualized family service plan]" [§300.24(b)(7)].

The need for counseling may be determined by any IEP team member, but referral is based on consensus. Parents may also request counseling or training. Typically, when determining the need for counseling, the IEP team will consider if the problem relates to assisting parents with gaining skills needed to implement the IEP or assisting with problem solving or referral to community resources that can help resolve the problem. The team also considers whether other measures have been taken and their effectiveness and if parent counseling and training services would promote a positive change. Assessment may include interviews with qualified personnel and teacher input. Again, parents can also initiate the process by requesting assistance or referral to develop skills to support implementation of their child's IEP. Service providers may include guidance counselors, psychologists, and social workers. Qualifications will vary from state to state. Service delivery may include counseling or consulting, be integrative and include the student, or be consultative by providing input and information on needs rather than providing actual services to the parents and child. The IEP team will determine the need, nature, frequency, duration, and intensity of parent counseling services.

Max has an emotional disability that affects his ability to learn. He not only requires a range of instructional supports and adaptations, but he also needs some help learning to deal with his feelings and interact more positively with others. A psychologist and/or counselor can help him process his feelings while learning alternative coping strategies. In addition, the IEP team may determine that his parents require counseling to learn to deal with their own feelings about Max's disability and to learn coping strategies so that they can do what they need to do to support him.

Physical Therapy Services

Physical therapy means "services provided by a qualified physical therapist" (§300.24[b][8]) and is intended to serve children ages 3–21 years old with a verified disability. Areas to be addressed may include gross motor skills, impaired mobility, and adaptive equipment and positioning needs that interfere with the child's educational performance. Some students may have a disability or impairment identified in a medical setting that does not interfere with their educational performance. Thus, the student may not require physical therapy through the educational program. Others may have a disability that greatly affects their educational performance. In this case, physical therapy may be needed in both medical and school settings.

Physical therapy focuses on helping a child achieve his or her optimum level of independence. The IEP team must identify if the child's disability relates to delay in gross motor skill development, delay in sensorimotor skills, difficulty with equipment used in the educational environment, or difficulty gaining access to school-related activities requiring gross motor skills. The team must also show that previous attempts to alleviate the problem were not successful and/or positive change would appear likely with physical therapy. Assessment must be completed by a physical therapist. Although many tests are available, there is not one test that evaluates the need for physical therapy as a related service.

Services are provided by a physical therapist, physical therapist assistant, or aide. The physical therapist usually holds a master's or doctoral degree in physical therapy and must pass a national examination to qualify for licensure in many states. Assistants and aides work under the supervision of physical therapists in accordance with state guidelines. Services may be direct, integrated, or consultative. It is important to note that these services are not mutually exclusive.

Alejandra is having problems with gross motor movements, such as walking, running, catching, and jumping. Two times a week a physical therapist spends an hour working with her to increase her functional abilities. Therapy is at different times of day, which enables the physical therapist to assess and work with Alejandra during typical activities, including normal transitions in the classroom and school. It also offers the physical therapist an opportunity to influence the way activities are planned to maximize opportunities for Alejandra to improve her motor skills associated with feeding herself.

Recreation Services

Recreation services include assessment of leisure function, therapeutic recreation services, recreation programs in schools and community agencies, and leisure education. They are intended to assist students with disabilities to plan ways to participate in inclusive environments. As a related service, recreation must assist children with disabilities with benefiting from their special education program. An assessment of leisure functioning is used to establish goals for the student. Goals might relate to developing knowledge and/or skills about use of leisure time, resources, communication, decision making, planning, and specific activities. For example, Milton receives recreation therapy twice a week. The goals of his program relate to improving his eye–hand coordination and socialization skills.

Services are provided by a trained certified therapeutic recreation specialist. The specialist usually has an undergraduate or master's degree in recreation therapy. Specialists do not have teaching credentials. In the public schools, a recreational therapist must be recognized and certified as related services personnel by state educational credentialing bodies. The therapeutic recreation specialist role will vary in educational settings, depending on the school's expectations and the size of the school, staffing patterns, organization or special education services, and familiarity with using recreation therapy services. Depending on student needs, the specialist may provide assessment services; individual or group-related services as designated by the IEP; consultation to teachers, parents, and other team members; or referral to community programs.

Rehabilitative Counseling

Rehabilitative counseling refers to

> Services provided by qualified personnel in individual or group sessions that focus specifically on career development, employment preparation, achieving independence, and integration in the workplace and community. The term also includes vocational rehabilitation services provided to a student with disabilities by vocational rehabilitation programs funded under the Rehabilitation Act of 1973, as amended. (§300.24[b][11])

These services are intended to serve students with disabilities ages 14–21 years. Rehabilitative counseling should help the student achieve independence and self-reliance through employment and education opportunities. Schools are responsible for providing rehabilitation counseling; however, the IEP team may identify an outside agency as the service provider. IEP goals, objectives, and activities should consider the student's transition needs for work experience, academic/vocational instruction, adult/daily living skills, and community resources. Formal and informal assessments are used to determine the needs of students with disabilities. Assessment should look at learning styles, vocational interest, functional skills, and abilities across work and community-based environments. Qualifications of professionals providing rehabilitation counseling services vary from state to state. Some states do not require licensure, whereas others require a master's degree and passing of a national examination to qualify as a rehabilitation counselor.

Sam will be exiting school in 2 years. His vocational rehabilitation counselor has arranged for him to participate in several community-based situational assessments so he can learn more about work. He will spend some time trying out various job tasks in a retail store, a hospital, and a military base. This will help him discern his interests and learn more about his abilities and potential on-the-job support needs.

School Health Services

School health services are "services provided by a qualified school nurse or other qualified person" (§300.24[b][12]) and are intended for students with chronic or special health conditions. The student must be qualified under IDEA 2004 and any state law, the service must be necessary for the child to benefit from special education, and the service must be provided if it can only be performed by a nurse or other qualified person (but not a physician).

Traditional related services such as those identified in Part A of IDEA 2004 include transportation, speech-language pathology, audiology services, psychological services, and physical and occupational therapy. The expansion of these traditional related services to include health services resulted from *Irving v. Tatro* (Rothstein, 2000), which dealt specifically with the issue of clean, intermittent catheterization (CIC). The judge's opinion was related services such as CIC, which enable a child with a disability to remain at school during the day, were just as important as transportation and school access.

Another case, *Cedar Rapids Community School District v. Garrett F.,* clarified medical services as those performed by a licensed physician and health-related services as those that could be performed by a school nurse, health aide, or trained layperson (Osborne & Russo, 2003). Examples of these school health services include suctioning, managing a tracheotomy, providing special feedings, positioning, and administering medicine (Downing, 2004). It is clear that administering medications is a school responsibility, but other issues are unclear, including liability, the personnel responsible for administering the medications, and inconsistency between state and local guidelines for health professionals (Cartwright et al., 2007).

Health services must be necessary during the school day and be needed for an appropriate education. If a child requires a health service to be able to attend school at all, then that health service is needed. School health is provided by a licensed and registered school nurse. The nurse develops the individualized health care plan and either implements or directs delivery of nursing care procedures in the school and other settings (e.g., internship, field trip).

Lanny, who has quadraplegia and cannot move from the neck down, needs health care services. He uses a wheelchair for mobility. In order to prevent pressure sores, it is important for him to shift his position in the wheelchair frequently. He receives assistance from a specifically trained specialist to help him with changing his position.

Social Work

Social work services include

> Preparing a social or developmental history on a child with a disability; group and individual counseling with the child and family; working in partnership with parents and others on those problems in a child's living situation (home, school, and community) that affect the child's adjustment in school; mobilizing school and community resources to enable the child to learn as effectively as possible in his or her educational program; and assisting in developing positive behavioral intervention strategies. (§300.24[b][13])

Social work services may be needed if there is evidence of emotional disturbance, abuse, or neglect to the child. These services may also be warranted if the child has behavior problems or if the child does not regularly attend school. The need for services is determined by the IEP team and evaluated by the social worker, in collaboration with family and others. Social workers develop a social and developmental history of the student that requires interacting with both the student and the family. This allows the social worker to learn how the family dynamics and home environment are affecting the student's learning and behavior at school. Social workers must comply with state regulations for certification. Service delivery should be developmental and use an ecological perspective.

Missy, a student with intellectual disabilities, was placed in a foster home when her mother became incarcerated. Due to this change, she has been enrolled in a new school. She has been experiencing a myriad of difficulties adjusting to the new school environment, so the social worker provides individual counseling to Missy once a week. She also meets with Missy and the foster family on a regular basis to help Missy adjust to the changes in her life.

Speech-Language Pathology Services

Speech-language pathology services include

Identification of children with speech or language impairments; diagnosis and appraisal of specific speech or language impairments; referral for medical or other professional attention necessary for the habilitation of speech or language impairments; provision of speech and language services for the habilitation or prevention of communicative impairments; and counseling and guidance of parents, children, and teachers regarding speech and language impairments. (§300.24[b][14])

Speech-language pathology services are intended to serve children with speech, voice, language, communication, and related disabilities. The child must have a disability in order to receive speech-language pathology as a related service. He or she must have a problem related to using speech or language that requires the expertise of an SLP, and the problem must interfere with the child's ability to participate in his or her educational programs. Certification will vary from state to state—some states require a master's degree or a doctorate. Only an SLP may assess the need for speech-language therapy, but an SLP assistant may aid an SLP. Service delivery changes as the needs of the student change. Services may include direct, integrated, and consultative services.

Tomika is working with an SLP to be assessed for an effective alternative communication device that will enable her to make simple requests in the classroom, such as asking to take a break, requesting a turn to talk, and making choices in recreational activities.

Transportation Services

Transportation services include travel to and from school and between schools, travel in and around school buildings, and specialized equipment (e.g., special or adapted buses, lifts, ramps) to provide special transportation for a child with a disability. Transportation services are intended for students who are unable to ride on the regular school bus and sit securely on the bus seat while the bus is in motion without specialized or adaptive equipment. The IEP determines whether the child qualifies for transportation services. Transportation providers must possess whatever vehicle operator's permit and additional training are required by state law.

 # Listening to the Experts

| Teacher's Perspective | I think that it is great that the IEP is a team and not just a reflection of what I was able to organize for Kathy. Oftentimes I do not have the answer for everything that we have to plan for regarding educational practices and transition services. When |

I think of related services and related services agencies, I think of the people who will be involved in solidifying the student's dreams and aspirations. Related services agencies and organizations are as vital to the IEP process as the teacher, student, and parent. For that reason, it is just as important to include, invite, and advocate for their participation in the meeting.

Kathy and I have discussed her plans for future employment. I cannot answer all of her questions or make a plan of action without the right resources, however. That is why it was important to discuss her options with a team of related services personnel. The Department of Rehabilitative Services; the Department of Mental Health, Mental Retardation, and Substance Abuse Services; and the occupational therapist from our public school all had a sense of responsibility in bringing together Kathy's dream. Although not all the agencies were able to make the meeting, they did send information and make other arrangements to make sure that Kathy understood what supports could be available to her as an adult. It was important for Kathy to see and understand the importance and purpose of these resources.

Student's Perspective

When Mr. Scott told me how many people could be on the list to invite to the meeting, I was shocked. I did not know so many people had a say or cared about what it is I do in school and when I graduate. I am glad that I have people who want to see me do well in the future. It feels nice.

Parent's Perspective

Now that she is getting older and getting closer to graduation, it is time that the team bring input for Kathy's future options. We need as many people as possible to make sure that she is successful.

Reflections on Kathy's Example

Mr. Scott worked with an occupational therapist to develop a way to help Kathy (and other students) make decisions about which related services personnel might be appropriate to invite to an IEP meeting. Table 10.1 was developed to help Kathy think through her options.

Tips and Strategies

The following tips and strategies help teachers bring different expertise and viewpoints to the IEP development process.

Table 10.1. Options for inviting related services personnel to an individualized education program (IEP) meeting

Problem area	Definitely invite	Consider inviting
Classes, assignments, and schoolwork	General education teacher, special education teacher	*Psychologist*—if help is needed to determine why there is difficulty with these tasks
		Speech-language pathologist—if the difficulties are related to listening to and following directions, asking for help, and communicating needs related to the assignments
		Occupational therapist—if the difficulties are related to managing fine motor skills, such as completing written work effectively and efficiently in both handwriting or typing; using necessary school materials, including lockers, notebooks, and staplers; using visual perception skills for organizing work or making sense of work that has more than one page
		Vision specialist—if there are problems with vision and this is causing problems with seeing the board, copying notes, and reading from books and worksheets
		Hearing specialist—if there are problems with hearing and this is causing problems with hearing lectures, explanations, and work assignments
Organization: organizing assignments, locker, materials, and notebooks; managing time and long-term projects	General education teacher, special education teacher	*Psychologist*—if help is needed to determine why there is difficulty with these tasks
		Occupational therapist—if fine motor or visual perceptual issues are related to organizing difficulties, such as limited strength to open a locker or use a stapler or other materials; losing papers and keeping work organized; and becoming easily lost in hallways
		Vision—if there are problems with vision and this is causing problems with finding a locker, getting around school, and being unable to use notebooks and organizers visually
		Hearing specialist—if there are problems with hearing and this is causing problems with hearing directions and organizing work
Behavior	General education teacher, special education teacher, psychologist	*Occupational therapist*—if problems seem to be related to sensory motor or sensory integration difficulties

Problem area	Definitely invite	Consider inviting
Participation in physical activities, recess, physical education (PE), and sports	Physical therapist, PE teacher, adaptive PE teacher	*School nurse*—if problems are related to medical or health-related conditions
Positioning and range of motion	Physical therapist and/or occupational therapist	*School nurse and/or physician*—if problems are related to medical or health-related conditions
Daily living activities (getting dressed, showering, brushing hair)	Special education teacher, occupational therapist, family	*School nurse*—if difficulty is related to medical needs or medical equipment
Instrumental activities of daily living (cleaning house, making meals, doing laundry)	Occupational therapist, special educator	*Physical therapist*—if problems are related to mobility, strength, and fatigue
Feeding: opening packages, using utensils, self-feeding, drinking, swallowing	Occupational therapist, speech-language pathologist[a]	*School nurse and/or physician*—if feeding issues are related to a medical or physical condition, particularly if related to aspiration
Medications: understanding when and how to take medication	School nurse, physician, family	None
Understanding/managing health needs, including catheterization, menstruation	School nurse, physician	*Occupational therapist*—if difficulty with managing health needs is related to motor and positioning issues

[a]Occupational therapists and speech-language pathologists differ on their skills in this area, so you need to talk to them about their skill level and expertise particularly related to feeding and swallowing.

- Be familiar with related services so students can receive help with thinking about possible related services to meet their needs and teach them to advocate for their rights.

- Find ways to involve related services personnel in the IEP process and tap their expertise. The fact that they are experts in their areas does not mean that is all they can contribute to the educational planning process. Seek their insight, and help students seek their insight throughout.

- Learn how to effectively follow up with related services representatives.

- Present pictures of the related services representatives to the student prior to the meeting and maintain this information in a booklet for the student.

- Provide related services providers with a one-page "IEP at a glance," stating the student's highest priority goals in simple language (e.g., working on answering *wh-* questions, increasing use of left hand). The student could be responsible for distributing the list to each related services provider on the team and providing updated lists as progress is made and priorities shift.

- Guide the student and his or her family to make an "about me" booklet to be shared with related services providers. Write the book in the first person and include information about expressive and receptive communication modes, likes and dislikes, adaptations (e.g., assistive devices, positioning, how to present materials), and tips on how the child learns best.

Conclusion

This chapter provided an overview of related services. As defined by federal law, related services are intended to address individual needs of eligible students with disabilities so they can benefit from education. Some of the various types of related services were also described. This included a description of who may provide the service and examples of what may be provided. Kathy's story showed how one student was assisted in choosing related services, and some tips from teachers were provided.

References

Board of Education of Hendrick Hudson Central School District v. Rowley, 458 U.S. 176 (1982).

Cartwright, J.D., Lipkin, P.H., Desch, L.W., Duby, J.C., Elias, E.R., Johnson, C.P., et al. (2007). Provision of educationally related services for children and adolescents with chronic diseases and disabling conditions. *Pediatrics, 119*(6), 1218–1223.

County of San Diego v. California Special Education Hearing Office, 93 F.3d 1458 (9th Cir. 1996), 24 IDELR 756.

Downing, J.A. (2004). Related services for students with disabilities: Introduction to the special issue. *Intervention in School and Clinic, 39*(4), 195–208.

Individuals with Disabilities Education Improvement Act (IDEA) of 2004, PL 108-446, 20 U.S.C. §§ 1400 *et seq.*

Levine, P., Marder, C., & Wagner, M. (2004). *Services and supports for secondary school students with disabilities: A special topic report from the National Longitudinal Transition Study-2* (NLTS-2). Menlo Park, CA: SRI International.

Osborne, A.G., Jr., & Russo, C.J. (2003). *Special education and the law: A guide for practitioners.* Thousand Oaks, CA: Corwin.

Rothstein, L.F. (2000). *Special education law* (3rd ed.). New York: Longman.

Taylor v. Honig, 910 F.2d 627 (9th Cir. 1990), 16 EHLR 1138.

Thomas, S.B., & Hawke, C. (1999). Health-care services for children with disabilities: Emerging standards and implications. *Journal of Special Education, 32*(4), 226–237.

U.S. Department of Education. (2002). *National Longitudinal Transition Study-2: Wave 1 student's school program survey.* Washington, DC: Author.

11

....

Transition Individualized Education Planning and Summary of Performance

Elizabeth Evans Getzel, Ann Deschamps, and Colleen A. Thoma

This chapter focuses specifically on individualized education program (IEP) meetings that involve transition planning and discusses the integral role that the summary of performance (SOP) plays in helping to gather information across the student's educational experiences to connect future goals with the supports, services, and instruction that the student has received while in school. All students with disabilities who receive special education and who are at least 16 years old should see a change in the focus of their IEP meetings. At this time, IEP goals, objectives, accommodations, modifications, and supports should not only address student academic and functional goals related to their disability, but they should also help attain their goals for an adult lifestyle. These goals can and should include a range of adult life domains including employment, postsecondary education, community living, transportation, recreation and leisure, and health care.

As students prepare for transition, the SOP is a critical piece in this planning process. In addition to a summary of academic and functional performance, this document provides an overview of the supports and services provided to a student throughout his or her educational history and can be used as a tool to share information and advocate for similar services from a range of adult service providers without having to repeat assessments and/or experiences. It provides essential information without requiring adult service providers to wade through years of IEP documents to find information critical to their own planning needs. This chapter introduces you to these important IEP requirements for transition planning and the role of the SOP in this process to help increase students' direction as they plan for their future.

Transition Planning and Services

The Individuals with Disabilities Education Improvement Act (IDEA) of 2004 (PL 108-446) lists specific requirements for transition planning and services. The term *transition services* refers to a coordinated set of activities for a child with a disability that:

- Is designed to be within a results-oriented process, that is focused on improving the academic and functional achievement of the child with a disability to facilitate the child's movement from school to post-school activities, including postsecondary education, vocational education, integrated employment (including supported employment); continuing and adult education, adult services, independent living, or community participation;
- Is based on the individual child's needs, taking into account the child's strengths, preferences, and interests; and
- Includes instruction, related services, community experiences, the development of employment and other post-school adult living objectives, and, if appropriate, acquisition of daily living skills and functional vocational evaluation (34 C.F.R. 300.43[a]) (20 U.S.C. 1401[34]).

Transition planning begins in the IEP when the student turns 16 (or earlier if determined appropriate by the IEP team) and is updated annually thereafter. IEP teams can determine if a student's disability requires additional planning time to ensure that appropriate postschool services are available, and, if so, IEP teams can decide to begin transition planning earlier than age 16. The transition plan includes the following:

- Appropriate, measurable postsecondary goals based on age-appropriate transition assessments related to training, education, employment, and (where appropriate) independent living skills.

- The transition services (including courses of study) needed to assist the student in reaching those goals. Transition services can be provided by the local education agency (LEA) or by an appropriate community services agency. If an agency is responsible for paying for and/or providing any of the necessary transition services for a student, then a representative of that agency must be invited to participate in developing that plan. Transition services will include instruction, related services, and community experiences. In addition, if appropriate, transition services can also include acquiring daily living skills and providing a functional vocational evaluation.

- Transfer of rights at the age of majority, including informing the student of his or her rights under Part B of IDEA 2004. The student must be informed of these rights beginning no later than 1 year before reaching the age of majority (IDEA, §614).

Much of the early research on teaching self-determination focused on active participation in IEP meetings as a way to provide opportunities to learn and practice self-determination skills, such as goal setting, problem solving, self-advocacy, and self-awareness/self-knowledge. Although this book focuses on student direction and involvement in the IEP process in general, IDEA 2004 is explicit about the need to involve students in the transition IEP process. If you are looking for resources to help organize student direction of transition IEPs, then you will certainly find a range of print, online, and multimedia resources. Some of these are included in the appendix of this book.

Helping Students
Identify Their Postsecondary Goals

Ask high school students to envision their adult lives, and you will get a range of answers. Some students will have detailed answers that are based on a clear understanding of who they are, detailing their strengths, preferences, and interests. Others will have an answer that is based on the adolescent need to establish themselves as separate individuals from their parents by making choices that are the exact opposite of what their parents would do (or what they believe their parents would do). An even greater number will have vague answers or will answer simply, "I don't know." It takes a great deal of knowledge to make wise decisions about one's adult life goals—knowledge about oneself, about the options available, and how to match one's strengths, skills, preferences, and interests with available options. Greene and Kochhar-Bryant (2003) identified five essential questions that can help students think about their goals and what is needed to reach them.

1. What are my school, work, and community living interests and skills?

2. Where do I want to go to school, live, or work after leaving high school?

3. What courses do I take to prepare for the future?

4. What are my strengths, and what do I need to improve?

5. What do I need to learn to make my post–high school goals happen?

Using these questions as a guide, there are a number of different options to help students make better decisions about their long-range goals. Most of the transition curricula, such as *The Next S.T.E.P. Curriculum* (Halpern et al., 1997) and *Choicemaker Curriculum* (Martin et al., 1996), have assessment processes to help students narrow down their options. There is also a computer version of the *Transition Planning Inventory* (Clark & Patton, 2009) that can be used for students who cannot complete paper-and-pencil assessments.

Some of the person-centered planning processes are also useful for helping students articulate their preferred transition outcomes and then use the information to target annual goals to include in the IEP. The Helen Keller Institute provides training to teachers of transition-age students who have sensory impairments, and their transition IEP materials build on the McGill Action Planning System (MAPS; Forest & Pearpoint, 1992). Figure 11.1 provides an illustration of how person-centered planning procedures can strengthen the transition IEP process and can inform the other individualized plans that come when students receive services from community support agencies. Figure 11.2 provides a step-by-step process for adapting MAPS for transition planning; Figure 11.3 is the transition planning addition to the MAPS process that is described in Step 3 of Figure 11.2. The appendix at the end of the book provides additional information about person-centered planning processes.

The SOP can play a key role during the assessment process. As students with disabilities learn more about themselves and determine their postschool goals, this information

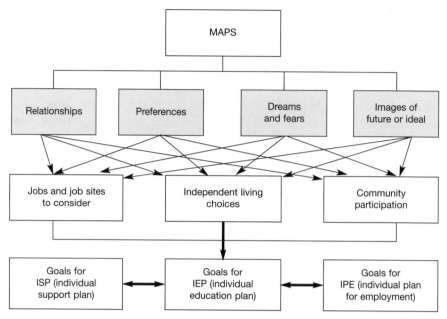

Figure 11.1. Using MAPS for transition planning. (Copyright © 2005 by N. Donta & B. Purvis, National Technical Assistance Consortium for Children and Young Adults Who Are Deaf-Blind; reprinted by permission.)

Step 1: Determine needs.

Ask, "What needs to happen to achieve the student's dreams?" and "How can we overcome the fears (or barriers) of the student, family, and team?"

List the needs; then, discuss and clarify them.

Transfer needs to the planning grid.

Step 2: Prioritize needs.

Look for common themes.

Prioritize needs important to all and/or critical to the student.

Step 3: Develop goals.

Create goals in each grid area (see Figure 11.3).

Use goals from the Education block for the IEP.

Use goals from the Employment block for the IPE (individualized plan for employment).

Use goals from the Independent Living block for the IEP and ISP (individual support plan).

Use goals from the Community Participation block for the IEP and ISP.

Step 4: Discuss next steps.

Share resources and strategies.

Generate ideas collectively.

Problem-solve collaboratively.

Step 5: Action plan.

Determine when to meet again and whether any subgroups need to be formed.

Include strategies for sharing information with others.

Identify someone to monitor the plan.

List tasks, assign role and responsibilities, and include time line.

Figure 11.2. Using MAPS for postsecondary transition planning. (Copyright © 2006 by B. Purvis, National Technical Assistance Consortium for Children and Young Adults Who Are Deaf-Blind; reprinted by permission.)

Planning grid

Education	Employment
Independent living	Community participation

Figure 11.3. Postsecondary transition planning grid. (Copyright © 2004 by B. Purvis, National Technical Assistance Consortium for Children and Young Adults Who Are Deaf-Blind; reprinted by permission.)

can be included in the summary for students to have as they move through the transition planning process and into the community. Specific strategies that teachers can use to work with students during the transition planning process to gather information and ensure student involvement include the following:

• Ensure that information within the school and county regarding transition is up to date. It takes students and parents a great deal of time and energy to identify the agencies to contact, and it can be discouraging to find that contact information is incorrect.

• Review with the student, family, and team members the transition planning expectations.

- Start with some simple questions about long-range outcomes and build on them over time. Students do not need to have answers for all transition planning domains before you can begin to help them plan for their goals.

- Get students involved in writing their own present level of performance to start to increase student direction of their transition IEP process.

- Do not assume that because a student is able to clearly articulate his or her goals in a one-to-one situation that he or she will be able to do so as part of the transition IEP meeting. There are a number of dynamics, not the least of which is the number of adults at the table.

Understanding the World of Adult Services and Community Agencies

As students with disabilities begin to identify their preferences for transition outcomes, the information gathered through the summary can help the IEP team determine what specific community agency supports and services are needed and what information in the summary can be useful to students with disabilities as they enter the community. IEP team members need to work with students and their parents to help them understand the adult service agencies and the different laws, policies, and guidelines that determine whether resources are available. Students and family members often realize that the adult service world is vastly different from the educational system. One of the most significant changes is that the system to educate students with disabilities is entitlement based, whereas employment and community services are eligibility based. For example, although a school must provide services for a student with disabilities and provide them at no additional cost for parents, there is no similar guarantee that services will be provided for free or at all after a student exits high school. In addition, some students may find themselves on waiting lists for years before receiving services.

The following sections provide advice and direction for students applying for adult services and aid. These topics include encouraging students and their families to apply for adult services early and to utilize the method of mapping community resources.

Encourage Students and Their Families to Apply Early for Services

Students and their parents should understand that adult services are provided under different funding mechanisms and by different agencies, such as vocational rehabilitation, the Social Security Administration, community disability services, and/or postsecondary educational offices. Students should begin with their goals for adult life and then identify the supports and services they will require to make those dreams a reality. Once supports and services are identified, students and the IEP team can identify the community agencies that could possibly provide them. Encourage the student to inquire about application processes and information needed, the waiting list to receive services and supports, and the costs (if any) to the student to receive them. Figure 11.4 provides a framework

Transition planning area	What do I want to do?	What supports am I getting now?	What supports will I need in the future?	Who could provide these?	How do I contact them?	What will I need to get their help?
Work						
Home						
Learning						
Health						
Friends						
Fun						
Getting around						
Money						

Getting the Most Out of IEPs: An Educator's Guide to the Student-Directed Approach by Colleen A. Thoma & Paul Wehman. Copyright © 2010 by Paul H. Brookes Publishing Co., Inc. All rights reserved.

Figure 11.4. Organizing student direction of adult supports.

that you can use to help students organize their information gathering about agencies that might be able to provide help and support to enable them to meet their goals.

Community Resource Mapping

Community resource mapping is a graphic representation of the various services, organizations, supports, and opportunities within a community (Crane & Mooney, 2005). Students and their transition team members choose a particular community (or section of a community/city) and investigate the resources that exist.

Max's transition team wanted to investigate the jobs that exist in his neighborhood, so they spent some time walking in the community, talking with business owners, and creating a map of the businesses and options that exist on the streets in his neighborhood as well as the service agencies that were nearby. This information was brought to the transition team meetings to help the team make decisions about what was possible.

This strategy is particularly helpful for transition teams who find that one of their challenges is knowing what is available for students in their own communities. Questions such as the reliability of transportation, available jobs, resources for health care, and accessibility of retail and grocery stores may only be answered by actually going into the community, asking questions, and gathering information on the ground. Information collected is then represented on a map that serves as a visual representation of what is available and can be used to identify additional supports that would be necessary for a student to meet his or her goals and inform the transition planning process. There are three steps to a community resource mapping process: planning, mapping, and summarizing.

Planning   Work with the student to decide on the purpose of the community resource map. Is it to learn more about all of the resources that are available? Or, is it to provide a more in-depth analysis of a specific area (e.g., employment, housing)? Identify the parameters of the mapping. How large of a community does the student want to target (e.g., one city, one neighborhood, one bus line)? Who does the student want to work with to collect this information? What resources will the student use to find what is available (e.g., walk through the neighborhood to collect information, use the Internet, use the telephone book, use a combination of these things)?

Mapping   Once you have a plan developed with the student, implement it. Walk around the community, talk with people, and gather information. Pay attention to the businesses that exist in the community. What jobs could someone do in those businesses? How friendly are people in general (e.g., Do they look out for one another, or are they indifferent)? What is the tempo of the community (e.g., fast, slow and interactive, fast but friendly)? How do people get around (e.g., biking, walking, riding buses, driving cars)? What is there to do for fun? Identify the agencies that provide support services in the community. What are they like? How welcoming are they? How easy is it to access (physically and interpersonally)? Pay attention to how comfortable the student seems to be in the community settings. What did the student seem to like, and what did he or she dislike? Take pictures and notes and collect artifacts (e.g., brochures, applications, pamphlets, web sites) or information about what you both find. Reflect on the information you collected to decide what additional information you still need to accurately portray the setting. What was missing?

Summarizing   It is important to put the information into a format that can be shared with other members of the transition planning team. A table can be used to summarize the information (see Figure 11.5). Students who have difficulty in reading might want to have a graphic representation of the resource map, such as a poster on which the student attaches pictures of the various businesses, agencies, and landmarks in their appropriate locations. Other students might want to make a web site version of their map with links to the businesses, agencies, and/or landmarks.

The information gained through person-centered planning, identifying community agencies, and community resource mapping is essential for the student's SOP.

Using the Summary of Performance in Transition Planning

So far, this chapter has emphasized that the SOP plays a critical role in transition. Ideally, the SOP is used as a tool in the transition planning process and reflects a student's academic and vocational skills and abilities. Most important, the summary identifies postsecondary goals with recommendations to reach those goals. Teachers can use the development of the summary as an opportunity for the student to articulate and explore his or her potential postsecondary goals over time. By the time the student is ready to graduate, his or her postsecondary goals accurately reflect his or her postschool plans and are more than just perfunctory words on a piece of paper. The SOP is defined in IDEA 2004 as:

> The public agency provides a summary of academic and functional performance, including recommendations to assist the student in meeting postsecondary goals, for students whose eligibility terminates because of graduation with a regular high school diploma or because of exceeding the age eligibility for FAPE under State law. (§300.305[e][3])

The IDEA 2004 requirement that LEAs provide students with a summary of their academic achievement and functional performance was intended to assist the student and family as they make the transition from secondary education into the community. Although the law does not provide specific guidance as to how this summary should be developed, it does identify three areas to be addressed.

1.   Academic achievement

2.   Functional performance

3.   Recommendation on how to assist the student in reaching postsecondary goal

Public school jurisdictions are left to their judgment as to what their SOP will look like. As a result, there is great variability among states as to how the SOP is developed and implemented. State education agencies must determine the best approach for creating a summary, and some provide templates for all school districts to use when developing the summary. Others provide guidance on its development but have given the responsibility to the local school districts to determine the design and process for

Restaurants			Sports and games	
a. Fast food			a. Participant	
b. Ethnic restaurants			b. Observer	
c. Eclectic food			Exercise/fitness	
d. Bars, grills			Theaters	
Computer training classes			Arts and crafts instruction or supplies	
Gas/auto maintenance			Transportation	
Tax assistance			Groceries	
Clothing stores			Hair cutting, styling	
			Clinics, emergency care	
Home furnishings			Veterinary clinics	
Child care			Dental care	
Bookstores			Home maintenance	
CDs/DVDs			Car washes	
			Convenience stores	
Public parks			Other places	

Figure 11.5. Community mapping results.

providing the summary to their students. For example, in some school districts, the SOP is part of the IEP, and in others, it is a separate document.

Some school districts identify the student's case manager as the individual responsible for completing the SOP, and in others, the district assists students in developing portfolios to collect information over time to include in the summary. Because of these different approaches in developing and implementing the SOP, educators, community organizations, students, and families often do not fully understand the intent and importance of the SOP and how to use the information as they make the transition into the community. The summary builds off of the transition planning process and provides a document for students to take with them as they exit secondary education. For this reason, it is critical for students to be involved in developing their SOPs. This involvement can empower students to learn about themselves in a number of areas and enable them to identify the services and supports needed to reach their long-term goals. The next section of this chapter focuses on what educators and community agencies are saying about the SOPs, along with ideas and strategies to assist in engaging students in their development.

What Educators Say About the Summary of Performance

In a series of facilitated discussions, educators were asked about the importance and benefits of the SOP (Deschamps & Getzel, 2007). Educators believed that the SOP provides closure for students with disabilities as they exit secondary education. The SOP offers opportunities to reflect on the progress of the student over the past years and helps remind him or her of the next steps to reach his or her goals. Educators also expressed the importance of providing something tangible to students when leaving school; a tool they can use for a number of purposes (e.g., information when seeking services, applying for a job, or entering postsecondary education or training). In addition to helping the student or family member, educators felt the SOP provides relevant information for community agencies.

Educators asserted that completing the summary is a team process. The student needs to be involved from the beginning for the document to be useful for the student. Frequently, there are also a number of other players involved in the process, however, including other teachers, parents, guidance counselors, and employers. All of these players in students' lives can provide information to help them complete their summary. Educators also emphasized the need to start gathering information early. Some school districts have developed portfolios to collect all the information for the summary starting in the eighth grade or the year of the student's first transition plan. When students reach their last year in school, the case manager and students can review the information in their portfolios to complete the summary. Keeping a "career" portfolio also ensures that important information, such as job references, career inventories, or assessment results, that are completed during the early years of high school do not get lost. Educators also expressed that, whenever possible, school districts should try to keep the summary simple and user friendly for students, keeping in mind that the intent of the summary is for them to have this information available for their transition to the workplace, postsecondary education or training, and the community (Martin, Van Dycke, D'Ottavio, & Nickerson, 2007).

Educators discussed some issues that have arisen around the SOP (Deschamps & Getzel, 2007). They felt that students, teachers, parents, and other stakeholders need information sessions or training about the summary and its purpose. The biggest hindrance to completing the form is students and other personnel lacking understanding about the summary. In order for the summary to serve a useful purpose, there needs to be an ongoing public relations campaign in schools so that all relevant parties understand the use of the summary and do not treat it as just another form to complete. Other continuing concerns expressed by educators on developing the SOP focused on the timing of its development (e.g., at what point during the student's final year to complete the SOP and give it to the student/family), providing SOPs to students with disabilities who dropped out of school, and ensuring that the student or family voice is reflected in the document.

What Community Agencies Say About the Summary of Performance

Community agency personnel expressed varying levels of information and knowledge about the SOP (Deschamps & Getzel, 2007). There are a number of reasons why community agencies are, for the most part, unfamiliar with the summary. One primary reason is the lack of understanding by students with disabilities and their families on how to use the information when meeting with community agencies. The summary can be used to communicate information about courses taken, specific skills learned, and accommodations proven effective. It is incumbent that teachers and transition professionals make sure students know this and utilize it accordingly. Community agency staff members also lack the training and understanding on how to use the summary to help determine appropriate services and supports. Collaborative training with school personnel and community agencies is needed to ensure that the receiving agencies understand the use of the summary. For those who were provided an SOP from a student and understood its purpose, agency staff expressed positive comments about the SOP and how the document saved the agency time in learning about the student, helping to prevent duplication of testing or assessments (Deschamps & Getzel, 2007).

Although a number of issues remain surrounding the SOP, due in part to its relatively recent inclusion as part of IDEA 2004 and the lack of federal guidance, it is essential that the process of information sharing and collaborative training occur among parents, school personnel, students, and community agencies so that the SOP truly becomes a usable and helpful tool to bridge the secondary and postsecondary worlds.

 ## Listening to the Experts

Teacher's Perspective

Because Kathy will not be graduating this school year, we did not have to finalize her SOP. However, when the time comes for graduation, I know that we are prepared to describe or summarize what her support needs are that will benefit her in the next program she enters. Kathy has been outstanding at taking ownership for what services she has and what services she will need that will support her educational and functional achievement. With the information that she has collected thus far, she is obtaining a better understanding of herself, which will help facilitate the important information to include in her SOP.

Kathy and her mother took a look at her prior coursework and her functioning skills and decided that she could benefit from an additional year in high school. By taking a step back and deciding what Kathy had and what she could still do to improve helped lead to the decision to spend an additional school year. The same attitude and perseverance it took to evaluate her strengths and needs will ideally be the same approach that will help in completing her SOP.

Student's Perspective

I am still learning about myself. I am still learning about my likes and dislikes and my needs. I am starting to learn about the people who can help me now and who will be the people that can help me in the future. I think this will help me describe what I need when it is time for me to graduate.

Parent's Perspective

Graduation is not here yet. It is right around the corner. I think it will be important for us to come together as a team near graduation to solidify the support and services that Kathy will need when it is time for her to graduate. We have a great start on defining and summarizing the support she will need once she graduates.

Reflections on Kathy's Example

Kathy is like most high school students—she has some concrete goals for the future but is not sure how to put the supports in place to make it happen. Mr. Scott worked with her to organize her transition outcome information on a "one-page summary form" (from Virginia Department of Education's web site, http://www.imdetermined.org), which she used as her invitation to her transition IEP meeting so those individuals planning to attend could have some basic information about her plans for the future as well as what she was currently doing in school. It helped facilitate and focus the discussions that occurred during her IEP meeting because everyone who came to the meeting had a better understanding of Kathy's strengths, needs, and long-range goals (see Figure 11.6).

During the IEP meeting, Kathy introduced this information and answered questions from the team members. They added their own information about Kathy based on her performance on assessments, in school, and on previous IEP goals to help the team target annual IEP goals that would help her work toward achieving those long-range plans

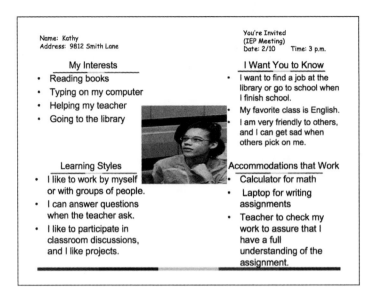

Name: Kathy
Address: 9812 Smith Lane

You're Invited
(IEP Meeting)
Date: 2/10   Time: 3 p.m.

My Interests

- Reading books
- Typing on my computer
- Helping my teacher
- Going to the library

Learning Styles

- I like to work by myself or with groups of people.
- I can answer questions when the teacher ask.
- I like to participate in classroom discussions, and I like projects.

I Want You to Know

- I want to find a job at the library or go to school when I finish school.
- My favorite class is English.
- I am very friendly to others, and I can get sad when others pick on me.

Accommodations that Work

- Calculator for math
- Laptop for writing assignments
- Teacher to check my work to assure that I have a full understanding of the assignment.

Figure 11.6. Kathy's one-page summary form. (Reprinted by permission from Mary Anne Huband.)

for her future. They used the information to help her choose classes for the next year and supports and services she would need, as well as educational goals.

Finally, Kathy, her mother, and a friend who lives nearby completed a community resource map as a way of investigating options for her long-range goals that exist in her neighborhood. She found a small branch of the public library nearby, identified bus stops near her home, and followed the routes to find which of her typical hangouts and friends' homes were accessible by bus (to decrease her reliance on her mother to drive her everywhere). They used the community resource mapping exercise to identify the nearest offices of the community support services agencies and pick up application and eligibility information. All of the information gathered by Kathy was placed in a portfolio to use when finalizing her SOP.

Tips and Strategies

The SOP can serve as a bridge for students as they exit secondary education and enter the community by documenting what has worked for the student in the past. The SOP also includes recommendations that support postschool goals (Kochhar-Bryant, 2007). It is important to not only focus on the actual document but also on how the SOP can become an important piece of the student's transition process. There are a variety of ways that teachers can integrate the summary into their work with students.

- Work with a group of students during a basic skills or English class to draft the SOP form and stimulate good discussion among the students about their respective postschool plans.

- Complete the SOP in a one-to-one meeting with the student. Complete the demographic parts of the summary at the beginning of the student's senior year and then complete the other parts with the student at different times throughout the year.

- Work on pieces of the summary a little at a time, all year long. For example, when students work on developing résumés, they can complete the job experience part of their summaries. Because students work on it steadily, they really own the document at the end of the process.

- Have students make drafts of the form on their own. Then, meet with the students to review the information to be filled in and discuss where they can find this information. After completing whatever they can do on their own, students then collect information by talking to teachers, guidance counselors, parents, and, in some cases, employers.

Using these and other methods, transition personnel in Fairfax County Public Schools in Virginia were asked to provide feedback on the process of completing the summary. They reported the following (Deschamps, 2006):

- "Completing the summary with the student helped clarify exactly what postsecondary resources the student needed. We were able to make connections before he graduated."

- "It helped to discuss postsecondary goals with students first and then work backward to complete the form. The students seem to take great pride in seeing how much they had learned and accomplished during high school."

- "It was easier and more time efficient to start completing the form with the whole class (in this case, an English class). Because we spent time doing résumés earlier in the year, the students could complete sections on work skills and experiences themselves. Once a draft was completed, students met with their case manager to go over the document and create a final version. Doing it this way really made it the student's document, not the school's."

- "It was amazing to me how completing the summary with students helped increase their awareness of how much they really have prepared for life after high school."

- "Completing the form with the student served as a reality check for the student. He realized that he really needed to get his act together and that it was in his best interest to take advantage of resources through the school before he graduates."

- "I was surprised how difficult it was for students to connect what they already know (skills and abilities) to what they are planning to do after they leave school. Going through the process of completing the summary of performance enabled them to make these connections. It is essential to start with the postsecondary goal(s) and work backward in order to make those connections."

- "This process crystallized the information for the students and helped them identify skills they have—it seemed to be a real confidence booster. It was the best conversation we had all year."

Educators identified other benefits of working with students as they develop their SOP. Students involved with their SOPs were able to practice self-advocacy skills, learn or reinforce their strengths and weaknesses, and take stock of their skills and abilities. Other benefits included reinforcing all of the students' accomplishments in secondary education as they relate to their postsecondary goals, practicing goal setting, and assisting students in focusing on what they really want after leaving high school.

Conclusion

This chapter outlined the transition planning process, including identifying postsecondary education goals, understanding the world of adult services, and completing the SOP. The ideas and resources are meant to assist the IEP team in working together with the student to engage in a variety of experiences to gather information to assist in developing postsecondary goals. An integral part of this transition process is the information gained by students on their abilities, interests, and career goals that can be incorporated into a SOP for them to use when entering a variety of settings in the community.

References

Clark, G., & Patton, J. (2009). *Transition Planning Inventory.* Austin, TX: PRO-ED.

Crane, K., & Mooney, M. (2005). *Community resource mapping.* Minneapolis: Institute on Community Integration Publications Office.

Deschamps, A. (2006, June). *Incorporating the SOP in Fairfax County.* Presentation at the Inservice Meeting of Career and Transition Services, Fairfax, VA.

Deschamps, A., & Getzel, E.E. (October 2007). *Summary of performance: One state's perspective on its implementation.* Presentation at the DCDT International Conference, Orlando, FL.

Forest, M., & Pearpoint, J. (1992). Everyone belongs: Building the vision with MAPS, the McGill Action Planning System. In D. Wetherow (Ed.), *The whole community catalogue: Welcoming people with disabilities into the heart of community life* (pp. 95–99). Manchester: Communities.

Greene, G., & Kochhar-Bryant, C.A. (2003). *Pathways to successful transition for youth with disabilities.* Upper Saddle River, NJ: Pearson/Merrill/Prentice Hall.

Halpern, A., Herr, C., Wolf, N., Doren, B., Johnson, M., & Lawson, J. (1997). *The Next S.T.E.P. (Student Transition and Educational Planning) Curriculum.* Austin, TX: PRO-ED.

Individuals with Disabilities Education Improvement Act (IDEA) of 2004, PL 108-446, 20 U.S.C. §§ 1400 *et seq.*

Kochhar-Bryant, C. (2007). The summary of performance as transition "passport" to employment and independent living. *Assessment for Effective Intervention, 32,* 160–170.

Martin, J.E., Huber-Marshall, L., Maxson, L.L., & Jerman, P.A. (1996). *Self-directed IEP.* Longmont, CO: Sopris West Educational Services.

Martin, J.E., Van Dycke, J., D'Ottavio, M., & Nickerson, K. (2007). The student-directed summary of performance: Increasing student and family involvement in the transition planning process. *Career Development for Exceptional Individuals, 30*(1), 13–26.

III

....

Implementing
and Evaluating the IEP

12

....

Goal
Implementation and Evaluation

Dawn R. Hendricks, Colleen A. Thoma, and Kimberly S. Boyd

Although participation in goal setting is a critical component of the student-directed individualized education program (IEP) process, goal setting by itself is not enough for students with disabilities. The IEP process does not end when the meeting is done. Many teachers feel a sense of relief once the IEP meeting is over and the document is signed. The work is just beginning, however, as the IEP continues to evolve. Implementing and evaluating goals is the crux of the IEP process (Wehmeyer, 1994). It is through implementing and evaluating goals that growth and learning ensue. Without this component, all you would have is a formal document with no lasting meaning or significance.

The IEP process contains three fluid components: premeeting, IEP meeting, and implementing and evaluating goals. The student-directed process should continue during this third component of the IEP. The student should have opportunities to provide input and/or direct this critical phase of goal implementation and evaluation. Instead of teachers taking full responsibility for determining what, when, where, and how a student will learn, it is necessary to ensure that students are actively involved in the decision-making process and are engaged in instructional delivery (Agran, 1997). Much of what happens in school is in the control of teachers and administrators. The student-directed process involves the student in all aspects of his or her educational program and places the responsibility for learning primarily on the student.

Continuing the student-directed process through the steps of goal attainment is also important because unless the student is involved in setting the path of study, there will be little motivation within the student to be successful. Involving students in this stage of the IEP process may result in increased goal attainment. German, Martin, Huber Marshall, and Sale (2000) found that students with mild and moderate intellectual disabilities increased the number of daily goals attained when given the opportunity to direct instruction. Zhang (2001) found similar results when students were actively involved in carrying out their education plan. Furthermore, the steps and procedures utilized in this process may teach students valuable life skills required in the postsecondary environment. Mason, McGahee-Kovac, Johnson, and Stillerman (2002) found that student-directed approaches resulted in increased student assertiveness and accountability. Active participation in goal implementation and evaluation prompts self-monitoring toward the desired outcome (Smith & Nelson, 1997). With self-monitoring, students learn to evaluate their own progress and identify when they meet or do not meet goals. Through this process, students tap into intrinsic motivation and see instruction as something they do with teachers, not something that is done to them.

Designing Action Steps to Promote a Student-Directed Process

Once the IEP is created and goals are outlined, an instructional plan is developed and action steps are implemented that will result in student learning. This requires educators to examine many facets of the educational program and make a number of pivotal decisions regarding IEP implementation.

- What is the progression for implementing instruction on IEP goals?

- Which curricula will be used to address IEP goals?

- Which specific skills and content will be used to address IEP goals?

- What resources will be used to address IEP goals?

- Where should instruction be provided?

- When should instruction be provided?

- How much instruction should be provided?

- What instructional methods should be employed?

Educators should enter into shared decision making with their students by collaborating to identify the key considerations for attaining each goal and defining the implementation and evaluation process. Students with a range of disabilities have demonstrated successful involvement in this stage of the IEP process (Test, Mason, & Hughes, 2004). The purpose of this model, just like any other model of instruction, is to promote student learning and growth. How this collaboration takes shape will vary according to the student. It is reasonable to believe that not every instructional strategy or activity implemented will be student directed. There are times when the most effective instructional strategy to achieve a skill will be a teacher-directed strategy. Furthermore, there are times when a needed skill will not be in the forefront of the student's thinking. It is important to emphasize that not all activities are student directed and not all students have the same level of input and control. Instead, the student is actively engaged in his or her planning and educational program to the greatest extent possible.

Involvement in this stage requires careful planning on the part of the educator and IEP team. Fortunately, there is an assortment of strategies available to promote a student-directed approach during the implementation and evaluation phase. These strategies can be implemented in isolation or, preferably, in combination to accomplish this goal. They are to be tailored to the individual in order to meet the desires and needs of the student;

address the specific skill; and fit the setting and materials that are germane to a specific class, school, or community. The following sections describe how to organize instructional and support activities through collaborative teaming and how to create meaningful learning activities.

Organizing Instructional Activities Through Collaborative Teaming

In order to organize the educational program in a student-directed manner, all IEP team members, including students, family members, educational staff, and community personnel, must be knowledgeable about and skilled in the tools and strategies used to promote student participation. Many of the IEP goals will require involvement from multiple service providers. A student-directed approach requires an effective and coordinated working relationship among all IEP team members. Furthermore, a student-directed approach requires all members to be working toward a common purpose. Research has found that the transition planning team does not always support student preferences and interests, even when the teacher and parent do (Thoma, 1999; Thoma, Rogan, & Baker, 2001). Ward stated that interactive educational planning "requires not only that people with disabilities develop inner resources, but that society support and respond" (1988, p. 2). To truly function as a team, all members must believe in and maintain the vision the student has for the future. Through collaboration and uniformity, IEP teams can enhance the quality of outcomes for students with disabilities. Members can work together to develop action plans and monitor progress as well as problem-solve and create solutions that will lead to ongoing goal attainment.

Creating Meaningful Learning Activities

As discussed in previous chapters, the student's preferences and priorities guide IEP goal development. As goals are implemented using a student-directed approach, the IEP team continues with this process by using the student's dreams to determine how best to provide instruction. This requires transferring IEP goals into meaningful learning activities that are both relevant and of interest to the student. The McGill Action Planning System (MAPS; Forest & Pearpoint, 1992) provides one strategy that can be used by educational teams to create germane instruction. With MAPS, educators use the student's individual characteristics, including interests, preferences, and needs, to guide the learning activities and instructional context. Figure 12.1 provides a visual depiction of how student characteristics lead to developing IEP goals and how these same student factors lead to implementing the goals.

Using the MAPS model, instruction is individualized based on the student and, whenever possible, is provided in natural community environments. Regardless of the student's disability, active learning opportunities in community environments, such as worksites, shopping malls, libraries, and cafeterias, appear to be the most functional (Wehman & Thoma, 2006). Table 12.1 provides an example of how a student's preferences translate into meaningful learning activities and locations in the areas of employment and leisure.

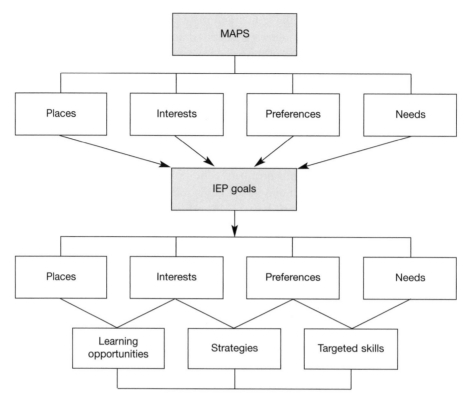

Figure 12.1. Using MAPS for educational planning. (Reprinted by permission from Barb Purvis.)

Students with disabilities face many obstacles and personal challenges that may negatively affect goal attainment. Circles of support can be created to address these needs and help the student reach his or her goals. This circle accompanies the student on the educational journey and provides needed encouragement and assistance. Creating a circle of support enables the student to realize his or her ambitions by gaining access to opportunities and supports that can lead to personal and educational development. It is recommended that each student have several circles, with each serving a different role in the student's life. Clearly, one of the circles will be the IEP team. Once the IEP is written, additional circles are created that help the student attain outlined goals; each circle serving a distinct purpose. For example, one circle may include peers, whereas a second includes parents and other relatives, and a third includes other significant adults or community members. The circles operate within a variety of community locations, providing support not only at school, but also during many pertinent activities and environments. Each circle of support plays a crucial role in assisting personal choice, developing goals, exploring interests, identifying strengths, and practicing self-determination skills. Perhaps one of the most critical roles is to expose students to various life experiences and help them learn about possibilities. It is not likely that students will formulate a dream and create appropriate goals that will lead to improved outcomes if they are not aware of the available options.

Table 12.1. Translating preferences into meaningful activities

Preferences	Possible activities	Possible worksite	Possible recreation/leisure site
Outdoors and animals	Gardening	Garden center	Garden center
	Landscaping	Farm	Home
	Horseback riding	Pet store	Farm
	Caring for animals	Animal care facility	Park
	Feeding birds		
Water	Swimming	Hotel	Pool
	Doing laundry	Restaurant	
	Dishwashing		
Music	Playing an instrument	Music store	Concert hall
	Listening to music	Concert hall	Outdoor arena
	Attending a concert	Instrument store	Music store
	Shopping for music		
	Organizing music		
	Cleaning a concert hall		
Walking and people	Delivering food	Coffee shop	Gym
	Delivering mail	Restaurant	Mall
	Bussing tables	Post office	Park
	Shopping		
	Walking on a treadmill		
	Walking at a park		

Fostering Self-Determination Skills

Although students with disabilities have been able to actively engage in the goal implementation and evaluation phase, it appears students need systematic instruction to gain the self-determination skills that will allow them to participate in a meaningful way (Allen, Smith, Test, Flowers, & Wood, 2001). *Self-determination* has been defined as "people controlling their own lives and their own destinies" (Wehmeyer & Schwartz, 1999, p. 76). Self-determination skills are important for students because these skills teach students how to make decisions and actively direct their own lives.

There is growing evidence that instruction to promote self-determination is important for students to achieve positive adult outcomes (e.g., Wehmeyer & Schwartz, 1997, 1998). Gerber et al. (1990) interviewed adults who were identified with a learning disability during their school years. Those who were successful exhibited high levels of self-determination skills. Wehmeyer and Schwartz (1997) provided a follow-up study of students with mild intellectual disabilities 1 year after graduation. Students with higher self-determination scores were more likely to be employed and earned significantly more per hour. In a separate study, Wehmeyer and Schwartz (1999) found that people with intellectual disabilities who were highly self-determined reported a higher quality of life. Based on extant research, it is clear that self-determination skills are an essential component of educational planning and a critical transition outcome.

Table 12.2.   Component elements of self-determination

Choice-making skills
Decision-making skills
Problem-solving skills
Goal-setting and attainment skills
Independence, risk-taking, and safety skills
Self-observation, evaluation, and reinforcement skills
Self-advocacy and leadership skills
Internal locus of control
Positive attributions of efficacy and outcome expectancy
Self-awareness
Self-knowledge
Self-instruction

Source: Wehmeyer, Agran, and Hughes (1998).

Wehmeyer, Agran, and Hughes (1998) have identified 12 key elements or skills that comprise self-determination (see Table 12.2). Also, these elements will be explained in further detail in the following sections. These skills comprise a wide diversity of behaviors, demonstrating the complexity of self-determination. By focusing on these skills, the construct of self-determination can be broken down into discrete, teachable units. It is easy to see how each of the 12 component elements is an essential ingredient of the goal implementation and evaluation phase of the IEP process. It is likely that a student with a disability, regardless of its severity, will require instruction on all 12 self-determination skills. It may not be feasible to deliver intense or equal levels of instruction in a timely and thorough manner. As instruction is provided, it is important to zero in on those skills needed by the individual for growth and learning. This requires prioritizing key skills and providing more instruction on high areas of need and impact. In addition, efforts to enhance self-determination should involve integrating a number of the component elements into one activity. Although each represents a specific behavior, they are interrelated and impact one another. This makes it possible to target multiple skills simultaneously through careful and considerate planning. The following sections briefly describe each element.

Choice-Making Skills

Choice making is the practice of picking from two known options in order to identify a preference. It is a relatively easy skill to incorporate throughout the school day and in a variety of environments. Educators can provide opportunities for choice making by having students participate in choosing what and how they learn (Kohn, 1993). These considerations include choosing the content of instruction, type of instructional strategy, materials, location, and potential learning partners or groupings. As choice making is encouraged, educators can discuss with students the consequences and limits that come with some choices.

Decision-Making Skills

Decision making is a lot like choice making, but it involves a more complex process requiring a wider set of skills. The decision-making process requires listing the options and identifying the consequences of each option. Then, the pros and cons of each consequence are assessed, and the best course of action is determined. Although decisions affecting the lives of individuals with disabilities are made multiple times a day, these individuals are often excluded from the decision-making process. Instruction targeting decision-making skills should be provided during familiar activities where meaningful issues can be addressed, such as career preparation classes, academic classes, extracurricular activities, or other functional educational activities (Field & Hoffman, 2002). Such instruction should not be an "add-on," but should be infused throughout the school day so students can demonstrate real-life application of the skill.

Problem-Solving Skills

Problem solving is a higher order process that occurs if a person does not know how to proceed to a desired goal (Goldstein & Levin, 1987). There are many approaches to problem solving, depending on the nature of the problem and the people involved. A typical approach involves a process similar to that used for decision making. This requires describing the problem, analyzing the cause, identifying resolution options, assessing each alternative, and choosing the best course of action. After this point, evaluation occurs to determine whether the problem was solved. It is important to introduce students to all of the steps necessary to solve a problem, including methods for searching out appropriate alternatives or solutions. Educators should provide adequate support and accommodations to students and should model this behavior by verbalizing the problem-solving steps used on a day-to-day basis (Wehmeyer & Schalock, 2001).

Goal-Setting and Attainment Skills

Goal setting involves establishing specific, measurable, and time-targeted objectives to achieve an end result. Goal setting involves not only determining a desired outcome, but also putting an action plan in place, implementing the plan, and evaluating its effectiveness. Involving students in goal setting should be relatively easy to accomplish because we develop IEP goals annually and create educational plans on the basis of these goals. It is a process of involving students in something that we already do regularly.

Independence, Risk-Taking, and Safety Skills

Independence is the ultimate goal we have for our students. Some students with disabilities may never be completely independent as they will always need ongoing supports and services. We must ensure independence is maximized and not stifled due to our own fears and apprehensions by allowing our students to take risks and experience the consequences of their choices. Of course, this excludes behaviors that would lead to injury or harm. Just as students with disabilities can be taught to make decisions and problem solve, they too can be taught to assess the level of risk associated with a given action or situation. In addition, students can be taught safety and health skills needed to live and work independently.

Self-Observation, Evaluation, and Reinforcement Skills

Self-observation, evaluation, and reinforcement strategies help students become aware of what they are doing and teach them to manage or control their own behavior at school, work, home, and in the community. Through these strategies, students learn to monitor their own behavior. They are taught to identify a target behavior, evaluate the presence or absence of this behavior, and provide self-reinforcement by delivering an appropriate consequence. For example, a student may learn to monitor the number of times he or she raises a hand to ask for assistance and obtains the opportunity to work on the computer when the desired number is achieved. The targeted behavior may be one that needs to be increased, such as greeting co-workers, or may be a problem behavior that needs to be reduced or eliminated from the student's repertoire, such as yelling out in class or throwing objects.

Self-Advocacy and Leadership Skills

Self-advocacy is the ability to speak up for oneself and may include voicing one's opinions, wants, or needs or defending a cause, person, or action. Students need to learn what to advocate and how to do so appropriately. Instruction should focus on teaching a student how to be assertive but not aggressive, communicate and listen effectively, negotiate, compromise, and navigate through relevant service delivery and community systems (Wehmeyer, 2001). Perhaps the most important area of instructional emphasis involves the education and transition process and the student's rights and responsibilities within that system.

Internal Locus of Control

Internal locus of control focuses on an attitude in which you believe you have control over the outcomes in your life and that your actions affect these outcomes (Wehmeyer et al., 1998). Students must believe that they can influence outcomes in their life if they are to set goals and work toward them. We can facilitate the development of internal locus of control by providing opportunities for students to demonstrate and learn about the relationship between their behavior and their performance. The relationship between studying for a test and achieving an *A,* practicing basketball and procuring a position on the team, greeting a peer and receiving an invitation to the football game, and arriving late to work and getting fired are all relevant examples. It is helpful to highlight such relationships during familiar and meaningful activities.

Positive Attributes of Efficacy and Outcome Expectancy

Self-efficacy and efficacy expectancy are closely related to internal locus of control. *Self-efficacy* refers to the belief that you possess the skills necessary to produce the desired outcome. *Efficacy expectancy* refers to the belief that using those skills will lead to this desired outcome. Students not only need to understand they have control over their life, but that they also possess important skills, and these skills are effective and can lead to meaningful outcomes. Again, an educational program that emphasizes choice making, decision making, problem solving, and goal setting should enhance efficacy in its students.

Self-Awareness and Self-Knowledge

To demonstrate *self-awareness* and *self-knowledge,* it is important for students to understand who they are and their own unique characteristics and attributes (Test, Aspel, & Everson, 2006). Students should be able to identify their interests, abilities, and limitations, including understanding the nature of their disability and its impact. Educators help students identify personal attributes through observations, interviews, assessments, and inventories. Information is infused into educational programming by providing opportunities for the student to articulate strengths and needs, develop goals, and make decisions that are appropriate and capitalize on his or her attributes.

Self-Instruction

Students will be expected to learn new things throughout their entire lives. They need to learn to teach themselves new skills or to identify resources for learning new skills. Typically, instruction is largely teacher directed in special education. There are advantages, however, to making the student a more active participant in educational decision making and instructional delivery. Not only does self-instruction lead to enhanced self-determination skills, but it also has resulted in improvements in rate and accuracy of performance and increased peer interaction as well as generalization to other skills (Agran, King-Sears, Wehmeyer, & Copeland, 2003; Grote, Rosales, & Baer, 1996). Educators can teach self-instruction through authentic learning experiences and provide practice opportunities during maintenance and generalization tasks (Test et al., 2006).

Providing Instruction on Self-Determination Skills

Self-determination skills are taught systematically through specific learning experiences in order to increase knowledge and use (German et al., 2000). Agran, Snow, and Swaner concluded that self-determination skills were an educational necessity, "one to be pursued as seriously and systematically as any other skill area we value" (1999, p. 301). Proponents of self-determination have struggled with the logistics of how, when, and where to teach self-determination. This is especially problematic given the current atmosphere of accountability that often creates conflicting priorities, such as preparing students for high-stakes testing.

So, where does instruction to promote self-determination fit into the curriculum for students with disabilities? Fortunately, instruction does not require a specific activity or location or even time of day. The self-determination elements discussed in this chapter are woven directly into the student's curriculum. For example, for students who gain access to the general education curriculum, many of the skills related to choice and decision making are easily linked to state standards and benchmarks. For those who benefit from an individualized or aligned curriculum, an experientially based program provides an

Table 12.3. Teacher requirements when incorporating self-determination skills

Recognize the importance of learning self-determination skills for students with disabilities.

Understand that self-determination means making choices that are important for the individual. It does not mean doing everything independently, nor does it mean that someone has to make the decisions that reflect our ideals.

Learn that opportunities to practice are as important as teaching the skill.

Listen to students regardless of what method they use to communicate.

Improve your communication skills with students, be aware of cues you give students about the "right" answer, and defer questions about student preferences to the individual student.

Hold high expectations for the student.

Spend time organizing the day to provide opportunities for students to learn what is most important to them, not just what fits neatly into a school day.

Give students responsibility and involve students in making plans.

Be willing to give up control to the student even if he or she might make a mistake or choice that you would not make.

Let students demonstrate their capabilities.

Source: Thoma & Held (2003).

ideal medium for instruction. Konrad, Trela, and Test (2006) provided an example of embedding self-determination skills into the language arts goal of writing a paragraph. Students wrote a paragraph about IEP goals. Results showed a functional relationship between self-determination instruction and IEP content and quality. By infusing instruction into typical curriculum content, teachers can ensure educational programs meet individual student needs in a meaningful way. Thoma and Held (2003) outlined beliefs and standards required of teachers when incorporating self-determination skills in the educational setting (see Table 12.3).

Self-Determined Learning Model of Instruction

In the preceding section, an overview of instructional and support activities that promote a student-directed approach during the goal implementation and evaluation phase was presented. Although each provides an effective way to increase student involvement, none of these strategies provide educators with a comprehensive model of teaching. Joyce and Weil defined a *model of teaching* as "a plan or pattern that can be used to shape curriculums (long-term courses of study), to design instructional materials, and to guide instruction in the classroom and other settings" (1980, p. 1). Models create the foundation for teaching and are designed to help educators be more effective and increase student learning. The appropriate model is selected based on content to be taught as well as learning characteristics of the student.

The Self-Determined Learning Model of Instruction (Mithaug, Wehmeyer, Agran, Martin, & Palmer, 1998) is designed to teach students to take control of their learning. It is based on the component elements of self-determination and provides a format for educators to engage students by actively teaching requisite skills needed to attain personalized goals and providing opportunities to incorporate these skills by directing educational activities. Through real-life experiences, students learn to be a causal agent in their own lives. This chapter provides an example of how the model was used to facilitate

Dwight's self-determination and self-directed IEP process. Many other resources offer more general information about the self-determined learning model of instruction (e.g., Mithaug et al., 1998; Wehmeyer, 2002).

Overview

The Self-Determined Learning Model of Instruction teaches students to employ problem-solving methodologies using student-directed instructional strategies in order to achieve individualized outcomes. The model teaches students to act on the environment and alter circumstances that pose obstacles to meeting their pursuits. Students with disabilities face many challenges. Through this model, they learn to regulate their problem-solving skills and resolve such difficulties. The Self-Determined Learning Model, therefore, is basically a problem-solving approach that can be used across multiple content areas to "solve" a variety of problems, including an academic problem (e.g., What do I want to learn in biology?), an academic skill problem (e.g., How can I improve my study skills?), an employment problem (e.g., What skills do I need to work as a dental hygienist?), a transition problem (e.g., Where do I want to live after high school?), and even a social problem (e.g., How do I ask someone out on a date?).

It is important to note that the Self-Determined Learning Model of Instruction is not a set curriculum. It does not require teachers to change the current curricula or to fit in new lessons that address specific ideas about self-determination. Rather, the Self-Determined Learning Model of Instruction allows teachers the flexibility to incorporate student-directed activities in the unique context of their classroom, using current educational programming. The model is specifically designed to allow educators and students to focus on what is important and to tailor the model to each student individually.

Understanding the Three Phases of the Model

The purpose of the model is to have students regulate their own problem solving to attain a self-selected goal. The model consists of a three-phase instructional process: 1) set a goal, 2) take action, and 3) adjust the goal or plan. Problem solving involves trial and error and sometimes repeating our actions in pursuit of our goal. We make our best guess on how to solve a problem using extant information, implementing the solution, and evaluating our progress. Often, we use that information to choose a better solution. At other times, we reach a goal that then leads to a new goal, and the cycle continues.

A problem is presented at each phase of the instructional process. A series of four questions designed to direct the student through the problem-solving sequence is provided for each phase. The students answer each question individually. The solutions to the questions lead to the sequence in the next phase. This sequence moves the student from where he or she is to where he or she wants to be by connecting his or her knowledge, needs, and interests to his or her actions. The four questions differ from phase to phase but represent similar steps in the problem-solving sequence. These steps include identifying 1) the problem, 2) potential solutions to the problem, 3) barriers to solving the problem, and 4) consequences of each solution designated.

It is important to remember that the questions are intended to create a dialogue between student and teacher and are designed to move the student through the process. Certainly, not all students with disabilities (or even all students without disabilities) will understand the questions or possess the life experiences required to fully answer each one. The questions may need to be modified or altered to ensure understanding and success. As questions are modified, wording changes should not alter the meaning of the question but remain true to its original intent of leading the student through a problem-solving sequence.

For each student question, there is a set of teacher objectives. These are objectives the teacher is trying to accomplish when implementing the model. They provide direction by outlining teacher actions that will enable the student to successfully move through the problem-solving sequence. Examples of teacher objectives include scaffolding instruction, using direct teaching strategies, and collaborating with students. In addition to teacher objectives, educational supports are identified for each instructional phase. Examples include awareness training, goal setting instruction, and communication skills training. According to Wehmeyer, Palmer, Agran, Mithaug, and Martin (2000), the educational supports are not a formal part of the model, but describe how the model is to be implemented. As teachers use the model, more teacher objectives and educational supports for individual students may be generated.

Phase 1: Set a Goal   We will reference Figure 12.2 throughout this section, incorporating how Dwight has worked through the Self-Determined Learning Model of Instruction. During the first phase of the model, Dwight outlines his goal. He works with his teacher to decide what the goal is, what he already knows about the goal, what he needs to change in order to learn what he does not know, and what he can do to accomplish his goal. We are using a single student example; however, this model is flexible. It can be used with both whole-class instruction using class goals or with individuals using individual goals. As the teacher, you will likely need to help the students through this process by reviewing the IEP goals and helping the students determine the specific goal they would like to target first. It should be clear that students can work on more than one goal at a time using this same process. It is important, however, to ensure that a specific goal is designated each time the process is implemented. Furthermore, it is critical for the goal to have a clear, measurable outcome. A well-written goal states not only what the student will achieve, but also is written in a way that the student can observe the achievement. The goal should include five essential parts.

1.   *Who*—Who will achieve this goal?

2.   *What*—What skill or behavior is needed to achieve this goal?

3.   *How*—In what manner or at what level can this goal be achieved?

4.   *Where*—In what setting or under what conditions can this goal be achieved?

5.   *When*—By what time or date can this goal be achieved?

Again, it is likely the teacher will need to help the student answer the questions involved in this step and help the student get to the heart of each question.

Phase I: What is my goal? *To control my own money*
Set a goal

1. What do I want to learn? *To pay bills*	3. What must change for me to learn what I don't know? *I need a bank account* *I need to learn about computer programs that can help*
2. What do I know about it now? *It costs money to buy things* *You pay for things with money or checks*	4. What can I do to make this happen? *I can work with my mom and teacher*

Phase II: What is my plan?
Take action

1. What can I do learn what I don't know? *I can have a math goal and a computer goal to learn how to pay bills* *I can take a class at the Credit Union*	3. What can I do to overcome these barriers? *Have a back-up plan*
2. What could keep me from taking action? *The goals might not work for this year*	4. When will I take action? *I will bring these goals to my IEP meeting scheduled next month*

Phase III: What have I learned?
Adjust goal or plan

1. What actions have I taken? *Mom and I set up a bank account* *I learned to use Quicken to pay bills*	3. What has changed about what I didn't know? *I know how to pay bills* *I can use the computer program and online banking*
2. What barriers have been removed? *I was able to work on these goals*	4. Do I know what I want to know? *Yes*

Figure 12.2. The Self-Determined Learning Model of Instruction for Dwight. (*Source:* Wehmeyer, 2002.)

Phase 2: Take Action Once Dwight's goal was solidified, and essential guiding information ascertained, he moved to Phase 2 of the model, which requires the student to take action. Dwight did this by creating a plan. First, Dwight and his teacher identified the best course of action, then outlined the specific steps delineating how he will accomplish his goal. Next, Dwight identified the barriers that he may encounter. In other words, what would keep Dwight from following through on the action steps he described previously? This is an important step and one that might require teachers to change how they typically interact with students. Although teachers generally focus on strengths and being positive, to successfully complete this phase, students do need to understand what has kept them from accomplishing goals in the past and the obstacles they might confront as they work on this goal. Action steps that address their barriers are added to the action plan. By identifying obstacles in the beginning, students can proactively address these barriers to success. The final component of this phase is for students to set a time line that depicts when they will incorporate the various steps of their action plan. This is also a critical step because it is important to ensure a time line is created that requires students to make steady strides toward their goal.

Phase 3: Adjust Goal or Plan as Needed The third phase of the model is for students to determine what they have learned and to adjust the goal or plan as needed. During this phase, Dwight evaluated his progress toward meeting his goal and determined what worked, what did not work, and what should happen next. The first question Dwight answered was, "What actions have I already taken?" Dwight followed his plan as outlined; however, this is not always the case. For some students, action steps may not have been incorporated. For others, the plan may have been altered for a host of reasons. Therefore, it is important to outline the actual actions that have been implemented prior to moving forward. In the next two questions, Dwight determined whether barriers were removed and change occurred. These questions required Dwight to determine whether he was effective at removing obstacles and changing circumstances that posed a threat to reaching his pursuits. In addition, Dwight had to determine what, if anything, changed. Specifically, students should outline new skills, new knowledge, or new directions they acquired through the process. These questions require student reflection and are instrumental in helping the students understand how their actions lead to change. In the final question, Dwight determined that the goal was met and he can redo the process with another goal. In general, students will determine if they know what they want to know or if there are new skills, new knowledge, or new goals they want to acquire. For students who encountered obstacles that prevented goal acquisition, they may wish to create further action steps to continue working toward this original goal.

Organizing Day-to-Day Implementation of Goals

As discussed throughout this book, there are three components to the IEP process: premeeting, IEP meeting, and implementing and evaluating goals. It is important to remember that the IEP process does not end once the IEP has been written and permission to implement it has been received. Often, once the meeting is over, there is an assumption that the IEP is being implemented appropriately. This is not always the case, however. There are typically multiple team members responsible for implementing various components of the IEP. Immediately following completion of the IEP meeting, a plan is to be created to ensure the IEP is implemented as agreed on and all team members are aware of their role.

Special attention should be given to the student. Students often feel overwhelmed asking questions about the IEP in a room full of adults, some of whom they may not know well. An IEP team member should have an individual meeting with the student to make sure he or she understands the IEP and provide the opportunity for questions. When meeting with the student, it is important to make sure he or she understands the ultimate goal of the IEP; its contents, including goals and objectives; and the reason he or she has an IEP. This includes understanding what his or her disability is and how accommodations and supports will help within the educational setting. The IEP team member should also discuss the role the student plays in its implementation. If the student does not understand what he or she is working toward and why, then the student cannot properly work toward goal attainment.

Each classroom setting, whether general education, collaborative, or self-contained, should incorporate elements into the curriculum to help the student meet his or her individual goals. In a general education classroom without supports, the general education teacher is responsible for incorporating the goals of a student with a disability into the daily lessons. Often, this requires more individualized integration as opposed to a whole classroom approach. In the collaborative classroom, the general education and special education teachers work together to ensure lessons are written to meet the needs of all learners, including those with disabilities. For students who receive services in a special education classroom, the special education teacher is primarily responsible. In addition, related services personnel such as speech-language, occupational, and physical therapists and transition specialists will be accountable for incorporating student goals.

It is essential for each team member to have a copy of the necessary components (e.g., student's disability, present level of performance, goals and objectives, classroom/testing accommodations) to help ensure everyone involved in implementing the IEP understands his or her responsibilities. A succinct overview of information can be provided as not to overwhelm anyone with too much information. A snapshot could be used for this purpose. A *snapshot,* which is sometimes also referred to as an IEP-at-a-glance, is a one-page summary of student goals, accommodations, and supports. The snapshot can be used by all team members to provide an efficient method for reviewing student information. It can also be used by students to advocate for entitled instruction, support, and accommodations. When using a snapshot or other form of documentation, it is important to remember to update and resend information when an amendment has taken place or when any of the information has changed. See the sample snapshot in Chapter 11 to see how to organize the implementation of an IEP.

Monitoring student performance and progress toward goals can present a difficult situation. The student's case manager (the educator responsible for overseeing and monitoring the student's educational program) will need an organized way to receive updates. Team members can report student progress to the student's case manager through a teacher monitoring form. A *monitoring form* is a document outlining student goals and objectives with a space to record information regarding performance. The teacher monitoring form (see Figure 12.3) should be updated at least four times a year (ideally prior to sending home progress reports) by all relevant team members. The case manager uses this information to report progress to parents via the progress report or report card. In addition, the case manager could meet with the student and discuss information the team members have reported.

Students need to be involved in the monitoring process as well. This can be done through a student monitoring form. This form can be similar to the monitoring form used for educators, but should be simple and easy for students to complete themselves. A "To Do List" is one way to structure the student form as it provides a concrete, organized format (see Figure 12.4). The student monitoring form is to be updated at least once a month and used to guide discussion between the case manager and student. Comparisons can be made between the educators' and student's summary regarding performance and progress.

At times, a student may determine that his or her IEP is not being implemented appropriately, or a student might not be receiving services as laid out in his or her IEP. When this happens, the student needs to know the appropriate steps to take in order to resolve the situation (see Figure 12.5). First, the student should contact the specific teacher with whom the problem is occurring. The student should attempt to tell the teacher what parts of his or her IEP are not being implemented. The student should also readdress the importance of the IEP and how it helps him or her educationally. If the student is unable to resolve the problem with the teacher, then the student should contact his or her case manager. The case manager should remind the classroom teacher of his or her requirements in regard to the IEP. The case manager should also ask the teacher if he or she still has questions about the IEP or if he or she needs extra assistance in order to continue implementation. Hopefully, this will be enough to solve the issue. If not, then the student should request that the IEP team reconvene. During this meeting, the IEP team should discuss why parts of the IEP are not being implemented and how the team can assist the classroom teacher. If there is still a problem, then the student should contact the case manager again and the case manager should contact the special education coordinator or special education administrator. At this point, the student and case manager have done all they know how to do and it becomes an administrative issue. It is important to remember that the parent/guardian should be involved in each step of the intervention as well, especially if the student is still a minor.

Listening to the Experts

Teacher's Perspective

It was important that Kathy had a say in what goals she thought would be appropriate for her to work on this school year. So, sitting down with her and deciding what goals she would work on allowed Kathy to take control of this process. It was imperative that I did not tell her what goals she would have to work on

School year: _____

Student: _____   Teacher: _____

Course: _____   Case manager: _____

The IEP progress report is provided to parents as a summary of student progress toward annual goals. It must accompany the quarterly report cards the day that report cards are distributed. Your response to the items below will be used to prepare that progress report. Please write the progress code and corresponding reasons in the same box. (Use goals/objectives sent with IEP information in September to determine/measure progress.) Thank you for your assistance.

Progress toward annual goal

SP: Sufficient progress to achieve goal
ES: Emerging skill, may not achieve goal
IP: Insufficient progress, may not achieve goal
NI: Not observed/taught in this class
M: Mastered goal

Reasons for limited progress
(ES or IP) *Indicate all that apply*

A. More time needed to reach goal
B. Excessive absences/tardies
C. Assignments not completed
D. Behavior impedes progress toward goal
E. See comments

Annual goals	Interim 1 due	Interim 2 due	Interim 3 due	Interim 4 due
Use of accommodations listed below *(Key: O,* often; *S,* sometimes; *N,* never; *R,* uses when prompted)				
Estimated grade				
Request meeting with case manager?				

First quarter comments: Date:	Third quarter comments: Date:
Second quarter comments: Date:	Fourth quarter comments: Date:

Figure 12.3. Monitoring form for IEP progress report. (Created by Patricia Butler, Clover Hill High School; reprinted by permission.)

Task	Anything needed?	Person(s) responsible	When?	Done
Determine date				
Determine location				
Invitations (create, distribute, follow up)				
Choose facilitator				
Choose recorder				
Gather supplies for meeting (newsprint, markers, tape)				
Purchase refreshments, if desired				
Prepare student-directed IEP information forms and/or support materials				
Set up room				
Clean up				
Type and distribute IEP				
Type and distribute action plan				
Oversee action plan				
Any others?				

Assignment	Person(s) responsible	Time line	Completed

Figure 12.4. To Do List. (Copyright © 2005 by N. Donta & B. Purvis; reprinted by permission.)

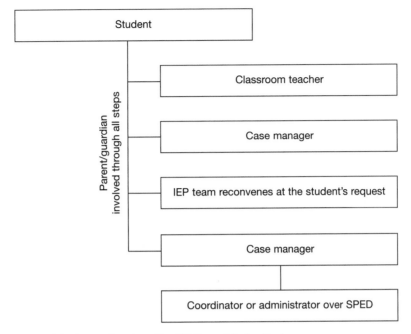

Figure 12.5. Intervention steps. (*Key:* SPED, special education.)

because it would be less important to her. Therefore, we used some guidance from the Self-Determined Learning Model of Instruction with choosing short- and long-term goals. In addition, the model provided direction for Kathy to implement her goal and evaluate her progress. These are critical components of the whole IEP process that often are forgotten.

Student's Perspective

After working through the activities of realizing what I wanted to work on this school year, I was able to choose some goals. I liked the goal of being able to work in the community. That goal will allow me to narrow down what I want to do when I graduate. I can see how choosing those goals were good for me both now and in the future. I also can see that what we decide in the IEP meeting has an effect on what I do every day at school.

Parent's Perspective

I was happy with Kathy's goals. They are going to work well for her. They seemed more specific for Kathy. Sometimes I will see goals that are very general and maybe hard for her to work on, so they have to be changed or they are always on her IEP. I think the goals that she has chosen are very realistic.

Reflection on Kathy's Example

Kathy and Mr. Scott used her one-page snapshot to help Kathy communicate with her academic teachers and related services personnel regarding her IEP goals. She used it to ask for the accommodations that she required to make sufficient progress and to help make the connection between what was happening in the classroom and what was required by the IEP.

Kathy and Mr. Scott also used the Self-Determined Learning Model of Instruction to help implement the goals identified in the IEP. Kathy found that the Self-Determined Learning Model of Instruction increased her interest in working on goals and helped her track her progress. Figure 12.6 is a goal for employment that was developed for Kathy using the Self-Determined Learning Model of Instruction.

 # Tips and Strategies

Teachers recommend that you help students identify easy, concrete ways for them to implement the IEP. It is also important to help students make the connection between what happened in the meeting with what happens in the classroom.

- Meet with the student one-to-one immediately after or the day after the IEP meeting, and answer any questions the student may have about what took place in the meeting.

- Give the student a copy of his or her IEP. Help the student remember the IEP goals and action steps by creating a hard copy that he or she can carry at all times.

- Meet with the student while writing the IEP to break each goal into small action steps. Write the steps in a list format and encourage the student to check the steps off as they are completed.

- Meet with the student while writing the IEP to prioritize the goals and develop a time line to implement each systematically.

- Meet with the student once a month to discuss progress toward goals, identify next steps, and define any needed accommodations and supports.

- Provide situations in which the student has to ask for an accommodation or support and has to explain why it is needed.

- Meet with educational team members as needed and discuss progress toward goals; determine modifications, accommodations, and supports; and answer questions.

- Provide a brief summary of the student for substitute teachers.

- Begin a self-determination club to help students learn to identify and articulate interests, strengths, and weaknesses.

- Help a student join or begin a club or organize an activity that focuses on his or her interests.

Next S.T.E.P.
My Employment Focus

1. **What is my goal? (Explain what goal you would like to reach, what information you currently know about it, and what you can do now to make this goal happen.)**

   I would like to work in a library. I can volunteer at the high school library or help out at the public library with the books. I want to visit and find out if I am interested in child care or restaurant work.

   Well, I know that you have to clean up the table in a restaurant, arrange silverware in a certain area, and put butter on tables a certain way. You have to wash the mirrors so they look nice. For the library, you have to organize books by author or title, water the plants, and alphabetize the books.

2. **Let's revisit. (Restate your goal, and list a few things you can do to work toward that goal.)**

   Work at a library. I can volunteer in the high school library. Or, I can help organize books at the public library: 1) study library database; 2) visit different libraries; 3) try to convince Mommy to sign me up to volunteer this summer; 4) visit and find out if I am interested in child care or restaurant work

   What or who can keep you from reaching this goal? (List people, circumstances, or challenges to reaching your goal.)

   Ms. Hobby, not doing my research.

   Let's discuss the action you took and how this action will continue. (Discuss the experience you had in the community and what you would like to continue to complete your goal.)

   I talked to Ms. Hobby because I like working with children, and I told her I wanted to try out the experience at the restaurant and child care center.

3. **What did you learn? (Let's discuss how much you learned and if you were able to reach you goal.)**

   Ms. Hobby took me to the restaurant and child care center, and all I had to do is ask.

   I helped out with setting the table, washing the windows, and taking butter to the tables. You had to know what side of the table things went on in the restaurant.

   At the child care I helped the kids with their work, watched them on the playground, and helped them out in music class.

   I learned that I like working with children. Working at the restaurant was okay.

4. **What has to happen next to reach your goal?**

   I have to convince my Mommy to let me volunteer over the summer, research the jobs I want to go to, and make sure I actually like the jobs I have chosen.

Figure 12.6. Kathy's goal for employment.

Conclusion

Continuing the student-directed process through the steps of goal implementation and evaluation is important as it may result in increased goal attainment and lead to better postsecondary outcomes. A student-directed process involves the student in all aspects of his or her educational program and places the responsibility for learning primarily on the student. The student can learn how to take action on his or her goals through a variety of self-determination strategies and supports. The Self-Determined Learning Model of Instruction provides a model of teaching that will help the student to take control of his or her learning. With this model, the student is the primary agent for making choices and decisions and implementing action steps that will lead to goal attainment. Through a student-directed process, measures and supports are employed that will lead to real change in fundamental areas for all students with disabilities.

References

Agran, M. (1997). *Student directed learning: Teaching self-determination skills.* Pacific Grove, CA: Brooks/ Cole.

Agran, M., King-Sears, M., Wehmeyer, M.L., & Copeland, S.R. (2003). *Teachers' guides to inclusive practices: Student-directed learning.* Baltimore: Paul H. Brookes Publishing Co.

Agran, M., Snow, K., & Swaner, J. (1999). Teacher perceptions of self-determination: Benefits, characteristics, strategies. *Education and Training in Mental Retardation and Developmental Disabilities, 34,* 293–301.

Allen, S.K., Smith, A.C., Test, D.W., Flowers, C., & Wood, W.M. (2001). The effects of "self-directed IEP" on student participation in IEP meetings. *Career Development for Exceptional Individuals, 4,* 107–120.

Field, S., & Hoffman, A. (2002). Preparing youth to exercise self-determination: Quality indicators of school environments that promote the acquisition of knowledge, skills and beliefs related to self-determination. *Journal of Disability Policy Studies, 13,* 113–118.

Field, S., Martin, J., Miller, R., Ward, M., & Wehmeyer, M. (1998). Self-determination for persons with disabilities: A position statement of the Division of Career Development and Transition. *Career Development for Exceptional Individuals, 2*(2), 113–128.

Forest, M., & Pearpoint, J.C. (1992). Putting all kids on the MAP. *Educational Leadership, 50,* 26–31.

Gerber, P.J., Schnieders, C.A., Paradise, L.V., Reiff, H.B., Ginsberg, R., & Popp, P.A. (1990). Persisting problems of adults with learning disabilities: Self-reported comparisons from their school-age and adult years. *Journal of Learning Disabilities, 23,* 570–573.

German, S.L., Martin, J.E., Huber Marshall, L. & Sale, R.P. (2000). Promoting self-determination: Using Take Action to teach goal attainment. *Career Development for Exceptional Individuals, 23*(1), 27–38.

Goldstein, F.C. & Levin, H.S. (1987). Disorders of reasoning and problem-solving ability. In M. Meier, A. Benton, & L. Diller (Eds.), *Neuropsychological rehabilitation* (pp. 87–109). London: Taylor & Francis Group.

Grote, I., Rosales, J., & Baer, D.M. (1996). A task analysis of the shift from teacher instructions to self-instructions in performing an in-common task. *Journal of Experimental Child Psychology, 63,* 339–357.

Joseph, L.M., & Konrad, M. (2009). 20 ways to teach your students to self manage their academic performance. *Intervention in School and Clinic, 44,* 246–249.

Joyce, B., & Weil, M. (1980). *Models of teaching* (2nd ed.). Upper Saddle River, NJ: Prentice Hall.

Kohn, A. (1993). Choices for children: Why and how to let students decide. *Phi Delta Kappan, 75*(1), 8–16, 18–21.

Konrad, M., Trela, K., & Test, D.W. (2006). Using IEP goals and objectives to teach paragraph writing to high school students with physical and cognitive disabilities. *Education and Training in Developmental Disabilities, 41,* 111–124.

Mason, C., McGahee-Kovac, M., Johnson, L., & Stillerman, S. (2002). Implementing student-led IEPs: Student participation and student and teacher reactions. *Career Development for Exceptional Individuals, 25,* 171–192.

Mithaug, D.E., Wehmeyer, M.L., Agran, M., Martin, J.E., & Palmer, S. (1998). The Self-Determined Learning Model of Instruction: Engaging students to solve their learning problems. In M.L. Wehmeyer & D.J. Sands (Eds.), *Making it happen: Student involvement in education planning, decision making, and instruction* (pp. 299–328). Baltimore: Paul H. Brookes Publishing Co.

Nolet, V., & McLaughlin, M.J. (2000). *Accessing the general curriculum: Including students with disabilities in standards-based reform.* Thousand Oaks, CA: Corwin Press.

Sale, P., & Martin, J.E. (2004). Self-determination. In P. Wehman (Ed.), *Functional curriculum: For elementary, middle and secondary aged students with special needs* (pp. 67–94). Austin, TX: PRO-ED.

Smith, D.J., & Nelson, J.R. (1997). Goal setting, self-monitoring, and self-evaluation for students with disabilities. In M. Agran (Ed.), *Student directed learning: Teaching self-determination skills* (pp. 80–110). Pacific Grove, CA: Brooks/Cole.

Test, D.W., Aspel, N.P., & Everson, J.M. (2006). *Transition methods for youth with disabilities.* Columbus, OH: Charles E. Merrill.

Test, D.W., Mason, C., & Hughes, C. (2004). Student involvement in individualized education program meetings. *Exceptional Children, 70*(4), 391–412.

Thoma, C.A. (1999). Supporting student voice in transition planning. *Teaching Exceptional Children, 31*(5), 4–9.

Thoma, C.A., & Held, M.A. (2003, February). *Facilitating self-determination: What to do before and after the transition IEP meeting.* Presentation at the Division for Developmental Disabilities Biennial Conference, Kauai, HI.

Thoma, C.A., Rogan, P., & Baker, S.R. (2001). Student involvement in transition planning: Unheard voices. *Education and Training in Mental Retardation and Developmental Disabilities, 36*(1), 16–29.

Ward, M.J. (1988). The many facets of self-determination. *National Information Center for Children and Youth with Disabilities, 5,* 2–3.

Wehman, P., & Thoma, C.A. (2006). Teaching for transition. In P. Wehman, *Life beyond the classroom: Transition strategies for young people with disabilities* (4th ed., pp. 201–236). Baltimore: Paul H. Brookes Publishing Co.

Wehmeyer, M.L. (1994). Perceptions of self-determination and psychological empowerment of adolescents with mental retardation. *Education and Training in Mental Retardation and Developmental Disabilities, 29,* 9–21.

Wehmeyer, M.L. (2001). Self-determination and transition. In P. Wehman, *Life beyond the classroom: Transition strategies for young people with disabilities* (3rd ed., pp. 35–60). Baltimore: Paul H. Brookes Publishing Co.

Wehmeyer, M.L. (2002). *Teaching students with mental retardation: Providing access to the general curriculum.* Baltimore: Paul H. Brookes Publishing Co.

Wehmeyer, M.L., Agran, M., & Hughes, C. (1998). *Teaching self-determination to students with disabilities: Basic skills for successful transition.* Baltimore: Paul H. Brookes Publishing Co.

Wehmeyer, M.L., Palmer, S.B., Agran, M., Mithaug, D.E., & Martin, J.E. (2000). Promoting causal agency: The Self-Determined Learning Model of Instruction. *Exceptional Children, 66,* 439–453.

Wehmeyer, M.L., & Schalock, R. (2001). Self-determination and quality of life: Implications for special education services and supports. *Focus on Exceptional Children, 33*(8), 1–16.

Wehmeyer, M.L. & Schwartz, M. (1997). Self-determination and positive adult outcomes: A follow-up study with mental retardation and learning disabilities. *Exceptional Children, 63,* 245–255.

Wehmeyer, M.L., & Schwartz, M. (1998). The relationship between self-determination, quality of life, and life satisfaction for adults with mental retardation. *Education and Training in Mental Retardation and Developmental Disabilities, 33,* 3–12.

Wehmeyer, M.L., & Schwartz, M. (1999). The self determination focus of transition goals for students with mental retardation. *Career Development for Exceptional Individuals, 21*(1), 75–86.

Zhang, D. (2001). The effect of "Next S.T.E.P." instruction on the self-determination skills of high school students with learning disabilities. *Career Development for Exceptional Individuals, 25,* 121–132.

13

....

Communicating with Team Members

Beth A. Bader, Marsha S. Tennant, and Pamela S. Targett

For some individualized education program (IEP) teams, a student's involvement and leadership is not new; for others, it is a novel idea. Active student participation in the IEP process requires continuous communication with and amongst the team members who are responsible for implementing various components of the IEP. For example, students need to be able to communicate their IEP goals as well as progress on achieving these goals to team members. They also need to solicit and receive feedback from team members about how well they are doing in using the goal-directed strategies and activities identified by their team during the IEP team meeting. Effective communication involves the capacity to listen, pay attention, perceive, and respond verbally and nonverbally to demonstrate that one has attended the meeting, listened, and accurately perceived the information from the meeting. These skills may vary among students with disabilities.

Regardless of the student's age or existing skill level, each student should be involved in communicating about his or her IEP goals and progress to the fullest extent possible. Often, for those students with severe disabilities, this communication will require some type of support. For example, individuals who cannot self-report data can still share information about the IEP when provided with the right type, level, and intensity of support. Under some circumstances, this might require using some type of assistive technology (AT) or involving their significant others to provide information that can then be verified through observing the students in environments where they are likely to produce the behaviors.

Students with high-incidence disabilities can be taught to use self-monitoring tools to illustrate their progress when communicating with team members. These self-monitoring tools can range from picture charts used by elementary-age students to computer-generated curriculum-based measurement graphs used by middle and high school students. Whether a student directly communicates with team members or needs the support of a teacher or instructional assistant, the communication needs to occur regularly and involve all IEP team members.

This chapter provides practical guidance for those looking for a place to start with involving students in the communication process. In addition, it is hoped that those who are already well schooled on how to get students involved in communicating with team members will find some new and creative ways to make sure this happens for all students. Communication strategies that can be used with students with the most severe disabilities are highlighted in this chapter.

After the IEP Meeting: Communicating During the Implementation Process

Many times after the IEP meeting, team members believe that the student's classroom teacher is their point of contact. It is only since the advent of student-directed IEPs that there has been a change in the communication flow during the entire IEP process. Communication is no longer the sole responsibility of the classroom teacher. If we believe in the concept of student-directed IEPs and are willing to support students to direct the IEP meeting, then we need to support students in communicating about the goals that direct their learning, the content of what they are learning, and the actual progress that they are making after everyone leaves the meeting room.

Simply being handed the IEP document to read and being given verbal instructions about its content could overwhelm any student and result in little learning or follow-through. Many students may learn best when they can have the contents of the IEP translated into everyday activities or if the content of the IEP can be paraphrased verbally to them. Other students, particularly those with significant cognitive disabilities, may pose entirely different challenges to the team. These individuals often require extensive intervention, one-to-one instruction, or support throughout their educational years. Combinations of teaching methods may be used to facilitate learning, such as verbal and/or signed instruction, hand over hand, pictorial or tactual cueing, and so forth. These students often have a slower learning curve than other individuals. Although an individual may be considered to have a severe disability, it is important for the team to recognize that he or she can still take an active role in planning and implementing his or her IEP.

How Can IEP Information Be Communicated to Elementary School Students?

Students at the elementary school level should know (at the very least) what an IEP is, why they have an IEP, and what their goals are for the next year. For these students to be able to communicate about their IEPs, they need to understand that the IEP is more than just a document, and they need to hear about what it is and why they have one more than just once a year. For very young children, this may mean that the words written on the IEP must be translated into pictures and symbols corresponding to what is taking place during their school day. Or, the information about the IEP could be condensed and transferred to simple phrases in a notebook with a photograph of the designated team member who is helping with the goal or activity. If an older elementary school student has access to a computer, then the information about the IEP could be placed online on a personal IEP web site with access restricted to the student, family, and other team members.

How Can IEP Information Be Communicated to Middle and High School Students?

The student needs to be involved in the IEP process at the middle school and high school levels. The student should be centrally involved in discussions to help develop an action plan for his or her future (Bassett & Lehmann, 2001). If the student has been an active participant in his or her IEPs prior to middle school, then the student should be able to recognize and articulate his or her own strengths, challenges, and goals. At this point, the student should assume a more advanced role in the IEP process rather than just attending the annual IEP meetings. Understanding and using information and technology in relation to the student's long-term goals should be central to a student's educational plan. The student can ask team members to assist in problem solving, collaboration, and interventions necessary to take him or her to the next level, but it is hoped that the student will initiate requesting this assistance rather than waiting for someone else to take control.

Making the transition from secondary education is a natural point when IEP communication and collaboration among the team becomes crucial. Assessments needed for transition planning are one way that teams can work together and brainstorm strategies and goals for the student. Because transition planning is life centered and not based completely on academics, it presents a method for expanding the capacity building tools of the student. Many products are available to assist with transition planning. For example, the *Transition Planning Inventory* (*TPI*; Clark & Patton, 1997) is an assessment that is used to help identify and plan the transitional needs of students. Information on transition needs is collected from the student, caregiver, and school personnel by using three separate forms that include student, home, and school components that incorporate a rating scale from each perspective. Assessments may reveal significant differences in perspective among the participants, but the resulting dialogue is critical and provides an excellent opportunity for the student to self-advocate and/or accept opinions of the other team members. Results of the assessment provide understanding of how the student is perceived by each team member and can be used to create individualized goals and benchmarks. Students can use assessments as a way to begin looking at long-range goals and the roles the team members can play. It is important that at the middle school and high school levels students understand where they are academically according to their IEP goals and what effect this path will have on them in postsecondary planning.

Communicating and Sharing Information to Evaluate Progress

Those involved in an IEP's implementation must get the student's input on many topics. The student should provide input on how to report progress on his or her goals and how information should be regularly reported to him or her. The plan for how to report progress should be developed soon after the IEP meeting takes place. Some students may want verbal updates from their team; others may need alternate types of updates or may need a combination of approaches to be used to communicate progress. To begin, the student should be given choices of how this information can be provided. Just as the student chooses to report progress to team members, team members can use similar strategies to communicate information to the student. Examples of ways to communicate information to students include using verbal or written communication, illustrations or photographs to communicate information pictorially, or a combination of these approaches.

To report on progress, a student must first have some idea of what he or she is trying to achieve (i.e., the goal). For each IEP goal, how the student will communicate progress on the specific learning objectives needs to be determined. Once again, the best way to do this will depend on the student's preferred method of communication. At the onset of academic and functional skills training, initial performance is documented to denote the student's current level of ability. Later, this baseline information can help illustrate the student's progress on specific goals.

How Can Team Members Report Progress to the Student?

Teachers must be able to measure student progress during community-based instruction. Often, this lends itself well to collecting task analytic data to document performance of certain activities. Under these circumstances, a teacher might be able to inform a student of progress by plotting data collected about how independently the student is performing on a graph. Or, the teacher might convert numerical data related to percentage of tasks performed correctly to some type of lettering system that denotes progress to the student (e.g., A: Awesome). For very young students or those with significant intellectual disabilities, a picture of the student goal could be posted at the top of a poster board with a picture of a bar graph under it. On a scheduled basis the bar graph is filled in to denote present level of performance toward reaching the goal. Depending on the goal, individual objectives may also be included. Using this type of communication device, the student understands once the bar is colored in, the goal has been met and it is time to celebrate. Of course, different strategies, other than those that are completely visual, must be created for students with low vision or blindness. These strategies would need to be sound based so that students could hear instead of see their progress toward achieving their goals.

In addition to choosing a strategy for reporting progress, a schedule for reporting must also be determined. For example, some students may opt for spontaneous progress on request, whereas others may be happy with predetermined intervals. Still others may desire a combination of the two. The method chosen to report progress must also concur with the desired schedule. For example, a student desiring spontaneous report on progress will need to have a method to request the information included in his or her daily communication repertoire. Again, this will require a functional analysis of where the activity (requesting for progress on goal) takes place. For example, Dwight, who uses AT to communicate, may need to have phrases preprogrammed into his laptop that provide a way for him to ask for progress. Or, he may be taught to use a certain gesture to communicate to others that he wants an update of his progress on demand. Once again, individualization and creativity is central to coming up with an effective system to report, request, and receive feedback on IEP goals.

Whatever method to communicate is chosen, the student should be taught how to use it in the natural environment. The skill must also be taught during the times of day when the student would normally use it. For example, rather than practicing using a communication board to request progress on goals in a meeting, a student could meet the speech-language pathologist (SLP) from the IEP team in various classes throughout the day to get immediate feedback.

Communicating with the Team to Evaluate Progress

Team members who are identified as having responsibility for implementing an IEP too often work independently with the student and/or classroom teacher without communicating with other team members outside of the annual IEP meeting. Not only do team members need to communicate directly with the student using the communication method chosen by that student, but they also need to communicate with each other on a regular basis.

The official student file is kept in a locked storage area and may be so large that using it to file periodic progress information for all team members to see may be prohibitive. Entering student-specific information in a classroom folder out in the open for everyone to access may not protect the privacy rights of the student, and it runs of the risk of getting lost on a teacher's desk. How then can individuals share information that is important for all IEP team members to know at any point in time in the implementation process?

The best way for team members to communicate with each other would be through the student. As mentioned previously, the student could maintain a communication notebook either in hard copy or on a secure Internet site. Only team members, the student, and family members would have access to the notebook. If a hard copy notebook is kept, then it should not be removed from a secure area in the classroom or resource room but could be viewed and information added by any team member. Of course, only having information shared in a single notebook runs the risk of the information being accidentally destroyed or lost. Therefore, consider copying the content in the notebook for each grading quarter and putting the copy in a secure area with the student's file.

If a secure Internet web site is chosen for communication, then passwords would be needed to enter the site, but it could be viewed and information entered from any computer having access to the site. Blackboard (http://www.blackboard.com) is an example of an Internet resource that could be used for communication among team members. Even with password-protected Internet sites, it is imperative that personal identifying information be kept at a minimum and that nothing be included in any notes that could be taken out of context or misunderstood by any team member. Accurate and timely sharing of information is imperative for all involved in a student's IEP process.

Max's teacher completed a "student snapshot" to assure adequate communication with his general education teachers about annual goals as well as the modifications and accommodations that were included on his IEP. The student snapshot could also be used for the general education teachers to communicate his progress on goals.

See Figure 13.1 for an example of a form used to compile a student snapshot.

Student name	Grade	Student number	Identification(s)	Case manager	Diploma type	Date sent to teachers	Date revisions sent

Present level of performance background and identification:

Additional case manager comments:

Accommodations:
- No accommodations
- Adaptive or special furniture
- Back-up copies of notes to supplement personal notes
- Braille/Brailler
- Break during tests
- Clarified directions
- Extended time—tests and quizzes
- Extended time—writing assignments
- Oral administration of tests and quizzes
- Preferential/proximity seating
- Read directions to student
- Shortened assignments
- Test administered in location with minimal distractions
- Use of calculator
- Use of a spell checker/spelling dictionary
- Use of word processor
- Written directions

Testing accommodations:
- No accommodations
- Audiotaped version
- Braille tests
- Environ. modifications
- Group size
- Mark in test booklet
- Respond by word processor or Brailler
- Scientific or graphic calculator
- Spelling aids

Class

Goals

Objectives

Figure 13.1. Form used to compile a student snapshot. (Created by Patricia Butler, Clover Hill High School; reprinted by permission.)

Developing Communication Skills for Students with Severe Disabilities

Cognition and language are interrelated. Thus, students with severe intellectual disabilities generally have more severe communicative disorders. In addition, this may be combined with some type of physical disability as in some cases of cerebral palsy. Even with intensive training, some of these individuals may only develop or regain minimal communication skills.

One way to help students with severe disabilities develop their communication skills is to perform an ecological assessment of their communicative abilities in multiple venues (e.g., school, home, work, recreation settings). Afterward, the information gained can be used to help determine goals for communication skills training or use an adaptive communication system. It is important to remember that no two students will have identical needs or solutions of communication. Thus, time must be taken to consider how each student will communicate his or her IEP goals as well as provide and receive information on progress across various settings.

How Can a Student with a Severe Disability Communicate Goals to Others?

A major goal of communication is for the communicator to gain control over the immediate environment. Two ways to enhance successful communication for students with severe intellectual disabilities include teaching the student to use multiple forms of communication and giving him or her control over a system if used. Rarely does a single form of communication work in all settings. Attempting to use a single form of communication in all settings can invite frustration. Instead, communication and communication systems must be functional to the circumstance and specifically relate to the individual's life activities. The student must have some means to be able to communicate, such as speaking in sentences, using words, making gestures, using signs, writing, or illustrating goals to share with others. For example, a student may be able to state his or her transition goal of working in the community using functional verbal communication skills and saying words such as *work, money,* and *me.* Another student could communicate his or her goal by pointing to a picture of a workplace and smiling. Someone else may write something associated with the goal by using words and symbols such as "$ is work." Still, another student could draw a picture of a stick figure with a smiling face entering a building to illustrate his or her goal. Another student could have photographs depicting goals to share with others.

Another option for a student who is nonverbal is to work with select team members and family members in cooperation with the SLP to develop a communication system specific to IEP-related activities. The system can be used to express a variety of concepts, including expressing and reporting progress on IEP goals. Such systems should be put in place in earlier years, thereby allowing plenty of time for the student to learn how to use them to express and report goals. Students with physical disabilities may need AT to help them use some communication systems. For example, a head pointer or switch may be needed to use an electronic communication board. Whenever AT is implemented, the student should receive training on how to use it.

As mentioned previously, the student's communication skills training must take place in the course of naturally occurring events or life activities for it to be meaningful. For example, instead of teaching a student to use a communication board to state his or her IEP goals in an office setting, the learning would take place in the home, in the school, or in other community settings (e.g., workplace, recreational activity, store). Teaching functional communication skills, such as stating IEP goals in the context of where the activity actually takes place, will help the student gain control over his or her immediate environment.

Jeremy is a student who has had difficulty developing speech and language due to a severe intellectual disability. As a small child he made sounds that were only understood by some people who knew him well. When he went to school, alternative communication systems were designed. This year, his transition IEP includes a number of goals, including going to work in the community, purchasing a meal at his favorite restaurant, and participating in a new recreational opportunity of his choice. He also has a goal of generalizing the use of a picture card communication system to express his IEP goals to three different team members. Under the goal is a series of objectives. For example, when arriving to work and at break, Jeremy will communicate his IEP goal by showing the correct picture card denoting that goal to his teacher/job trainer with 100% accuracy for 5 consecutive days.

Jeremy's story is a good example of how a student with a severe disability can communicate progress. He is able to express his opinion related to goals at the IEP meeting using a series of pictures that are taken on the job. See Figure 13.2 for an example of Jeremy's communication board.

One of Jeremy's goals is to independently purchase the snack of his choice at break time. The first of a series of pictures illustrates Jeremy on the first day of work and the teacher/trainer instructing him on how to operate the soda machine. For related school personnel, every few weeks another picture is taken. The next one illustrates the teacher has faded her instructional prompt from hand-over-hand physical guidance to the use of gestures (i.e., pointing to where the money is inserted and drink choice).

The next picture shows Jeremy buying a drink on his own. At select intervals Jeremy is assisted with e-mailing the photos depicting his progress to his IEP team members. They know this means in return they are to reinforce Jeremy for the progress he is making at work. Each one prints off the picture. The next time one of them sees Jeremy, they reinforce him for doing a good job while pointing at the picture. Jeremy wants his family to have information more often. A picture is taken and sent to his mother's telephone once a week. When he arrives home, she reinforces his work.

At the IEP meeting, Jeremy pushes the button on the computer to advance pictures that illustrate the progress he has made. He also uses a communication board specific to his IEP meeting that includes symbols representing a number of things, such as the participants' names; activities; and phrases, including I LIKE THIS and I DO NOT LIKE THIS.

Figure 13.2. Jeremy's communication board.

Once initiated, it is not unusual for the selected strategy to need modification. For example, too many symbols on a communication board can be confusing. It is important to evaluate these systems and their effectiveness. Changes should be made to existing systems so they will be current and useful.

Communicating and Reporting Goal Progress for Students with Severe Disabilities

Sometimes the student and teacher can use the same method to communicate and report progress on goals. For example, Jeremy and his teacher developed a portfolio that illustrates his progress on the job. The teacher reports on progress by taking Jeremy's picture while he is performing certain tasks at select times and then assists Jeremy with putting these photographs in an album. Jeremy then communicates his thoughts by including a picture of him looking happy next to the activities he likes. Both he and his teacher have an album that can be shared with others.

Finding ways to assist some students with severe intellectual disabilities with expressing, reporting, and soliciting feedback on their IEP goals will require extra creativity. When ideas on how this might be accomplished are not readily available, an IEP team may want to try using a creative problem-solving model to help them come up with some potential ideas. The steps involved in the creative problem-solving model discussed in this chapter include reformulating the problem into a question, holding a brainstorming session, reducing the list of options, evaluating remaining ideas, and making a more precise judgment. These steps are outlined in more detail in the following sections.

Reformulate the Problem into a Question   Searching for a solution is more productive when you have a destination in mind. State the presenting issue as a problem, and then formulate it into a question. For example, "Jeremy does not report progress on his IEP goals to team members." Reformulate this statement into a question. Now the question reads, "How can we ensure Jeremy is able to report progress on his IEP goal to team members?" Now a goal or end result is in mind.

Hold a Brainstorming Session   Quickly go around the group and ask each person to provide an idea or option on how to resolve an issue. All thoughts have merit no matter how ridiculous they may sound at the time. Let the ideas flow during this brainstorming session until you have come up with a list of options.

Reduce the List of Options   Now there is a list of possible solutions or options for the student. Reduce the list by combining similar ideas. Reformulate ideas as necessary.

Evaluate the Remaining Ideas   The next step is to evaluate those remaining ideas by using an evaluation criterion. For example, each group member could simply give each idea a positive or negative vote. The top two or three ideas with the most positive votes will remain on the list. This can be graphically represented through the use of a "decision tree" that helps students differentiate between the various choices and the evaluation of each option.

Make a More Precise Judgment, and Choose Your Top Idea   Group members make a more precise judgment on the final top-ranking ideas. Each member is asked to prioritize the ideas, and the student is given the choice and asked to choose what he or she would like to try.

Max's teacher used this approach to help him communicate with others. Max is not a student who would typically need a communication support in place because he has an emotional/behavior disorder. He does need to learn problem-solving skills, however, and his teacher used this approach to help him learn to handle frustrations more productively as well as to communicate his goals for IEP meetings. (See Figure 13.3 for Max's problem-solving process.)

 # Listening to the Experts

Teacher's Perspective

Communicating with the members of the IEP team is impera-tive. We must all take responsibility for our roles and responsi-bilities both during and after an IEP has been completed. There should be discussion and effective communication among team members so there is no confusion as to who will be accountable for what is discussed at the IEP meeting. It is also important that accountability is discussed with the student and family so they, too, are aware of what the next steps are for collecting informa-tion needed after the meeting and who they can count on to complete the different tasks discussed.

Since completing Kathy's IEP, there have been increases in com-munication between all IEP team members. I relate the increase in communication to them all having a closer understanding of who Kathy is and what her needs are. This can all be credited to her directing her IEP meeting. Kathy has taken an active role in staying involved in following up with team members and with her goals. For example, she has often been able to verbalize that something she is working on is related to a goal or objective in her IEP. She has reminded me on several occasions, when I would forget, that I should be following up with a teacher or other professional about an accommodation that she needs. She even wrote a note to me as a reminder to contact her occupa-tional therapist to format a typing program onto her laptop, which was discussed at the IEP meeting.

I try to be supportive to Kathy as her confidence and motiva-tion for becoming independent increases. Initially, Kathy would never save me any of her schoolwork, but now she can't wait to collect data that she thinks is related to her goals. I still communicate with her teachers and other staff about

Step	Options	Best option
What is the real problem?	I was kicked out of the library. The librarian is unfair. I wasn't doing anything. I didn't follow the rules. If I can't go back to the library, I will not be able to do homework using the Internet.	I was not following the rules and was caught. The librarian followed her rules and kicked me out.
Which options could result in my ability to return to the library?	I could do nothing. I could yell at the librarian. I could cause damage to the library to communicate my anger. I could apologize. I could go back to the library and hope that I won't be in trouble. I could file a complaint with the librarian's boss. I could have someone else talk with the librarian.	
What would be the most likely result of each of the options?	Apologize—She might accept it and I could return. Go back—The librarian would remember me and the chance that I could return might be reduced. Complaint—Nothing since I don't really have any complaint other than I don't like the outcome. Someone else talk for me—Librarian might accept it.	Apologize: has best chance for success.

Figure 13.3. Max's problem-solving process.

225

her needs, but quite often she is able to let them know what her needs are.

Student's Perspective	I like that I now know and had a chance to choose goals that I can work on during the school year. It helps me remember what I need to be doing. I can easily remember that I should tell my teachers to save what I'm working on, or I should give what I'm working on to Mr. Scott because it is related to my IEP. I also like to track my typing skills. It makes me try a little harder.
Parent's Perspective	Kathy is excited about school. She likes to come home and tell me what she worked on. She will tell me that she has given her classwork that was related to her IEP to Mr. Scott.

Reflection on Kathy's Example

Kathy and Mr. Scott spent a great deal of time working to increase her ability to communicate with her team members after the IEP meeting was held. Premeeting preparations focused on helping Kathy communicate during the meeting, but Mr. Scott knew that these efforts were not sufficient to ensure that Kathy (or any student) was ready for the ongoing communication with team members necessary to advocate for supports, services, accommodations, and modifications. Mr. Scott took a two-tiered approach; first, he developed a lesson plan to help teach self-advocacy skills (see Figure 13.4), and then he developed a resource list that Kathy could use to identify the appropriate team member to contact depending on her needs (see Figure 13.5).

 **Tips and Strategies**

The following information contains some tips and strategies for teachers.

- Make sure action plans and notes are created in a format that students can see and read. Students who are blind or have low vision will need notes and action plans in an accessible format (e.g., large print, braille). Often, sending materials in a CD/DVD format allows the student to use his or her own computer with these preferred settings in place.

- Have students who use American Sign Language meet with team members using a video relay telephone, which can be provided free of charge.

- Have each person on the team discuss his or her role and how he or she will assist the student and family after the IEP meeting.

- Give the student a form that contains team members' contact information.

- Hold a conference with students every week. If there is information that parents may want to be aware of, then they are invited to attend.

Stepping up to advocate

Target group: *Secondary students*
Target curriculum: *STEPS*

Objective/purpose:

Teacher will review students' self-advocacy and communication skills. Students' self-advocacy, leadership, and self-determination skills will be assessed and advanced for the purpose of learning about themselves.

Materials:

Stopwatch, tape recorder with cassettes, poster, magazines, photo of students, self-reflection opportunity, glue, and scissors

Procedure:

1. Teacher and students will review what it means to have proper communication skills. Students will brainstorm what skills you must use to communicate effectively with others. Teacher will pair students in groups of two and practice the following skills that are often used in communication. Have each group use a stopwatch for the 1-minute interval.

    *   **Eye contact**—students will practice communicating back and forth with each other and holding eye contact for approximately 1 minute. Allow students to practice with each other for approximately 5 minutes.

    Students will relax after the 1-minute eye contact exercise. Students will review with each other if they did a great job with this exercise or how they can improve. Students will then move on to the next skill for communication.

    *   **Sitting up straight**—students will practice and reflect on sitting up straight in their chair when communicating with others. Students and teacher will model examples of how to do so.

    *   **Tone of voice**—while students are in their groups or pairs, the teacher will record students' conversations using the tape recorder and cassettes. The teacher will then play back students' conversations so that they may hear the tone, quality, and manner in which they were speaking with each other. Students will then reflect as a group on the tone they have taken with each other and how they may make improvements for effective communication.

    This activity of reviewing proper communication skills will continue, as the teacher will choose two additional skills that students have brainstormed in the earlier session. The teacher will allow students to practice the two additional skills before moving to the next set of procedures.

2   After reviewing how they can effectively improve their own individual communication skills, students will verbally review what they believe the term "self-advocacy" means.

    *   After students have had the opportunity to reflect on what they believe self-advocacy means, the teacher will review the definition with students: *self-advocacy—managing one's own life; being in charge of one's own life; speaking up for yourself and controlling your own destiny.*

3. Students will be given photos of themselves along with a poster board and several magazines. Students will be given the opportunity to place a photo of themselves in the center of the poster board. Students will then be instructed to look through the magazines and focus on photos and articles that will help share information about themselves in the areas of communication and self-advocacy. Students will be asked to review magazine photos for things that connect with what they believe is their style of communication (eye contact, sitting up straight, tone) and how they currently advocate for themselves or would like to advocate for themselves. Students will cut out the photos and articles and glue them around their photo on the poster board.

Evaluation:

4. When students have completed the poster assignment, each student will have a chance to present their findings. Students may choose alternative methods for presenting this information. For example, if students would like to type a brief paragraph to summarize their findings—they may do so; if students would like to orally present their findings—that would be appropriate! Students may have the option to present this information in different formats based on their communication skills, which they may have just discovered.

Figure 13.4.   Lesson plan to teach self-advocacy skills.

Know who to run to with your questions?

If you have questions about the following topics	Then you may call or contact
What is in your IEP?	Mr. Scott
Transportation	Mrs. A. Sanchez, CARE van
Computer/technology	Mr. Sullivan, occupational therapist
Grades/classwork	Classroom teachers
Activities at school	Mr. Donald Federer, principal
Graduation	Mrs. J. Davis, guidance counselor
Resources in the comunity	Mrs. Richardson, case manager
Volunteer positions/ transition after high school	Mrs. Davidson, transition coordinator

Figure 13.5.   List of Kathy's IEP team members.

- Reflect with the student on how to best communicate and what modes could be used for the student to communicate with team members after the meeting.

- Identify the team members' schedules, and navigate the communication process with the student.

Conclusion

If we as professionals support the reality of student-directed IEPs, we must also learn to support student-directed communication about the IEP process. Students need to learn how to communicate with their IEP team members and understand why this is important. In turn, team members must respect the student's choice of how information is being communicated and the content of what is being communicated. No matter the severity of their disability, students can learn to communicate what their IEP goals are and be able to recognize and communicate the progress that they make toward meeting these goals. The student, family, and team all need to agree to, and participate in, a communication process that allows timely and accurate information to be shared throughout the year, and not just during IEP meetings.

References

Bassett, D.S., & Lehmann, J. (2001). *Student-focused conferencing and planning.* Austin, TX: PRO-ED.

Clark, G.M., & Patton, J.R. (1997). *Transition Planning Inventory: Assessing transition needs.* Austin, TX: PRO-ED.

14

....

Evaluating
Progress Toward Goals

Pamela S. Targett and Paul Wehman

Special educators use assessment and measurement tools to evaluate whether a student is making progress in meeting annual goals. Educational assessment is aimed at answering questions such as, "Is the student making meaningful progress toward a goal?" "Why or why not?" and "Is it time for the student to move on to the next level of learning?" Although educators traditionally initiate and conduct most assessments, students with disabilities also need to take an active role in evaluating their progress toward their goals. Motivation for learning that leads to meeting annual goals can be continued or increased when students are informed of their progress. Feedback confirms accurate understanding of performance, provides knowledge of mistakes, and corrects learning. By receiving feedback, the student is encouraged to continue to learn.

Many teachers wonder how students with disabilities, particularly those with severe disabilities, can make data-based decisions about their progress in meeting annual individualized education program (IEP) goals. This chapter explores ways to empower students to evaluate their progress toward achieving their goals. Examples of simple tables, graphs, and self-monitoring strategies that can help organize this process are also included in this chapter.

Using Self-Determination
Skills to Evaluate Progress

Self-determination refers to the ability to make choices and decisions and be a causal agent in one's own life. Over the years, many materials and methods to promote student self-determination have emerged (Field, Martin, Miller, Ward, & Wehmeyer, 1998; Wehmeyer, Agran, & Hughes, 1998). In addition, evidence that self-determination is important for students to achieve positive adult outcomes has come to light (Wehmeyer & Schwartz, 1999). The methods and materials of the Self-Determined Learning Model of Instruction focus on teaching students to set goals, make decisions and choices, solve problems, and self-advocate (see Chapter 12 for more information on this model). There are three phases to the Self-Determined Learning Model of Instruction: 1) setting a goal, 2) taking action, and 3) adjusting the goal or plan.

During the third phase, students are encouraged to self-evaluate their progress toward achieving their goals (Wehmeyer, Palmer, Agran, Mithaug, & Martin, 2000). If they determine that progress is inadequate, then they evaluate whether the lack of progress was due to an inappropriate goal, ineffective plan, or failure to implement the plan for a sufficient amount of time. Based on this analysis, students may revise their goal, change their action plan, or keep working on the goal. Teaching self-determination skills plays a critical role in empowering students to take greater control and responsibility for their own learning and to become causal agents in their lives.

Self-determination skills should begin at an early age for students. Sale and Martin (2004) stated that self-determination activities in the early elementary years should focus on teaching students helpful strategies for setting goals, planning to achieve goals, and self-evaluating performance. During the elementary years, students should have repeated practice for these activities. An example of an annual goal and sample activities specifically related to developing self-evaluation skills for an elementary student is included in Table 14.1.

In middle school, self-determination activities should focus on refining strategies for setting goals, planning ways to achieve goals, and self-evaluating performance. It is during these years that students will begin to focus more on goals that extend beyond both middle and high school (Sale & Martin, 2004).

Activities in high school should focus on teaching self-determination through student leadership of the IEP process. This will not occur if the student does not actively participate (to whatever degree possible with support) in the IEP meetings and collaborate with educators and others to develop his or her goals, interventions, and self-evaluation strategies. These are also the years when students will focus on developing and refining the self-determination skills needed to be successful in adult life.

Opportunities must be created across elementary, middle school, and high school programs for students to exercise self-determination, and self-determination oriented goals, including self-evaluation, need to be part of each student's IEP. When teaching these and other skills, educators must assist students with developing ways to and the skills needed to monitor their progress toward meeting annual goals. The remainder of this chapter provides examples of how to develop skills needed to monitor this progress.

Table 14.1.   Developing self-evaluation skills for an elementary-age student

Annual goal

To increase Susan's knowledge of how to self-monitor and evaluate progress toward goals

Sample activities

Susan will write a goal for her academic work to be achieved over the next month.

Susan will select a way to illustrate her daily progress toward meeting her goal.

Susan will chart her daily progress toward meeting her goal.

Susan will review the charted information with her mother and brother each day.

Susan and the teacher will meet weekly to review her progress and determine if her goal has been met or needs adjustment.

Susan will meet with her teacher to establish a new goal.

Ways to Monitor Progress

There are numerous ways that students can track progress toward their annual goals, and they are described in the following sections. The approach that should be used for the student will depend on a number of factors, such as the student's ability and preference, the support needed, and the nature of the goal being measured. Simple graphs, tables, and other self-monitoring tools can help students evaluate their progress toward annual goals. It is important to note that to successfully monitor progress, students will not only need to learn about possible options to track progress, but must also be instructed in their use and how to interpret the results.

Graphs

Graphs display behavior measurements to provide an overall visual impression of when and how frequently a certain behavior occurs. Graphs are usually drawn between two lines that are joined to form an L shape. The vertical line (up and down) is the *ordinate* and is usually used to indicate the rate or amount of behavior. The horizontal line (left to right) is the *abscissa* and is usually used to indicate the time when the behavior occurred. Each entry on the graph is a dot that simultaneously records two facts: the amount or rate of the behavior and time that the behavior occurred. The dot records these facts by being placed directly opposite the value of the vertical line that corresponds to the amount or rate of behavior and directly above the value of the horizontal line that corresponds to the time that the behavior occurred.

When making a simple graph (only one condition), you will have two major decisions to make: how long to make the lines and how they will be labeled. Each graph label should be as short as possible while still describing the number being recorded. The horizontal line should include a label that includes a time factor such as hours, weeks, or days. The vertical line should use a word that documents the nature of the behavior being recorded.

Alejandra's annual goal read: "Alejandra will demonstrate interpersonal skills necessary to participate in group activities." Her teacher established a number of short-term objectives to monitor Alejandra's progress toward reaching this goal, including the following: "Alejandra will demonstrate appropriate turn-taking skills (is quiet and does not interrupt others) when participating in the daily group task." Alejandra chose to use a graph to help self-monitor her progress toward reaching this goal. (A conventional graph of the results is shown in Figure 14.1.)

Graphs can be used to monitor many types of behaviors, including homework scores, time percentage of on-task behavior, frequency of positive statements, timeliness to class, or amount of work completed. Graphs may be charted on the computer, on paper, or on a combination of the two. Students with more significant disabilities are likely to need support to use graphing to monitor progress. For example, illustrations or symbols may be needed to label and better convey the graph's purpose, or the student may require physical guidance or hand-over-hand assistance to plot data points.

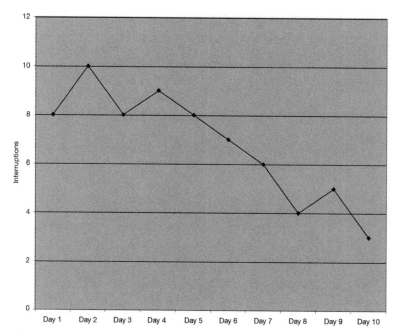

Figure 14.1. Alejandra's frequency of interrupting others.

Tables

Tables present summarized data in columns and rows. Tables can be used to present numerical values. Figure 14.2 shows how a student summarized weekly scores that reflect the average percentage of time he stayed on tasks during community-based vocational training into a weekly table. Titles and labels for tables are always placed at the top of the

	Bagging groceries	Pulling expired stock
Week one	25%	40%
Week two	25%	50%
Week three	45%	65%

Figure 14.2. Time spent on task.

table. Titles and labels for figures are always placed below the figure. All tables and figures must include the units of measurement involved.

Observation Checklists and Rating Scales

Observation checklists and rating scales can also be used to help students monitor progress. These scales can be used to assess students' abilities, attitudes, or performance in process areas such as communication skills, linguistic skills, and extent of participation or interest in the topic. They may also be used to assess the extent or degree to which specific concepts, skills, processes, or attitudes have been acquired.

The primary difference between an observation checklist and a rating scale is that the checklist observes whether the criteria is met or not usually met by means of a yes or no response, such as a checkmark or plus sign (+) for *yes* or an *X* or minus sign (–) to denote *no*. A number is often given on a rating scale to ascertain the level to which the student has achieved the aim of the activity. For example, a rating scale may require a student to select the statement that best describes his or her perception of performance, such as a *3,* which indicates the student has achieved the objective; a *2,* which shows that the student has some understanding but needs more time or assistance to learn the objective; or a *1,* which denotes the student has not achieved the objective. Figures 14.3 and 14.4 illustrate portions of this type of instrument.

Portfolio

Students can also map progress by putting together portfolios of completed work. The portfolio is a tool for organizing a collection of meaningful activities carried out by the student over a given period of time. Putting together a portfolio requires students to acknowledge the steps they have taken and the reflection that led them to select each piece

Basic computer use	Yes	No
I logged on the computer on my own.		
I logged off the computer on my own.		
I used the computer on my own.		
I closed the programs on my own.		

Figure 14.3. Rating scale illustrating student's use of basic computer skills.

Objective	My objective has been achieved	I have gained some understanding but need more time or assistance to learn	I have not learned the objective
Demonstrates the basics of file management (saves documents, opens and saves files, creates folders to organize files)			
Knows how to use e-mail (composes and sends e-mail, organizes e-mail folders for saved messages, deletes messages)			

Figure 14.4. Rating scale showing perception of performance.

of work. This collection demonstrates student proficiency in a particular area, the steps taken to bring about improvement, and the progress in his or her learning. It will contain evidence of student's work with a view to an improved monitoring of his or her learning and an eventual appraisal of final achievement. For example, a student participating in a community-based vocational training program may develop a photo album illustrating the various job tasks he or she learned. Or, the portfolio could include examples of written activities, teacher's comments about progress toward goals, or self-reflection on how well the student is doing. The portfolio could also include charts, tests, audio recordings, or videotapes.

The student should be supported to manage the portfolio. Depending on the student's needs, the teacher should support the collection and organization of the samples. Students are encouraged to collect samples regularly and systematically, and class time should be allotted to keep the portfolio up to date.

Using Technology to Monitor Progress

There are a number of reasons to use technology to help students track their progress and goals. For example, this will help motivate and inspire the student and teach and reinforce basic skills such as how to self-monitor. Perhaps most important, technology also helps promote student progress and celebrate achievement. Some students would not be able to participate or independently self-monitor progress toward goals without using technology. The following sections discuss using electronic organizers and computer software programs that can help students self-monitor their progress toward reaching IEP goals and objectives. We conclude with a listing of some other self-monitoring tools that can be used across a variety of settings and skills.

Electronic Organizers

Electronic organizers are electronic devices that allow an individual to download important information such as names, telephone numbers, e-mail addresses, and dates. They might have alarms/cues that will remind the individual of deadlines, meetings, and so forth. For example, personal digital assistants (PDAs) can help students organize their time and activities by storing a wealth of information, including contact information, personal calendars, interactive memos, "to-do" lists, and so forth. Most also have built in alarms or reminders to prompt or cue that an event is coming up.

Today's traditional PDAs are descendents of the original PalmPilot and Microsoft handheld PC devices. Palm devices run the Palm OS (operating system), and Microsoft Pocket PCs run Windows Mobile. The differences between the two systems are fewer than in the past. Selecting one over another depends primarily on whether there is a need to have the device's file formats compatible with the student's computer operating system. For example, Windows-based PDAs have Microsoft Word built in, and this helps if the student needs to take notes away from the computer and then download them for further writing and editing. Information can be entered into a PDA using either a stylus to write on the screen or an on-screen keyboard. Some PDAs even have a tiny keyboard built in that will dock into an external keyboard. Both types of PDAs support other downloads. This includes games, organizational tools, and reference programs. When additional memory is installed, PDAs can accomplish complex tasks comparable to computers. Electronic organizers are commercially available at retail stores and e-stores that sell small electronic equipment.

Organization is one of the learning challenges that some students with disabilities face. This is often an abstract concept, so it is helpful for these students to develop strategies to support the need to be organized. Entering information related to goals and tracking progress of these goals using a PDA can be very useful for some students. A goal to support this may be: "The student will keep a daily 'to-do' list of specific tasks related to accomplishing (specify IEP goal here) with 80% accuracy, as measured by the teacher."

Software

Computer software programs can be used to develop self-monitoring tools. The end result should be a simple method, such as a contract, checklist, or graph, that a student can use to keep track of his or her progress toward reaching the IEP goals and objectives.

For example, word processing software can be used to develop contracts that can help the student develop, evaluate, and adjust a plan. Typically, the contract would include what the student plans to do and a completion date. Afterward, questions are answered to help him or her gage progress and make adjustments as needed to finish the plan.

A checklist is another tool that can assist students with monitoring progress on their goals. The checklist should be kept in a place where the student will have access to it, such as in a computer file or a hard copy in a folder. Whenever an activity is completed, it is checked off as completed or deleted from the list.

In addition, a graph could be created using the table feature in Microsoft Word software or another computer word processing program. It could also be charted on a handheld device. Microsoft Excel creates spreadsheets that students can use to track their progress. The teacher may have to design the charts, depending on the student's ability and the complexity of the task. Afterward, the student should be able to enter data to graph his or her progress with or without support.

An Internet search will reveal an abundance of software templates that are also available. Some are specifically related to self-monitoring performance. For example, the KidTools Support System (KTSS) is a federally funded project to provide performance support software for children ages 7–13 who have learning disabilities and/or emotional and behavior problems. The software includes easy-to-use templates to assist children in self-managing, problem solving, and making plans and contracts.

KidSkills are planning and organizational tools to help children use learning strategies for success. The KidSkills resources program provides information about tools for adults. Both programs can be downloaded at no cost. More information on these software programs can be found by searching the Internet.

Other Tools

An array of effective self-management tools exist, and Table 14.2 presents examples of tools that support students to self-monitor their behavior and evaluate their performance.

Table 14.2. Tools that support students to self-monitor their behavior and evaluate their performance

Option	Brief description	Example
Electronic device (alarm watch or beeper)	Electronic device vibrates or makes noise at intervals or set times to prompt the person to implement a self-management strategy	Capri sets an alarm on a pager to vibrate 15 minutes before the end of each school day to remind her to chart her progress on the computer each day.
Self-talk	Students are taught to state prompts and questions to encourage self-monitoring	Ray states, "Have I marked off what I completed today on my chart?"
Recorded message	Student records message to listen to at a later time to prompt task completion	Tape recorded message states, "Have I marked off what I completed today on my chart?"
ACT-REACT	Six-step strategy that students are taught to help self-monitor performance. Steps are modeled and students self-record productivity.	Steps include: *articulate* goals, *create* a plan, *take* pictures, *reflect* using self-talk, *evaluate* progress, and *act* again
K-W-L chart	Three-column chart created to record information about what student *knows*, *wants* to know, and *learns* about a topic. After lesson, training that was learned is recorded. If the student does not learn what he or she wanted, then new ways to acquire the information are examined.	Jose wants to know how to send an e-mail. *K* column states, "I know how to turn on the computer." *W* column states, "I want to send an e-mail." After engaging in one-to-one instruction on how to send an e-mail, he records what he learned under the *L* column. "I can send an e-mail to my sister."

Listening to the Experts

| **Teacher's Perspective** | The motivation and excitement for being successful is there with Kathy. She is becoming more aware of herself, which is allowing her to make better decisions about what is best in her life. It is important that I try to help Kathy make important decisions about her IEP. Some of those decisions are often based on the data that team members (including Kathy) have collected. It can be difficult to understand how data is collected, formulated, and how to follow up on the data, but teaching her to understand will help with evaluating her progress. |

| **Student's Perspective** | I know that I am getting faster with typing. I can get printouts of my speed from my computer. My computer will tell me that my typing speed was either faster or slower than before. I also know when I am doing well with some of my other goals because my grades in class will show that. |

| **Parent's Perspective** | I think that it is difficult for all of us, not just for Kathy, to understand what all the reports, data, and assessments mean. She is definitely excited about working on these items, but sometimes knowing where to go and what to do with all the facts and figures may be hard to understand. |

Reflections on Kathy's Example

Kathy and Mr. Scott developed a form that she could use to document her progress on weekly goals (see Figure 14.5). She is responsible for collecting the information in each class, and at the end of each week, they find time to discuss her progress and any necessary action steps. For example, one week she did not work on a goal in math class. They discussed how she could advocate for the time to do so and what steps she might take if the teacher failed to implement the IEP goals.

Tips and Strategies

Here are some strategies for teachers to use when helping students monitor progress on their goals.

- For nonconventional readers, illustrate goal(s) using photographs or line drawings of steps the student must take to reach his or her goal. Review with the student, and allow the student to select pictures of what has been accomplished or what still needs

Weekly school report

Check if you have completed classwork, quizzes, homework, and other assignments for each class.

Name: _____   Week from: _____ to: _____

Grade: _____

Subject	Period	Classwork	Homework
English	1		
STEPS I	2		
History	3		
Math	4		
Biology	5		
Study hall	6		
Computer application	7		

Comments: _____

_____

_____

Figure 14.5. Weekly school report.

to take place. Students with limited mobility can do this through gestures or eye gaze. It will be important that a team member familiar with the student and his or her preferred communication method be involved.

- Have students self-monitor their progress and needs across settings.
- Review with students the outcomes of effective data collection.
- Make clear the instruction for data collection with students and make it meaningful to them.
- If you plan to reward students' progress, then make the rewards related to their IEP.

Conclusion

Special educators must be prepared to teach students how to self-assess, evaluate, and monitor progress toward their annual goals. This means teachers need to know some common types of data collection tools, such as those described in this chapter; understand when to recommend the use of various tools; understand what the student should do when gathering data to help create a create meaningful record; and be prepared to offer supports needed to ensure all students, including those with severe disabilities, have the opportunity to participate in evaluating their progress on meeting IEP goals and objectives.

References

Field, S., Martin, J., Miller, R., Ward, M., & Wehmeyer, M. (1998). Self-determination for persons with disabilities: A position statement of the Division of Career Development and Transition. *Career Development for Exceptional Individuals, 2*(2), 113–128.

Nolet, V., & McLaughlin, M.J. (2000). *Accessing the general curriculum: Including students with disabilities in standards-based reform.* Thousand Oaks, CA: Corwin Press.

Sale, P., & Martin, J.E. (2004). Self determination. In P. Wehman (Ed.), *Functional curriculum: For elementary, middle and secondary aged students with special needs.* Austin, TX: PRO-ED.

Wehmeyer, M.L., Agran, M., & Hughes, C. (1998). *Teaching self-determination to students with disabilities: Basic skills for successful transition.* Baltimore: Paul H. Brookes Publishing Co.

Wehmeyer, M.L., & Schwartz, M. (1999). The self determination focus of transition goals for students with mental retardation. *Career Development for Exceptional Individuals, 21*(1), 75–86.

Wehmeyer, M.L., Palmer, S.B., Agran, M., Mithaug, D.E., & Martin, J.E. (2000). Promoting causal agency: The Self-Determined Learning Model of Instruction. *Exceptional Children, 66*(4), 439–453.

15

....

Developing Next Steps

Ronald Tamura, Judith E. Terpstra, and Colleen A. Thoma

So far, this book has addressed all of the elements and procedures for developing a student-directed individualized education program (IEP). Regardless of the level of support needs, students can facilitate and direct an IEP team in some manner to promote the development and implementation of their own IEP.

This chapter provides information to help you determine what next steps logically follow implementing the students' IEP goals. After all of the requirements have been met, the IEP becomes a legal document and has to be implemented as written. Beyond implementing the IEP, there must be a clearly delineated assignment of responsibility to the stakeholders to follow through.

What can you do after the meetings are finished and you have the IEP document that has been put into action? How do you find time to stick with student-directed IEP processes? How do you help the students build on current skills to move up on the continuum? How will you build support among the IEP team, and how will you iron out any glitches? What resources are available to make the IEP work, and how can you find these resources? How will you develop next year's IEP? These are some of the questions that this chapter answers.

Finding Time

Now that you have the skills and steps to implement a student-directed IEP process, how do you go about finding the time for engaging in this process? The student-directed IEP process is one that you will need to be aware of and plan for throughout the school year. As you have read in the previous chapters, it is a process that requires careful planning and implementation, including ensuring the skills and levels of continuum in the IEP for the student, assessing procedures, and collaborating with others (e.g., administrators, related services, parents, outside agencies). Here are some strategies that can be used to find and save time when engaging in the IEP process.

- Start the process early in the year, well before the IEP is due.

- Evaluate which level of the continuum the student is on by determining the amount of involvement the student typically has had in his or her IEP meeting.

- Meet with the team at the start of the year to develop questions regarding evaluation and assessment outcomes prior to the IEP meeting.

- Gather and conduct assessments, portfolio information, videotape documentation, and work samples.

- Identify what supports are necessary for the student to participate in this process at his or her level or an advanced level.

- Develop a time line with benchmarks for you to complete as well as a time line for the student (with monthly, daily, and weekly benchmarks; see Figure 15.1).

- Explore using universal design for transition (Thoma, Bartholomew, & Scott, 2009) to incorporate strategies and methods that need to be taught to your student for a successful student-directed transition IEP.

Time management

Month	Activity	Person responsible
September	• Identify students on caseload • Evaluate level on continuum for each student • Meet with teams to identify evaluation process • Set up monthly team meetings • Set up monthly meeting (or more frequent if needed) with student	Case manager initiates and IEP team supports
October	• Begin to gather and conduct necessary assessment • Have team meetings • Develop supports needed before, during, and after student-directed IEP process	IEP team
November–May	• Continue to conduct assessments • Have team meetings	IEP team
May	• Conduct student-directed IEP	IEP team, including student and parents

Figure 15.1. Sample time line. (*Key:* IEP, individualized education program.)

A section presented later in this chapter addresses overcoming building and administrative barriers that will also allow additional time and support for this process.

Skill Building

The seven stages of a student-directed IEP continuum are important components of the student-directed IEP process (see Table 1.2 in Chapter 1 for an example of each stage of the process). How do we get Dwight, Alejandra, Max, Susan, and Kathy to increase their participation at their own IEP meetings? You should first identify the strengths and needs of each individual student to determine where on the continuum he or she is able to participate. After the student is placed on the continuum, you can do the following:

- Identify the skills and competencies that the student will need to improve or maintain at his or her current level of participation.

- Identify supports or accommodations that will be put in place for maximum participation at the student-directed IEP. These supports should include communication systems and any other assistive technology options that may be required.

- Identify any other materials that may be needed at the student-directed IEP meeting for presentation of material, assessments, and student choices, including laptop computers, projectors, PowerPoint software, and prerecorded messages. The material needs to be identified early so that you and the student will have the opportunity to learn to use and practice implementing the materials. See Chapter 9 for additional resources and information on technology and materials.

- Identify skills needed for the student to reach the next level of participation. In your plan, benchmarks for achieving these skills should be included. Once identified, these skills should be incorporated into the curriculum and lessons throughout the school year to support the student in participating at a higher level in the IEP process.

This book has guided you through the skills and steps necessary to implement the required skills for effective participation in the student-directed IEP process. Figure 15.2 provides a tool for you to organize your efforts to increase student direction of the IEP process. Because the goal is to facilitate more student direction of the process when possible, this tool can help you plan the instruction, supports, and/or technology supports you might need to make it a reality. Remember to review the different examples, figures, and tables included in previous chapters of this book for ideas.

Building Support within the Team and Ironing Out the Glitches

When building team support, it is important to align the stakeholders to implement the IEP. Service delivery and goal implementation are key components of the IEP. Using an action plan or a responsibility chart to determine the responsibilities of each stakeholder

Student: _____

Current continuum level: _____

Skills/competencies needed at current level	Supports or accommodations in place (including AAC and AT options)	Other materials needed	Skills needed for next level

Figure 15.2. Student skill matrix for continuum. (*Key:* AAC, augmentative and alternative communication; AT, assistive technology.)

(e.g., student, parent, teacher, related services provider, outside agency, friends, family) is a good way to ensure accountability. The implementation plan template (see Figure 15.3) is a way to assign responsibility to the stakeholders who have been identified in the IEP. The template allows the stakeholder to document and be responsible for knowing 1) the individual goal or service area, 2) who is responsible for the implementation, 3) who is responsible for data collection, 4) the focus of the goal area, 5) what resources and supports are needed and available to support the implementation, and 6) whether the goal or service was implemented and why.

This type of system would also allow the students to have a permanent product or recording of their goal and service areas. This system would also provide information if a goal and/or service area was or was not being implemented as written in their IEP.

There are many types of accountability systems existing in the education system. The important point is there should be a system to align the stakeholders (whether it be a plan similar to the one in this chapter or one that is created specifically for the student) to ensure that goals and services are being implemented.

Implementation plan

1. **Goal or service area:**

   Who is responsible for implementation?

   Who is responsible for taking data?

   By when and how often?

   What is the focus of the goal area?

   Resources and support (available/needed)?

   How will we know if it was implemented?

   Was it implemented?   Fully   Partially   Not at all

   If not fully, why?

2. **Goal or service area:**

   Who is responsible for implementation?

   Who is responsible for taking data?

   By when and how often?

   What is the focus of the goal area?

   Resources and support (available/needed)?

   How will we know if it was implemented?

   Was it implemented?   Fully   Partially   Not at all

   If not fully, why?:

Figure 15.3.   Implementation plan template.

It is important for both you and the team to be well organized and well prepared to make the student-directed IEP process effective. Support within the team and within the building will help to facilitate this process. As with any process, however, it is possible that you and the team will experience some challenges in developing and implementing the student-directed IEP. Every collaborative process involving more than a few people, especially from different physical locations, can contribute to these challenges. You will need to be able to recognize and be prepared to address any challenges or "glitches" in this process as they occur.

A challenge may include scheduling issues with parents or administration, including last-minute schedule changes by a parent or other team member. Another challenge may occur when a well-prepared student suddenly freezes and does not want to continue at the current level of participation. Technology that has been determined to be necessary for the presentation and meeting may not be working effectively at the correct time or may not be present as required. Developing an effective team at the beginning of the process will help overcome these common barriers. Effective teams have clear goals, all members' needs are met, each team member has individual accountability, and team members have leadership skills (Friend & Cook, 2007). Effective teams are flexible and prepared for adversity. Documentation is another component to overcoming common barriers. Documentation is essential to ensuring that you and the team members are accountable to the IEP process. As the teacher and facilitator of the student-directed IEP process, it is also important to have an effective and appropriate back-up plan. In the case of a well-prepared student who suddenly becomes too nervous to participate or "freezes" during the meeting, you must know the student and the situation well enough to make an immediate plan of action that will empower the student to continue at an equal or adjusted level of participation. It is important that you do not dismiss the student's nerves or concerns and "take over" the meeting. As a part of the student-directed IEP process, you must be well prepared in advance to overcome these common obstacles and any other challenges that you may face during the process.

Developing Teacher Groups

You may find that it helps to develop your own support group as you begin to implement student-directed IEPs with students for whom you are responsible. Eisenman, Chamberlin, and McGahee-Kovac (2005) found that teachers benefited from participation in a teacher work group where they shared their strategies, lessons, tips, and other resources that they found independently. As the authors were researching student-directed IEP strategies being used in classrooms across Virginia, they found that teachers were interested in participating in focus group interviews; it was a way that they could not only share what they were doing, but they could also learn from others.

If you are the only teacher in your building who is implementing student-directed IEPs, then it will be more difficult to find others who might be willing to come together to share those ideas and strategies. If you do not know of any state or local efforts to implement student-directed or student-led IEPs, then you might employ the following strategies to find others who might be willing to participate in a teacher work group.

- Contact a local or state professional organization such as the state chapter of the Council for Exceptional Children (CEC) or subdivision group. Ask if they know of any local efforts to implement student-directed IEPs in your area.

- Search the Internet for student-directed IEPs to determine whether there are groups near you that are actively working in this area.

- Look on your state or school district's web sites under special education to see if they have a coordinated effort. You could also look at the web site of neighboring school districts.

- Spread the word through teachers you know, university faculty, and/or parents.

- Start your own blog or web page and make a prominent announcement that you are looking for others to share their expertise and experiences.

Finding Resources

By now you have found time, helped your students build on current skills, created an organizational plan, and built support within your team and building. How do you use your creativity to make this process work? You can use Figure 15.4 as an addition to the skills matrix to list and organize additional resources (e.g., web sites, reproducible materials, books, data collection tools, assessments). To get started, the end of this book includes an appendix of resources that you can use to help support the student-directed IEP process in your educational setting.

Student: _____

Current continuum level: _____

Resources needed:

Figure 15.4. Finding resources to support levels of continuum.

Developing Future IEPs

There are a number of things that you and the student should consider when thinking about developing future IEPs.

- A list of accommodations that have been used to facilitate success in all environments in the form of a matrix (see Figure 15.5)

- Progress reports from the student, teachers, service providers, and parents or guardians

- A list of past and current interests (because interests change within the course of a year)

Matrix area of concern	Successful use of accommodation/modification
Visual perception	Seated up front in all classes English and history—notes provided if needed Use of laptops for model of concepts in science Use of laptops for map work and visuals related to history
Memory difficulties	Notes provided—all classes as needed Study guides—all classes
Language difficulties	Repeat directions as needed—all classes Study guides that are vocabulary only—history and English
Abstract reasoning	English and history—graphic organizers for inferring meaning from the text One on one assistance with comprehension questions in all classes
Adaptation difficulties	None
Vocabulary and major concepts	Preteach vocabulary for all subjects English and history terms are provided in different formats (visual and auditory)
Other	None

Figure 15.5. Sample matrix for programming.

- A set of personal goals developed by student to include academic, social, and postsecondary areas

- A portfolio or samples of the student's work (using a variety of media)

- Any appropriate transition assessments (Sax & Thoma, 2002)

- Implementation plans (see Figure 15.3)

- Previous IEPs (should have at least the last 3 years to determine educational benefit)

- Any other relevant information that will provide insight when developing the IEP

 # Listening to the Experts

Teacher's Perspective

It is important to follow up on Kathy's progress so that everything that has gone into the IEP process will not be in vain. It is my duty to ensure that her teachers are informed and are following through with her IEP. It is also my duty to ensure that the stakeholders follow through with services, goals, and implementing the IEP. I will often send out reminders throughout the school year to team members, Kathy, and her mother to see where we stand and how can we continue to push forward with goals and services.

If there is a need to reconvene to discuss rewriting a goal for whatever reason, then that is something that we will do to ensure effective follow through. Fortunately, we do not have to wait until the IEP end date (a year out) to meet and discuss progress. An IEP meeting or a general conference is appropriate to set up whenever the time is needed.

Student's Perspective

Sometimes I do not know what to do next, but I'm reminded that we can come together as a team at any time. I know that keeping up with the things that I'm working on may help me reach my goals faster. When I meet my goals, I know that I can build on them for the next IEP. I'm glad that the goals will not just end.

Parent's Perspective

Determining what steps are next is significant if we are going to keep the ball rolling on her progress. She has to be aware of her goals and what happens after she reaches her goals because it can serve as a reward for all of her effort. If she meets a goal in 2 weeks, then she has to know that it doesn't end there; we can meet and rewrite her goal so that she can continue her progress.

Reflections on Kathy's Example

Kathy and Mr. Scott used the time for preparing for next year's IEP to reflect on what Kathy had accomplished in the past year. She found that she had a clearer idea of what the IEP could do and how to more actively participate in the entire process after going through it the first time. Mr. Scott used a checklist to help with their discussion (see Figure 15.6). The questions on the checklist helped to determine what worked as well as what could be improved in the meeting and throughout the IEP process (premeeting, meeting, and implementation/follow-through).

 ## Tips and Strategies

The teachers that we spoke with recommended that you think of ways to build on a student's first student-directed IEP meeting to expand his or her level of involvement, more easily share information with others in the next year's IEP meeting, and chart progress over time.

- Think about ways to fit all of this into an already busy day.

- Find those small moments of time to talk about preferences, careers, or IEPs.

- Find ways to work with teachers of academic content to combine two different goals (academic and transition).

- Find ways to identify after-school activities, community activities, or family activities to increase self-advocacy skills and skills that can be used in a student-directed IEP meeting.

Conclusion

This chapter has provided information for helping students determine next steps. The responsibility for implementing the IEP goals does not rest solely on the student. Dwight, Alejandra, Max, Susan, and Kathy will need different levels of support to facilitate and direct their own IEP team to promote the development and implementation of their own IEP. Your own students will also need different levels of support depending on where they are on the continuum of student-directed IEPs. We hope that the book has provided the tools and the understanding to offer that support and engage your students to move toward leading their IEPs.

How did my IEP go?

Date of IEP: _____

I worked hard to get ready for the IEP meeting by learning to speak up for myself and be a good team leader/member. After the meeting is over, I will look at the following checklist to help me decide what I need to improve for next time (remember, there is always room for improvement), and what I need to do in the post-meeting follow-up.

Yes No Item to consider

☐ ☐ Were all the people I invited to the meeting there?

☐ ☐ Was I introduced to everyone I didn't know?

☐ ☐ Did I make sure everyone else at the meeting was introduced?

☐ ☐ Did I have a chance to do all of the meeting that I practiced/ prepared?

☐ ☐ Did other team members listen to me?

☐ ☐ Did I get to talk about the things I like to do? About things I don't like to do?

☐ ☐ Did I get to talk about my goals for the future?

☐ ☐ Did I talk about the things I do well? About things I don't do well?

☐ ☐ Did we find ways to help me address my learning needs/challenges/ struggles?

☐ ☐ Did I talk about academic accommodations and adaptations?

☐ ☐ Did I address my access to the general education curriculum?

☐ ☐ Did I address my transition goals (if I'm at least 16 years old)?

☐ ☐ Did I have a say in who was invited to the meeting?

☐ ☐ If not, are there people I would like to invite to the next meeting?

☐ ☐ Does my plan have goals for all the things I think are important?

☐ ☐ Is this the best IEP plan for me at this time? *(To determine the answer to this question, answer the following questions first.)*

Do I like the classes I am taking?

☐ Am I learning new things in my classes?

☐ Am I learning how to do things in the community?

☐ Am I taking classes with my peers?

☐ Am I learning what I need to become more independent?

☐ Am I learning things that will prepare me for what my life will be like as an adult?

☐ Am I learning how to get along with others?

☐ Am I learning how to work with others?

☐ Am I learning how to speak up for myself?

☐ Am I learning how to solve problems?

☐ Am I learning how to set goals?

☐ Am I learning how to decide if I'm getting where I want to go?

☐ Do I know what I'm good at and can I tell others?

☐ Do I know what kind of help and support I need?

☐ Can I tell others what I need and want?

What supports do I want in my next student-directed IEP meeting?

Support	Keep	Discard	Add
Premeeting (assessment, logistics, organization, practicing, invitations)			
Meeting			
After meeting (share, implement, evaluate, prepare)			

Getting the Most Out of IEPs: An Educator's Guide to the Student-Directed Approach by Colleen A. Thoma & Paul Wehman. Copyright © 2010 by Paul H. Brookes Publishing Co., Inc. All rights reserved.

Figure 15.6. Checklist to determine what worked as well as what could be improved in an individualized education program (IEP).

References

Eisenman, L.T., Chamberlin, M., & McGahee-Kovac, M. (2005). A teacher inquiry group on student-led IEPs: Starting small to make a difference. *Teacher Education and Special Education, 28*(3/4), 195–206.

Friend, M., & Cook, L. (2007). *Interactions: Collaboration skills for school professionals* (5th ed.). Boston: Allyn & Bacon.

Myers, A.J., & Eisenman, L.T. (2005). Student-led IEPs: Take the first step. *Teaching Exceptional Children, 37*(4), 52–58.

Sax, C.L., & Thoma, C.A. (2002). *Transition assessment: Wise practices for quality lives.* Baltimore: Paul H. Brookes Publishing Co.

Thoma, C.A., Bartholomew, C.C., & Scott, L.A. (2009). *Universal design for transition: A roadmap for planning and instruction.* Baltimore: Paul H. Brookes Publishing Co.

Appendix

....

Resources

Mark Richardson and Colleen A. Thoma

There are a number of resources available that can help you organize your student-directed individualized education program (IEP) process, and this resource list is designed to provide a starting point. Start with one or more of these available resources and make it work for yourself, the students who will be directing their IEP process, and the other key stakeholders.

Student Self-Determination Curricula

Many of the curriculum packages developed originally in the late 1990s to teach self-determination skills to transition-age students with disabilities included a student-led or student-directed IEP process as part of their materials. Some of the more popular self-determination curriculum packages that are still commercially available include the following:

- *Next S.T.E.P. (Student Transition and Educational Planning) Curriculum* http://interact.uoregon.edu/NEXTStep/NextSTEPintroduction.html
- *Choice Maker Self Determination Curriculum and Lessons* http://web.uccs.edu/education/special/self_determination/cmcr_curriculum.html
- *Dare to Dream, Revised: A Guide to Planning Your Future* http://www.fldoe.org/ese/pdf/dream.pdf
- *Tools for Change: A Video-Based Curriculum Building Skills and Knowledge in Self-Advocacy and Disability Rights* http://www.selfadvocacy.com
- *Self Determination Synthesis Project* http://www.uncc.edu/sdsp/sd_curricula.asp

Student-Led IEPs

These resources include online resources and printable guides that can help you organize and help students run their own IEP meeting. Many of these resources focus on transition IEP meetings, but some also include a much broader IEP focus.

- *Helping Students Develop Their IEPs: Technical Assistance Guide* http://www.nichcy.org/InformationResources/Documents/NICHCY%20PUBS/ta2.pdf

This guide is written for parents and teachers who would like to help students with disabilities become involved with developing their own IEPs.

- *A Student's Guide to the IEP* http://www.nichcy.org/InformationResources/Documents/NICHCY%20PUBS/st1.pdf

This guide represents a comprehensive step-by-step strategy for students who want to become more involved with developing their IEPs.

- *Vermillion County School District's Information on Student-Directed IEPs.* http://www.vermiliontpc.com/iep/student_directed_iep.htm

Many of the examples in this book came from the work of one of their teachers, Sandra Martin, and her colleague, Jane Collins, who were recipients of the 2009 Iva Dean Cook Teachers of the Year from the Division on Career Development and Transition for their work in student-led IEP development.

- *I'm Determined* http://www.imdetermined.org

The *I'm Determined* project is a student-led IEP process developed by the Virginia Department of Education. The web site includes a variety of resources that teachers can use to organize student involvement in their IEP meetings including lesson plans, templates, assessments, checklists, brochures, and PowerPoint training slides.

- *Can I Go to the IEP Meeting?* http://www.bridgerlandliteracy.org/newReaders/CanIGo.html
- *Student-Led IEP Meeting: Planning and Implementing Strategies* http://escholarship.bc.edu/education/tecplus/vol3/iss5/art4/
- *Resources for Involving Students in Their IEP Process* http://escholarship.bc.edu/education/tecplus/vol3/iss4/art1/
- *Student-Directed IEP: A TOTAL Project* http://www.vermiliontpc.com/iep/student_directed_iep.htm
- *Glen County SELPA: The Self-Directed IEP Meeting Step by Step* http://www.glenncoe.org/_programs/_special_education/documents/SelfDirected_IEP.pdf

Person-Centered Planning

Although not technically a student-directed IEP process, there are student-centered planning processes that have been successfully used to increase the level of involvement of students and their parents in the IEP process. These strategies may be useful to help you organize your student-directed IEP process for students who are in elementary or middle school or those who require a great deal of support to be involved in their IEP process. Following are some books, planning guides, and other resources on person-centered planning.

- *Reach for the Dream! Developing Individual Service Plans for Persons with Disabilities* http://www.trninc.com
- *The Guide to Future Planning: Planning the Next Steps to Adult Life for Students with Disabilities* http://www.peatc.org/NEXT_STEPS/Intro/brief.htm
- *The McGill Action Planning System (MAPS)* http://www.ric.edu/sherlockcenter/publications/MAPS.pdf
- *It's My Choice* http://www.mncdd.org/extra/publications/choice/Its_My_Choice.pdf
- *Increasing Person Centered Thinking: Improving the Quality of Person Centered Planning* http://www.rtc.umn.edu/docs/pcpmanual2.pdf
- *Person-Centered Planning: Finding Directions for Change Using Personal Futures Planning* http://www.capacityworks.com/
- *The Person Centered Planning Educational Site* http://www.ilr.cornell.edu/ped/tsal/pcp/index.html

Other Resources

- *Career Planning Program (sample Action Plan)* http://www.careers.ed.ac.uk/CPP/Making_Plans/Action_Plan.pdf
- *Career Development and Guidance: Worksheets, Handouts, Planning Tools, and Workbooks* http://www.khake.com/page95.html
- *Institution for Community Inclusion (ICI)* http://www.communityinclusion.org/
- *TASH* http://www.tash.org/index.html
- *Beach Center on Families and Disabilities* http://www.beachcenter.org/families/person-centered_planning.aspx
- *Quality Mall* http://www.qualitymall.org
- *Oregon Technical Assistant Corporation (OTAC)* http://www.otac.org
- *National Consortium on Leadership and Disability for Youth (NCLD)* http://www.ncld-youth.info

Resources for Related Services

The following web sites offer information on related services.

- *American Counseling Association* http://www.counseling.org/
- *American Foundation for the Blind* http://www.afb.org
- *American Occupational Therapy Association* http://www.aota.org
- *American Physical Therapy Association* http://www.apta.org
- *American Psychological Association* http://www.apa.org
- *American School Health Association* http://www.ashaweb.org
- *American Speech-Language-Hearing Association* http://www.asha.org
- *American Therapeutic Recreation Association* http://www.atra-tr.org
- *Educational Audiology Association* http://www.edaud.org
- *National Association of School Nurses* http://www.nasn.org

- *National Association of School Psychologists* http://www.nasponline.org
- *National Consortium on Deaf-Blindness* http://www.nationaldb.org
- *National Dissemination Center for Children with Disabilities* http://www.nichcy.org
- *National Institute of Deafness and Other Communication Disorders* http://www.nidcd.nih.gov
- *National Resource Center for Paraprofessionals in Education and Related Services* http://www.nrcpara.org
- *Rehabilitation Engineering and Assistive Technology Society of Northern America* http://www.resna.org

Note: In addition to other resources, the information presented draws from copyright-free resources from publications of the National Dissemination Center for Children with Disabilities (NICHCY).

Index

Page numbers followed by *f* and *t* indicate figures and tables, respectively.